Creative Responses to Child Sexual Abuse

of related interest

Creating a Safe Place
Helping Children and Families Recover from Child Sexual Abuse
NCH Children and Families Project
ISBN 1 84310 009 6

Child Protection Work
Beyond the Rhetoric
Helen Buckley
ISBN 1 84310 075 4

Play Therapy
Where the Sky Meets the Underworld
Ann Cattanach
ISBN 1 85302 211 X

Childhood Experiences of Domestic Violence
Caroline McGee
ISBN 1 85302 827 4

Making an Impact – Children and Domestic Violence
A Reader
Marianne Hester, Chris Pearson and Nicola Harwin
ISBN 1 85302 844 4

The Child's World
Assessing Children in Need
Edited by Jan Horwath
ISBN 1 85302 957 2

Helping Families in Family Centres
Working at Therapeutic Practice
Edited by Linnet McMahon and Adrian Ward
ISBN 1 85302 835 5

The Early Years
Assessing and Promoting Resilience in Vulnerable Children 1
Brigid Daniel and Sally Wassell
ISBN 1 84310 013 4

The School Years
Assessing and Promoting Resilience in Vulnerable Children 2
Brigid Daniel and Sally Wassell
ISBN 1 84310 018 5

Adolescence
Assessing and Promoting Resilience in Vulnerable Children 3
Brigid Daniel and Sally Wassell
ISBN 1 84310 019 3
Set ISBN 1 84310 045 2

Creative Responses to Child Sexual Abuse

Challenges and Dilemmas

Revised Edition

Edited by Sue Richardson and Heather Bacon

Foreword by Frank Cook MP

Jessica Kingsley Publishers
London and Philadelphia

First published in the United Kingdom in 2001 by
Jessica Kingsley Publishers Ltd
116 Pentonville Road
London N1 9JB, England
and
325 Chestnut Street
Philadelphia, PA 19106, USA

www.jkp.com

Copyright © 2001 Jessica Kingsley Publishers

Second impression 2003

Library of Congress Cataloging in Publication Data
A CIP catalog record for this book is available from the Library of Congress

British Library Cataloguing in Publication Data
A CIP catalogue record for this book is available from the British Library

ISBN 1 84310 147 5

Printed and Bound in Great Britain by
Athenaeum Press, Gateshead, Tyne and Wear

Contents

Figures and tables

Figures

Tables

*This book is dedicated to the children, adults
and protective parents who have kept alive our commitment
to advocacy on their behalf.*

Acknowledgements

We are especially grateful to the following people for being there and for helping to change what has been a lonely landscape. We would like to thank Stewart Mottram for his invaluable subediting; Becky Rayner for help with preparing the manuscript; Jan Aldridge, Maggie Ambridge and Pauline Colledge for reading the manuscript and helpful suggestions; Pauline Colledge for editing and support with Chapter 5; Chris Bacon for painstaking editing; Cath Delaney and Linda Walker for assistance with Chapter 7; Nicholas Malton, Archivist, NSPCC Library for tracking down a missing source; Dorothy Heard for her interest-sharing and support.

Foreword

Whenever we are confronted with the nakedness of abuse there is the tendency in all of us to want to cover it up. The fact that the vast amount of sexual abuse will go on in families, carried out by adults the children trust, is something that is always hard for us to accept. It is much easier for society to demonise the monster who prowls in the shadows, abducting and abusing our children.

Abuse goes on in secret. Its perpetrators seek to avoid being discovered. They do not want to face the consequences of their actions and therefore they need not only to control the children they abuse but also to control the environment in which they abuse. A society where the main focus on abuse is the stranger leaves children vulnerable. The child's problem is exacerbated if, when the focus is on the family, there is a tendency to disbelieve. The discussions about abuse and society's attitude to the offender show clearly how angry people are when children are abused. Adults will do anything to protect children. If this is so, why in the area of intrafamilial abuse is there a tendency to have policy, legal systems, media attitudes and community responses to the family that are ineffective? As a result, children are left unbelieved and professionals are often castigated. Removing a child leads to condemnation. So does leaving the child in danger. Neglect and physical abuse can often be seen. The problem with sexual abuse is that despite the damage that it does, it is very difficult for our legal system to deliver justice.

With this book we are confronted with the reality of abuse. With children bearing the secret pain alone. With children, and the professionals who are trying to help them, becoming victims of systems. Systems that would appear not to put the paramount interests of the children first. Cleveland is mentioned in most chapters as each author explains their role in working within systems that according to them were and are still not working in the best interests of children.

Cleveland was a watershed. For most people the word conjures a wide range of thoughts and feelings: *Isn't that the county that wrongly took all those children into care?* Whatever your belief, this book brings information from the professionals who were involved. It looks at the follow-up studies and the implications of Cleveland on our understanding of child sexual abuse today. In doing so it opens up a picture, a different picture from the one often read about in the papers.

As an MP who gave evidence to the Butler-Sloss inquiry and who has spent many years involved with charities that work with sexual abuse, I am fully aware of the debates, of the concerns and of the pain both for those who are abused and those who are accused. I believe that this book gives new insights and understanding and continues the debate as to how we resolve the dilemmas, the confusions, and the ignorance and prejudice that prevent unspeakable truths being told.

Frank Cook

Introduction

Sue Richardson and Heather Bacon

> The challenge is to be able to honour the past and to embrace the future
> without doing an injustice to either. (Walrond-Skinner 2000, p.2)

This book explores some of the journeys travelled by sexually abused
children, adult survivors, protective parents, professionals and the wider
community in the post-Cleveland era. The 1987 Cleveland child abuse crisis
was part of a paradigm shift in the societal recognition of child sexual abuse,
initiated more than a decade earlier by women survivors and feminists. The
report of the Cleveland inquiry (Butler-Sloss 1988) opened its conclusions by
saying:

> We have learned during the Inquiry that sexual abuse occurs in children of
> all ages, including the very young, to boys as well as girls, in all classes of
> society and frequently within the privacy of the family. The abuse can be
> very serious and on occasions includes vaginal, anal and oral intercourse.
> (Butler-Sloss 1988, p.243)

At the same time, the traumatic impact of this recognition led to the fragmentation of the child protection system and to the loss of a coherent narrative of
the events in Cleveland. Forms of resistance to the new paradigm included the
scapegoating of professionals (Richardson 1993b) and allegations of false
memory (for a discussion of the latter, see Mollon 1998; Sinason 1998).

Two competing versions of reality have since developed. The first version
emphasises family support, suggesting that conflicts of interest between
adults and children can be resolved. It has became embodied in
post-Cleveland legislation and procedures directed at children where the
abuse has already come to light because the child has made a disclosure. The
second version holds that the majority of sexually abused children are trapped

in silence, unable to disclose and unable to get over the hurdles imposed by the investigative and legal systems. Such children were helped in Cleveland by paediatricians making a medical diagnosis of child sexual abuse. The loss of this medical window (Wyatt and Higgs 1991; see also Wynne, Chapter 6), and that of the narratives of children and professionals who advocated on their behalf in Cleveland, were essential components of constructing the first version of reality. Those who do not accept that the first version of reality provided for all children in need of protection have found themselves without a voice. One significant effect of this has been to reduce the numbers of children entering the child protection system.

An appraisal of what happened to children and professionals in Cleveland can be found in Butler-Sloss (1988); Campbell (1997); Itzin (2000); Richardson and Bacon (1991a). This book takes Cleveland as its starting point as an example of a wider phenomenon – the crisis of recognition of child sexual abuse and subsequent fragmentation of knowledge – which includes Nottingham, Rochdale and Orkney. It goes beyond Cleveland by bringing together a range of perspectives about continuing challenges and dilemmas for the protection of sexually abused children.

We asked all the contributors to comment on the personal and/or professional impact of Cleveland on them and to consider the needs both of sexually abused children who can disclose, and those who cannot. The interest of our contributors in being part of this book indicated a new desire for dialogue about the difficulties of child protection. From their different perspectives, all the contributors can see the limitations of the first version of reality in respect of children unable to disclose. Some, by virtue of their role, have addressed primarily the needs of children who have disclosed (see McLouglin, Chapter 7; Palmer, Chapter 9). Others highlight the dilemmas of working with children who find it hard to join this group (see Ambridge, Chapter 10). Those outside the child protection system make a forceful challenge to the status quo (see Tate, Chapter 1; Brooks, Chapter 5; Ambridge, Henry and Richardson, Chapter 11; Richardson, Chapter 12).

Commenting on the impact of Cleveland was inevitably more difficult for most of the professionals working in child protection. Initially, some of the contributions illustrated the fragmented and unprocessed nature of the experience they had been left with. As the book progressed, the material did become more coherent in this respect. In response to the continuing difficulty of connecting with Cleveland, we have not tried to make the collective narrative more coherent than it actually is.

Our own process as editors and co-authors has been one of consolidating the outcome of our long and difficult journeys post-Cleveland. We have had to recognise continued areas of professional difference. For example, our different ideological perspectives made the task of writing and editing Chapter 3 an arduous one. In attachment terms, we consider that we have moved from conflicting states of mind to a more coherent narrative of our own. We value our supportive companionable interaction, recognise our capacity to dominate or submit when under stress, and struggle in different ways to meet our needs as professionals for appropriate care (see Richardson and Bacon, Chapter 2).

In addition to trauma theory, we have found an attachment framework useful to the integrative thinking needed both to understand the problems of child sexual abuse and to repair the massive disruption it brings to the holding environment for children, carers, adult survivors and professionals. The chapters reflect different levels of awareness and understanding of attachment issues and a range of perspectives in its application. At the same time, attachment issues are a feature of all the contributions. Chapter 5 for example, describes children who disclose to a trusted attachment figure – their mother. Not only did these children receive no protection from the system, but also their attachment relationships were damaged, disrupted or severed. We also make links with developments in the study of dissociation (see Bacon, Chapter 3; Ambridge, Henry and Richardson, Chapter 11).

The book addresses some difficult areas of theory and practice which are unresolved in respect of work with children and protective parents (see Bacon, Chapters 3 and 4; Brooks, Chapter 5; Ambridge, Chapter 10). Rather than provide answers, our aim is to stimulate thinking and an exchange of views. We are committed to tackling the challenges inherent in working with child sexual abuse, an issue where, for many reasons beyond the scope of this book, the 'authoritarian insistence for obscurity over enlightenment' (Summit 1988, p.45) still hampers and threatens good practice.

CHAPTER I

Unspeakable truths
Child sexual abuse and the media

Tim Tate

Mid-morning 5 April 1994

Several million viewers in homes across Britain are watching the BBC. On pastel-coloured sofas, Anne Diamond and Nick Owen are hosting *Good Morning* – their daily mix of news, chat and celebrity gossip. This particular morning in April, Diamond turns to the camera and announces:

> Seven years ago, parents throughout the country were stunned when hundreds of allegations of child abuse were revealed in the county of Cleveland within a few weeks.

From there, she and Owen take turns in reading the script from their autocue.

> Owen: In all 121 children were taken into care in less than two months and experts feared a nationwide pattern of abuse had been uncovered.

> Diamond: The Cleveland Case became the most notorious child abuse dossier of the decade. But soon many of the allegations were proved to be little more than rumours and suggestions.

> Owen: A judicial inquiry found many of the allegations were made by confused children under intense questioning from social workers and that medical methods used to reinforce them were new and untested in this country.

> Diamond: The massive Inquiry drove hundreds of families apart and some are even now trying to get their children back so they can start lives together again.

The camera then cuts to a shot of a middle-aged couple sitting on a sofa, opposite Diamond and Owen.

> Owen: June and Donald ... [*although Owen named the couple we have chosen not to*] had their son, Andrew, taken away from them at the height of the scandal seven years ago. [*The screen is filled with the school photograph of an 11-year-old boy.*]
>
> Diamond: Although they were shown to be innocent of the abuse that their son Andrew was subjected to, they believe they are still now being punished for it ... [*she turns to the couple*]. Most people would find it amazing: you were cleared of the allegations of sexual abuse towards your son and yet you've still not been able to see him.

What must have been the reaction of Anne and Nick's mid-morning audience? What emotions were they trying – for be in no doubt they have been trying – to stir? Shock? Sympathy? Anger, even?

There is one problem with this, one flaw in the entire script and the interview with the couple that followed it: barely a word of it was true.

High Court, Family Division, Middlesbrough, 3 February 1988

Mr Justice Sheldon is giving his verdict in a case brought by the couple who would – six years later – sit on Anne and Nick's pastel sofa, pleading for the return of their son. But this morning in February, Mr Justice Sheldon is far less sympathetic than Diamond and Owen.

The couple have sued Cleveland County Council for the return of their son, Andrew, and his younger sister. Both sides are represented by counsel. Both sides have put their case, and the judge has had the benefit of considering all the evidence, written, verbal and medical – including statements from both of the children which describe extreme acts of sexual abuse by the father, sometimes in front of the mother.

But the judge begins by recalling an earlier court hearing:

> The father, on 30 June 1981 at the Guisborough Magistrates Court, pleaded guilty to two offences of indecent assault on an 8 year old girl and asked that a third similar offence should be taken into consideration – offences in respect of which he received a sentence of six months imprisonment suspended for two years. They were committed ... in, by his own written admission, circumstances of gross indecency.

Next, Mr Justice Sheldon moves on to the present case:

Having listened to all the evidence and having seen and heard [the father] in the witness box ... I am left in no doubt whatever that [he] has sexually abused his children substantially as they have described ...

The father was more than a difficult and domineering man: I found him to be dishonest, untruthful and a hypocrite ... I found myself unable to accept anything that he said unless it was confirmed by other cogent independent evidence.

For the mother ... it is plain in my opinion that she was not, and is not, equipped mentally to withstand the dominance of her husband ... and that even though she may have disliked what he was doing to them and may not have known all the details all the time, she was well aware that he was sexually interfering with them and that at times actively acquiesced in what was happening.

This, then, was the couple who sat demurely on Anne and Nick's cheerful sofa; this was the couple to whom the BBC gave a platform for the following exchange:

Diamond: He [*the son*] could be watching now. What do you want to say to him?

Father: I want to say, wherever you are ... come home and get away from those very evil people who have got you in captivity.

How could it be that a convicted paedophile – a man denounced as a liar, a hypocrite and an abuser by a High Court judge – could be given such unquestioning support by the world's most respected public service broadcaster?

The answer lies in the attitude of the media towards the notion of sexual abuse, an attitude that was formed – in a fundamentally distorted fashion – during the 1987 Cleveland child abuse case.

It is, at heart, a discordant attitude – simultaneously professing anger at sex beasts who abuse children while denouncing or reviling those who dare to protect children by removing them from abusive families. But it is an attitude that has, in the years since Cleveland, shaped public opinion and government policy – rarely to the benefit of abused children.

In 1997 I produced and directed a documentary film re-examining the Cleveland crisis ten years after the events. I have made documentaries and written books about what adults do to children for more than fifteen years and believed I had come to understand the particular dynamics of public opinion about the subject. But nothing in my previous work had prepared me for the experience of reinvestigating Cleveland.

It is worth – given the passage of time – recalling the basic architecture of the crisis: 121 children from many different and largely unrelated families had been taken into the care of Cleveland County Council in the three short months of the summer of 1987.

Behind these headline statistics were decades of neglect and/or misunderstanding of the issue of child sexual abuse, a long-running dispute between police and paediatricians over who should have primacy in the investigation of such cases and the presence of two dedicated paediatricians at Middlesbrough General Hospital.

Dr Marietta Higgs and Dr Geoffrey Wyatt had both understanding of, and training in, recognising the physical signs that a child's body had been abused. One of these signs was – and still is – reflex anal dilatation (RAD): a simple clue which is suggestive of anal penetration from outside. It had been recognised as a valuable weapon in the armoury of doctors examining children for many decades and was endorsed by both the British Medical Association and the Association of Police Surgeons.

Drs Higgs and Wyatt brought other qualities to the investigation of child sexual abuse: they believed children should be protected from it. More than thirteen years after the 1987 crisis this simple belief has a ring of almost *faux naiveté*, yet in Cleveland in the late 1980s it was a breath of air to the social workers tasked – by law – with protecting children.

Yet by July 1987, the paediatricians were at the centre of a national storm of outrage – denounced by politicians, press, television and public opinion. The parents of the 121 children taken into care were lionised for their courage or portrayed as the victims of a monstrous witch-hunt. Their voices – sometimes their faces – dominated news-stands and television bulletins.

When the courts seemed to be returning all their children to them, the nation seemed to breathe a sigh of relief, while simultaneously demanding the scalps of the paediatricians and social workers.

When I began researching the documentary film about Cleveland, what struck me instantly was the one-sided nature of almost all the Cleveland story as presented to the public – whether by press or politicians – in the print or broadcast media. Cleveland had entered the English language as shorthand for irresponsible and over-zealous child protection workers (be they doctors or social workers) who broke up happy families in their pursuit of what appeared to be an almost mythical creature – child sexual abuse.

I had trouble with this one-dimensional coverage for two very simple reasons. The first was that I had interviewed Marietta Higgs for Independent Television News back in 1988. The second was that I had read the entire report (Butler-Sloss 1988) of the official judicial Inquiry into Cleveland. Neither the interview nor the report – for all its elliptical language – supported the public image of Cleveland. And so two colleagues and I set out to re-examine the facts of Cleveland rather than the rhetoric or the myth.

Then I worked for Yorkshire Television, one of the most respected producers of documentary films in the world. I warned my managers that we might run into 'turbulence' along the way, so powerful were the emotions still surrounding Cleveland. I clearly did not grasp just how powerful the public myth had become, or how much had been invested in maintaining it. I certainly underestimated the power of this myth to resist re-evaluation.

When we began researching the film on behalf of Channel 4, which had commissioned and paid for it, the response from individual child protection workers inside and outside Cleveland was universally positive. Everyone we met wanted what they saw as the true (and hidden) story of Cleveland to be told at last: the story of how very young children – many of them pre-verbal – had been abused, first sexually by an adult, then systemically by courts and lawyers who returned them to abusive families.

Each of these workers had knowledge of individual children from the crisis. Some were still working in the Middlesbrough area. Yet none had any contact with the families, none had been allowed to retain documentation and none knew of any official child protection agency that had tracked what happened to the children after the three fraught summer months of 1987.

The key to resolving the puzzle of Cleveland was the children. What had actually happened to them? Had they been abused – or had the paediatricians and social workers (as public opinion held) been over-zealous and plain wrong?

Curiously – particularly given its high profile, year-long sittings and £5 million cost – this was the one central issue never addressed by the Butler-Sloss judicial Inquiry. For all its painstaking recording of testimony and sifting of internal evidence, the inquiry's remit did not require it to answer the main question.

Ten years after the crisis, my colleagues and I set about reconstructing the records of the 121 children at its heart to determine exactly what had happened to them. There was a certain inevitability in the official refusal to co-operate. Many of the children had been wards of court, which imposed severe legal restrictions on the dissemination of information about them. And all had a moral right to privacy. Furthermore, Cleveland County Council had been disbanded by government edict two full years before we began our investigation.

Unearthing the information on the 121 children without official assistance proved to be enormously difficult. For one thing it was potentially unlawful: my co-producer and I found ourselves in the unusual position of needing to risk the wrath of the courts simply to determine how well – or badly – the courts had protected the Cleveland children.

The information itself had been thoroughly dispersed: from one unitary county council, the Cleveland children had now fallen under the aegis of four individual local councils – if, indeed, they had become the responsibility of any child protection department at all.

Eventually, though, we did assemble the data given to the Butler-Sloss Inquiry. This divided into two categories: the confidential material, presented in camera, and the transcripts of public sessions of the hearings. Putting the two together we assembled our own database on the children – each identified only by the code-letters assigned to them by Butler-Sloss.

When it was finished, this database told a startlingly different story from the public myth. In every case there was some prima facie evidence to suggest the possibility of abuse. Far from the media fiction of parents taking their children to Middlesbrough General Hospital for a tummy ache or a sore thumb and suddenly being presented with a diagnosis of child sexual abuse, the true story was of families known to social services for months or years, histories of physical and sexual abuse of siblings and of prior discussions with parents about these concerns.

In several of the cases the children themselves had made detailed disclosures of abuse; many of the pre-verbal children displayed severe emotional or behavioural symptoms consistent with sexual abuse. There were even some families in which a convicted sex offender had moved in with mother and children.

All of this information had been presented to the Butler-Sloss Inquiry. Virtually none of it had emerged from that inquiry into the public arena and certainly not into the vitriolic media coverage of Cleveland. To my colleagues and me this seemed initially impossible to comprehend: how could this have happened? How could truth have been turned on its head so completely? And why, given the apparent strength of the evidence, did the courts come to close their minds to these children's cases?

It is often said that Vietnam was the first television war. By the same token, Cleveland was the first war over the protection of children to be fought not in the courts, but in the media. By the summer of 1987 Cleveland had become above all, a hot media story. The *Daily Mail*, for example, had seven reporters, plus its northern editor, based in Middlesbrough full time. Most other newspapers and television news teams followed suit.

What were all the reporters looking for? Not children at risk. Not abusing adults. Aggrieved parents were the mother lode sought by these prospecting journalists. Many of these parents were only too happy to tell – and in some cases, it would appear, *sell* – their stories. Those stories are truly extraordinary. In many cases they bore almost no relation to the facts. Parents were allowed – encouraged – to portray themselves as the innocent victims of a runaway witch-hunt – and these accounts were duly fed to the public.

Nowhere in any of the reporting is there any sign of counterbalancing information from child protection workers or the organisations that employed them. Throughout the summer of 1987 newspapers 'reported' what they termed a national scandal of innocent families torn apart. The claims were repeated in Parliament and then recycled as established 'facts' by the media. The result was that the courts themselves began to be paralysed by the power of this juggernaut of press reporting – 'journalism' which created and painstakingly fed a public mood which brooked no other version of the story. My own family was extremely hostile when I explained that I was to re-examine Cleveland. The power of the very word 'Cleveland' to bring to the surface extreme anger and fear was remarkable – ten years after the events in question.

Perhaps then, it should not have been such a surprise to discover that the courts were also affected. No matter what legal textbooks say, judges are only human and can be influenced, and they appear to have been. Given that most of the hearings took place out of sight of the press, the following examples are taken from the recollection of child protection workers present in court.

In one case, during a controversy that centred fundamentally around disputes over the meaning of RAD, a judge refused to allow 'any evidence about children's bottoms' in his courtroom.

A second judge – hearing an application to have their children returned by parents about whom social services had grave worries – told the assembled lawyers that, as she lived in the area, she could not help but be influenced by what she read in the press.

Hardly surprising then that child protection workers soon found courts not hearing their applications, cutting them short, or loosely supervising informal deals which allowed children to be sent back to parents, even in cases where there was explicit evidence of apparent abuse to be explained and dealt with.

In the film we dealt with several of these cases. One case concerned one of the first families to be 'reunited' – the word, the very loaded word, used by all newspapers and television covering the case – with their children. Yet the social services file – not apparently considered by the courts – makes very uncomfortable reading.

It shows that the family – mother, father and three children – had been known to social services for some time prior to the 1987 crisis.

- All three children were said to have behavioural problems – including an incident in which they dug up the floorboards and set fire to the family home.

- They were listed as having an alarming number of bruises and scars on their young bodies.

- All were seriously underweight.

- They had contact with a close family relation who was recorded as having abused other children as an adolescent.

- One of the children had drawn a picture for a National Society for the Prevention of Cruelty to Children (NSPCC) officer working with him – a picture of an adult man apparently buggering a boy.

- At least one of the three children had expressed extreme reluctance to return home.

This information and the risk to those children it implies was never properly tested in court. Faced with the juggernaut of press reporting and public opinion, the protection of children took a back seat.

Sue Richardson, the child abuse consultant at the heart of the crisis, watched as cases began to unravel:

> All the focus started to fall on the medical findings; other supportive evidence, mainly which we held in the social services department, started to be screened out. A situation developed where the cases either were proven or fell on the basis of medical evidence alone.

> Other evidence that was available to the court, very often then, never got put. We would have had statement from the child, the social workers and the child psychologist's evidence from interviewing. We would have evidence of prior concerns, either from social workers or teachers, about

the child's behaviour or other symptoms that they might have been showing, which were completely aside from the medical findings. (Channel 4 1997)

Ten years after the Cleveland crisis, Sue Richardson was adamant that evidence relating to children's safety was not presented to the courts which subsequently returned those children to their parents:

I am saying that very clearly. In some cases, evidence was not put in the court. In other cases, agreements were made between lawyers not to put the case to the court at all, particularly as the crisis developed. Latterly, that children were sent home subject to informal agreements or agreements between lawyers. The cases never even got as far as the court. (Channel 4 1997)

Nor is Richardson alone. Jayne Wynne, one of the Leeds paediatricians who had pioneered the use of RAD as an indicator of sexual abuse and who subsequently had detailed knowledge of many of the Cleveland children, remains concerned by the haphazard approach of the courts to their protection.

I think the implication is that the children were left unprotected. The children who were being abused unfortunately returned to homes and the abuse may well have been ongoing. (Channel 4 1997)

As my colleagues and I worked our way through the database of all 121 children we saw this disturbing picture emerge again and again. One of the cases that sticks – immovably – in my mind is the fate of the first two children in the crisis.

These two little girls – aged 5 and 3 – had been taken into care from parents known to have abused them physically on previous occasions. The elder girl had more than 60 small bruises on her body when she was taken into care. The child had also made a clear disclosure of sexual abuse by her father.

Heather Bacon, the consultant psychologist involved in many of the cases, had no doubt about what had happened to the children:

There was one young child in that household who did make what I thought was a very clear statement. She said that daddy had put a toy in her bottom and when she was asked what the toy was, she said, it was an 'extra leg' on daddy.

I thought that was pretty graphic and believable and yet I understand that that evidence was never presented to the court because the medical evidence was disputed at the trial and the case was finished without the disclosure evidence being heard. (Channel 4 1997)

In the midst of the media firestorm evidence like this was frequently never presented to the courts. It became – quite literally – unspeakable.

Those two children, like many others, were simply sent home. Unprotected. But the parents did get their story, their triumph, in the press once again. And a grateful tabloid, allegedly, paid them £40,000 for the privilege. Additionally, Cleveland County Council paid them – and others like them – compensation, despite having strong prime facie evidence that they were guilty of abusing their children.

As one of the mothers who did protect her children (and of course got neither publicity nor cash) told us:

> It was all about the parents and no one thought about the children at all. A lot of people were shouting about how Dr Higgs had diagnosed the children and was splitting the families up. To me it was more a vendetta against Dr Higgs and the fact that the child abuse had been discovered. Nobody thought about the poor children.

This woman – Jean – discovered the abuse only because of intervention by the paediatricians and child protection workers. Her husband had interfered with all three of their daughters – all at 8 years old – on evenings when she was out of the house, and had then pressured them never to speak about it:

> The eldest one closed up. She wouldn't say anything to anybody, she wouldn't say anything. The middle one … we tried to find out off her if anybody had been doing anything they shouldn't and all she kept saying was that the eldest one had a secret and the eldest one would hit her if she told us the secret.

> I don't think really in her own mind, she wanted to believe that the daddy that she loved had done this to her. She didn't want to believe it had happened.

> I praised Dr Higgs all the way through. I was grateful to her for diagnosing my children so early on and I just think she saved quite a few children from being abused.

Jean is a willing and convincing witness. Her children still live with her; her husband was charged with abusing them but committed suicide while awaiting trial. Yet Jean's story is not one which has been told in the press: her story – that of children being saved from continuing abuse by the intervention of the Cleveland child protection workers – is not one that matches the popular myth. It, too, has become an unspeakable truth.

And what of the Butler-Sloss Inquiry – the official and judicial investigation into Cleveland, its causes and its lessons? The year-long inquiry simply did not address the question of how many children were actually abused – but it did come to some very interesting conclusions:

1. Anal dilatation was 'abnormal and suspicious and requires further investigation' (Butler-Sloss 1988, p.193) for possible sexual abuse having occurred.

2. 'It was entirely proper for the two paediatricians [Dr Higgs and Dr Wyatt] to play their part in the identification of sexual abuse' but they were to be criticised for not recognising that 'the certainty of their findings in relation to children diagnosed by them posed particular problems for the police and Social Services' (Butler-Sloss 1988, p.245).

3. There was 'no evidence … that any social worker has acted in anything other than good faith' (Butler-Sloss 1988, p.85).

4. Stuart Bell MP – the chief spokesman for the parents and leader of the media campaign – had 'talked of social workers looking for "child fodder"' and had made 'intemperate and inflammatory remarks on television and to newspaper reporters which had a part in exacerbating an already difficult and sensitive situation. We are sad that he was unable to withdraw or modify allegations which could not be substantiated' (Butler-Sloss 1988, p.168).

The inquiry report made absolutely no finding on whether or not any of the children had been abused, but overall suggested that the Cleveland crisis had arisen because of a backlog of unaddressed cases, a bitter 'turf war' dispute between police surgeons and paediatricians (with each claiming they knew better than the other about the incidence and detection of child sexual abuse), and a media frenzy centred around inaccurate reporting of both the RAD issue and individual cases. Hardly then, a damning verdict on the child protection workers or on Dr Geoffrey Wyatt and Dr Marietta Higgs.

But what were the headlines the next morning? 'Sack Her' – the lead on one mass-market middlebrow tabloid – summed it up. The Cleveland myth was protected and no one from the child protection services challenged this blatant pack of lies. In defence, the management of these organisations would argue that they have a statutory duty to maintain confidentiality and it is an appropriate and laudable duty. Unfortunately, it doesn't protect children.

By taking their complaints to the media, had not these parents effectively released social services and the health authorities from their duty of confidentiality? I am not arguing that these organisations should identify the families: but if the battle for the children is being fought in the court of public opinion (however distasteful we find that) the public has to have enough of the true story to trust child protection workers to do their job.

My co-producer and I were several months into the film before the most astonishing revelations about Cleveland emerged. It appears that – despite the media myths – in only 28 of the 121 cases did the courts effectively rule that the children had not been abused. For the rest, orders were put in force that, either specifically or by implication, recognised that abuse had occurred.

Then there was the question of what happened to those children next. We received documents – anonymously – which showed that at least 5 of the Cleveland children (and by implication, children who had been returned home at the height of the crisis) had subsequently been re-referred on suspicion of having been sexually abused.

Cleveland County Council, which was monitoring all the 121 children, reported this to the Department of Health. It had been closely involved with the cases from early in the crisis. Very quickly the department instructed the council to cease monitoring the Cleveland children as a unified group. All records of them as a category of children appear to have been destroyed at this point.

Today no official agency has any idea how those 121 children fared in the years after the crisis. Cleveland County Council was subsequently disbanded and its successor authorities say they have no means of identifying any of the Cleveland children and therefore have no means of knowing whether any of the children on its abuse registers might be from the Cleveland families. Intrigued, my colleagues and I began examining the way this material had been suppressed. Perhaps we were a little naive at this point. Although I fully expected the going to get rough I hadn't anticipated what would happen next.

The night before we were to begin filming, I was informed that Yorkshire Television no longer wanted to be associated with the film – even though Channel 4, which had commissioned it, was still very keen to receive it. I was to be allowed to make the film using my own independent production company, but for reasons of principle – which apparently meant not causing new distress in Cleveland – Yorkshire Television would not be associated with it. By coincidence, the Middlesbrough MP – who had championed the cause of the parents in the press, on television and in his own book but who had been heavily criticised by the Butler-Sloss Inquiry – had written to Yorkshire Television to voice concern that the film was being made. (Within a year the management of Yorkshire Television would change and the executives who took the decision to abandon the film left the company.)

Simultaneously, all current and former child protection workers with whom we were in contact were told not to speak with us. If they did so they risked dismissal. Even Sue Richardson, the former child abuse consultant, who now worked for an entirely unrelated organisation, the National Children's Home Action For Children, was told that if she appeared in the film she risked dismissal. Sue chose to resign rather than be silenced.

In 20 years of journalism and film-making I had never come across such blatant attempts to silence professionals whose only 'crime' was to speak up for children at risk.

Just what was being protected here? Why should our film – subsequently broadcast – be headlined by *TV Times*: 'Is this the film which should never have been made?' and why is this myth on 'innocent families' torn apart by child protection workers so powerful? Official explanations for the Cleveland crisis ranged from (not unusual) tensions and disagreements between police and social services, the stubbornness of the paediatricians in not slowing down their efforts once the system became clogged and the inevitable difficulty of being the first major case where abuse on a large scale was reported over a short period of time.

In the years since Cleveland the pattern has been repeated. Nottingham, Rochdale, Orkney – and the ever-lengthening list of revelations of systematic abuse of children within care homes. Behind the headlines is one eternal truth: adults' voices are always louder than children's. Since abused children find it harder to find their voices than others, adults are needed to step in to protect them.

But recognising child sexual abuse, especially on a large scale, is a dangerous business. Once identified there is a legal – not to mention moral – imperative to do something about it. In a political climate hostile to additional public expenditure and conditioned to distrust allegations of abuse, the instinctive reaction of the public is to shoot the messenger rather than listen to the message.

Ultimately the key is the media. Those who control press and television in any civil war have public opinion in the palm of their hand. Political imperatives tend to follow the dictate of public opinion.

As Sue Richardson had cause – and ultimately, time – to reflect:

> The protection of children depends on the climate of public opinion. The courts are not immune from it. It's the crucial deciding factor really as to whether child sexual abuse will be dealt with or not, and the way in which the public hysteria was whipped up by the media meant that the cases didn't have a chance, really. (Channel 4 1997)

CHAPTER 2

Piecing the fragments together

Sue Richardson and Heather Bacon

This chapter explores the way in which the discourse concerning the 1987 Cleveland child abuse crisis has been accompanied by a loss of a coherent narrative of events. It shares the personal and professional impact of the crisis on the authors as an example of the difficulty, for both individuals and professional systems, of reconnecting in the aftermath of the events of 1987, which, by their traumatic nature, were deeply fragmenting of relationships and of professional endeavour. We share some key aspects of our respective professional journeys of reconnection and outline the theoretical models which we have found helpful. An attachment framework is used to explore the needs of professionals as caregivers and the ways of reconciling competing narratives.

Background: the 1987 Cleveland child abuse crisis

Between February and July 1987 in Cleveland, two consultant paediatricians, Marietta Higgs and Geoffrey Wyatt, made a medical diagnosis of child sexual abuse in respect of 121 children. The medical diagnosis was the result of increased awareness among professionals (Hobbs and Wynne 1986). Although but a fraction of Cleveland's child population of approximately 140,000 was involved, the numbers of children suspected of having suffered sexual abuse rose to an unprecedented level. The agencies responsible for investigation and intervention were overwhelmed by the task of investigation. Parents, the media, influential public figures and some professional groups reacted with shock and disbelief. The situation polarised and led to a public inquiry lasting over five months chaired by Lady Justice Butler-Sloss.

A particular feature of the controversy was that a significant number of the children concerned had made no complaint of abuse prior to the diagnosis. The social services department responded in the same way as they did to children with a diagnosis of non-accidental injury: the children were admitted to hospital or foster care on a statutory basis for further investigation. This action fuelled multidisciplinary conflict, public and media outcry and led to a call for the children to return home.

The Official Solicitor, whose officers interviewed a number of children reviewed by the Cleveland Inquiry, concluded that:

> One of my lasting impressions will be the accounts, often extremely harrowing, of sexual abuse at the hands of often trusted adults and the frequently expressed gratitude and relief at the intervention of the medical experts and Social Services in Cleveland. (Hinchcliffe 1989, p.89)

At the same time, the two paediatricians and Sue Richardson, the child abuse consultant employed by Cleveland Social Services Department, were singled out for attack by the media and those parents, public figures and professionals who did not accept the diagnosis. In the public arena, events were described in dramatic and partisan terms. The parents were seen as the innocent victims of the professionals, who were presented as the ones responsible for abuse via their intervention. Some cases were upheld by the courts. Many others were settled in response to the controversy and the children returned home without the facts being established. In the longer term, the community has remained fearful or confused and has been unable to move to a genuine resolution (see Tate, Chapter 1; Richardson, Chapter 12, this volume).

Cleveland: a re-evaluation

The 1987 crisis, in which we each had a key role as child abuse consultant and child psychologist respectively, left us with more questions than answers. In the wake of the Butler-Sloss inquiry, we began an intensive process of re-evaluation from our respective social work, psychotherapeutic and psychological perspectives. We reviewed our roles, our professional relationships, our connections with the community and wider networks and the needs of sexually abused children and their carers. This became a continuing task for our professional alliance. We published the initial outcome (Richardson and Bacon 1991a) in which we tried to explore and disentangle the process of professional intervention and how it might be matched against the processes the children were going through both internally and in their families. We hoped that this would lead to a constructive and healing dialogue with colleagues and with those by whom we had felt misunderstood and rejected. Through this dialogue, we hoped to see the emergence of a new and better informed societal willingness to tackle the problems of sexually abused children. We also cherished the hope expressed by Butler-Sloss (1988, p.245) that professionals in Cleveland would be able to work together on behalf of children in the future.

Making meaning: the development of a cognitive framework

With our paediatric colleagues, we identified two groups of sexually abused children: Group A and Group B (Wyatt and Higgs 1991). Group A are those children who choose to make an alerting disclosure about their abuse which triggers action by the child protection system. Group B are children who present with alerting signs and symptoms of sexual abuse but are unable to make a disclosure: the abuse is a well-guarded secret, accessed by adults (such as paediatricians) before the children can act in any way for themselves (Richardson and Bacon 1991b). The differences between the two groups led us to conceptualise disclosure as an interactive process on a continuum on which children can make a journey towards disclosure or remain trapped in silence. We began to identify some of the factors which influenced which group individual children would fall into, and how we might help those in Group B to move into Group A. We also identified, on a continuum of professional survival, how the dynamic interaction of forces such as support versus silencing could influence practice in a child or adult-centred direction (Richardson and Bacon 1991c, pp.145–6).

Search for dialogue

Publication and contributions to many conferences did not lead to the dialogue we had hoped for with our colleagues and with policy makers. We noted that in the aftermath of Cleveland, the impetus of legislation, procedures and public and professional awareness was directed at children in Group A. We considered that even children in this group were ill served by the child protection system, that the dilemmas of children and adults in Group B remained unaddressed and that both were usually left to find their own way along the continuum of disclosure.

We sought to understand whether or not what had happened to us in the professional system when the Cleveland crisis escalated might in some way parallel the process for the sexually abused children. We saw the task of processing as essential, not only for our own healing process but also to enable us to contribute to that of the wider system. We have both experienced a continual internal tension between the need to engage with and the need to break free from what we perceived to be a stuck system, paralleled externally by attempts to engage with our colleagues and the wider system in a dialogue that would promote understanding.

Our respective clinical work has confirmed that there is a complex process going on for any child or adult who has to struggle with the meaning and effects of child sexual abuse. Butler-Sloss (1988, p.25) notes that: 'The Official Solicitor reported to the Inquiry that the children's stories reflected variously: misunderstanding, mistrust, discomfort, anger, fear, praise, gratitude and sheer relief'. This varied response to intervention, which puzzled us at the time, is now much more understandable. Since 1987, our description of the process of disclosure – or non-disclosure – has been validated and expanded by many other clinicians (e.g. Gonzalez *et al.* 1993; Sorenson and Snow 1991; Swann and Ralston 1997; Wade and Westcott 1997; Woodward and Fortune 1999) and researchers (e.g. MacLeod 1999; Wattam 1999). As a result of theoretical advances in our knowledge of child development and human response to trauma, there is now a much more developed framework for understanding the clinical phenomena of children in Groups A and B seen in Cleveland.

Efforts at co-operative inquiry

We saw ourselves as taking part in a process of co-operative inquiry (Heron 1981) from different perspectives which would enable us to debrief, put our narrative together, recover lost fragments and integrate them into a coherent story. Rowan (1981) describes Esterson's (1972) theory of a 'new mental stance' in research tasks of this kind, with three stages:

> first, a reciprocity between the observer and the rest of the social field, next, a temporary nihilating withdrawal from active participation, third, a negation of the withdrawal and a return to the reciprocity with the rest of the social field. (Rowan 1981, p.168)

The second stage, where an observer relates primarily to him or herself, is the most painful, and the most crucial in the process of discovery.

Although we could not establish the kind of reciprocity described by Esterson (1972) with our immediate colleagues, an attempt to link with sympathetic 'outsiders' was relatively well supported and successful. Using the help of two attachment-based psychotherapists (Richardson 1995), we moved painfully into the second stage.

We used the model of a trauma response cycle (Duncan and Baker 1989) to understand the impact of its stages of anxiety, guilt, anger and grief on ourselves as professionals and in the community in Cleveland. For example, we were struggling to grieve; tremendous anxiety had been induced in the community by the collapse of assumptions about the nature of family life. This approach enabled us to grasp the enormity of what had happened and provided a context within which to focus on our individual stories. It highlighted the importance of finding maturational exits from the trauma response cycle via information, affirmation, protest and mourning (Duncan and Baker 1989). This marked a significant step towards mourning and renewal. It helped us to re-establish some of our personal and professional boundaries but it was only a beginning.

We then shared our stories with other groups of similarly traumatised professionals, forming alliances with those in other countries (Richardson 1994) and with those engaged in battles in the fields of ritual and organised abuse. This process served, however, to increase our sense of isolation both from the mainstream and from other colleagues in Cleveland. We had no secure nurturing base as professionals, one which could not only encourage and support us to examine our own behaviour but also reflect on its own responsibility as the caregiving system, and on ways to support professionals engaged in the risky task of child protection. Essential to the informed caregiving we needed was an understanding that: 'Unlike ordinary frontiers of discovery, child sexual abuse provokes an authoritarian insistence for obscurity over enlightenment' (Summit 1988, p.45). Summit's view highlights that fact that the support needs of professionals in this field are different from other areas of practice which have a more secure public and political mandate: careful attention and support is needed for exploration. The absence of informed, exploratory caregiving and any shared processing with our colleagues and the wider child protection system left us with only our efforts as individuals. This led to painful differences of perception in which, according to our attachment style, we blamed others (and sometimes each other), experienced unnecessary guilt, took too much responsibility for things we were powerless to change, and became increasingly alienated from the wider system.

Professional isolation and loss of professional confidence were two of the most crippling aspects of this process. The more we scrutinised and questioned our actions and beliefs (for example our belief in the need for advocacy for children in Group B), the more we were caught in the double bind of retaining our original beliefs, while recognising ever more clearly that they were not necessarily shared by those with whom we tried to establish new working relationships. Fear about re-traumatisation, and sensitisation to any triggers for repetition of painful situations, also made it difficult to build a basis of trust with colleagues in new situations.

We found it difficult to gain access to a community of interest-sharing peers in order to resolve these persistent dilemmas and our own relationships in our professional networks. For Geoffrey Wyatt, Marietta Higgs and Sue Richardson in particular, this amounted to professional exile. Sue Richardson found herself living with what Hollander (1998) refers to, in a different context of exile, as the 'paradox of loss and creativity', i.e. the way in which the psychological crisis of separation and irreparable loss is worked into a different sense of the self and transformed creatively. For example, Sue has taken on a new professional identity as a psychotherapist and has integrated her knowledge and experience of abused children into work with traumatised adults. Heather eventually decided to leave Cleveland and has since set up a specialist child sexual abuse project. It was difficult to frame these as positive choices at the time: it felt like abandoning something that should have been possible to salvage. In hindsight, our respective choices enabled us to develop our practice and to find a few like-minded colleagues.

We were aware that our struggles were part of a wider process that leads to the defensive exclusion of unspeakable truths about child sexual abuse (see Tate, Chapter 1; Richardson, Chapter 12). We came to realise that for this to be transformed into holding difficult information in awareness, including our findings from Cleveland about children in group B, the fragmented narrative of professional endeavour in this field needed to become more integrated and coherent. Drawing on research and clinical practice with victims of sexual abuse trauma, we saw parallels between the need for traumatised children to move from fragmented states towards integration and the need for the professional system to deal with its own fragmentation.

Attachment theory and the construction of a narrative

Bowlby (1969) saw attachment as a behavioural system in which the goal of obtaining care could not be achieved without the co-operation of a caregiver. This system is both goal-directed and goal-corrected, that is attachment behaviour is stimulated by the goal of receiving care and ceases when this goal is met by the right degree of proximity to an attachment figure. Attaining this goal restores the exploratory system, which is overridden during any threat to well-being.

Heard and Lake (1997) have extended Bowlby's model of behavioural systems which maintain proximity and exploration. As part of this extension, the authors have introduced the concept of two major alternative patterns of relating: supportive companionable (SC) and dominating and submissive (D/S). Supportive companionable forms of relating promote the goals of exploration and interest sharing. Supportive companionable relating depends on the availability of responsive, attuned and empathic caregiving. In the face of a threat to well-being, the impact of fear means that dominating or submissive forms of relating are likely to be employed in self-defence and exploration ceases. The latter is maintained or restored by responsive caregiving.

To construct a coherent narrative of our own, we found that, in addition to trauma theory as a vital component of our understanding, an attachment framework was helpful in two important respects. First, it shed light on how children cope with extended periods of abuse by caregivers and how they are likely to react to the impact of intervention on their attachments. Second, it helped us to explore ourselves as professional caregivers. For example, the work of Heard and Lake (1997) has helped us to understand some of the difficult responses in our respective professions and in the community because of the way in which our work aroused fear and anxiety. We could understand better some of our own defensive responses such as anxious care-seeking as part of a bid to continue our explorations. These insights have enabled us to obtain more effective caregiving, to adopt an exploratory, less blaming stance towards the systems we need to understand and towards events which remain unprocessed and to increase our 'autobiographical competence' (Holmes 1993).

The application of attachment theory to our experience as professional caregivers

In exploring the application of attachment theory to professional systems, we pay attention to the kind of caregiving needed by professionals to enable them to deal with threats to well-being and to restore impairments to supportive companionable relating and exploration (see Richardson, Chapter 12). We take into account the way in which the professional's attachment system is likely to be aroused by exposure to work with trauma. In our view, not only high-profile cases like the Cleveland crisis, but also the field of child protection as a whole, operate in a difficult and often threatening environment. As a regular occurrence, the systems of self-defence will tend to be activated and exploratory behaviour will be at risk of being inhibited.

In exploring our respective experiences as child abuse consultant and child psychologist, we discovered that we had been in the same war but on separate battlefields. Sue's professional role meant that she had an overview and a knowledge of events to which Heather did not have access. In turn, Heather's clinical role meant that she could access the internal worlds of some of the children in a way which Sue did not have the opportunity to do. Sue's battle fronts were in the interdisciplinary and public domains – she was a key target for attack by professionals and others with different perceptions, and by the media. Although public and professional perceptions have become better informed, Sue has remained a long-term target of campaign groups. Heather's struggles were less public. She was not targeted in the media: her battle front was alongside the children struggling to resolve their dilemmas. This became a source of long-term stress in her continuing advocacy for children in the courts and the child protection system. The differences in outcome for us as professionals initially threatened to be divisive. We also suffered a great deal from the loss of one another as working colleagues. As a psychologist, Heather was able to maintain her professional autonomy and identity. As a social worker and an employee of the local authority, Sue took the full force of public and political mayhem and was effectively ejected from her professional role. Our stories reflect this difference.

The professional caregiver in Cleveland: Sue Richardson

The post of child abuse consultant which placed me at the centre of the Cleveland crisis had been created as an organisational response to the threat to well-being posed by the Jasmine Beckford Inquiry (London Borough of Brent 1985). This was one of a series of child deaths and subsequent inquiries which aroused public censure in response to the failure of child protection. As a result, the child protection system was bound to be fearful and inclined to self-defence. Several of my peers pointed out the potential danger of accepting a role which they perceived as a defensive shield for the organisation. I did not allow their warnings to influence my decision to accept the post: I felt secure in my attachment to my professional base and as a professional caregiver; I was supported by a network of interest-sharing peers; my exploratory system was operating at a high level; I was full of energy for the task; my self-defence was low. I saw exploratory activity – keeping abreast of current thinking and striving to be at the cutting edge of practice – as the best means of protection for both me and the organisation. The Director of Social Services made it clear that he wanted no scandals as a result of failure to protect children and I took this as my mandate. I did not place much emphasis on my own needs for care: I was accustomed to a professional and organisational culture in which this was usually provided by only a few close colleagues and friends.

The importance of discovery of child sexual abuse and the support provided by like-minded peers initially protected me from responding defensively. I welcomed the discovery of a medical window into the abuse of often very young children and initially perceived the crisis primarily as one of resources. I believe that, had it been possible to protect professional boundaries, the conflict between paediatricians and police surgeons could have been resolved: a new protocol for medical examinations and investigation was being negotiated when the situation finally erupted in the public domain. In the unsupportive and hostile environment which followed, fuelled by the media and the intervention of public figures, the ability of the whole system from government downwards to join in exploration was impaired. Defensive reactions were stimulated by fear of public controversy and of the issue itself. At a local level, this led to the management of the crisis being taken over by the chief executive, to the protection of children not being pursued assertively in the courts and ultimately to a financial settlement with aggrieved parents. At government level, it led to the setting up of a judicial inquiry and to the restriction of professional autonomy via guidance such as the *Memorandum of Good Practice* (Home Office and Department of Health 1992), which was not attuned to the interests of the most vulnerable children in Group B.

Once the inquiry was announced, continued interest sharing with colleagues in other disciplines was seen as a threat. My reluctance to adopt a purely self-protective stance led to arguments with my legal representatives. I invested hope in the inquiry as a means of establishing the truth. Butler-Sloss emphasised that no one was on trial and appeared to want to be genuinely exploratory. However, the adversarial nature of the legal system and of the responses of organisations under scrutiny meant that the Inquiry fell far short of the truth commission I had hoped for.

I found the Inquiry's limited brief to examine arrangements for dealing with suspected cases of child abuse intensely frustrating. My well-being began to suffer. Despite some personal and other support, I became an anxious care seeker. At the same time, I was besieged by demands for care from other anxious care-seekers such as social work colleagues exposed to traumatised children. My professional caregiving capacities were stretched to breaking point. All existing caregiving and care-seeking part-nerships between colleagues were placed under severe stress. For example, the two paediatricians were instructed by their barristers not to associate with me at the Inquiry and numerous attempts were made in cross-exami-nation to split colleagues from one another.

My professional systems and the local community which had previously provided me with a secure base became both frightened and frightening. The traumatic impact of the discovery of widespread child sexual abuse was uncontained. At every level – the professionals, their employers, the community, family and friends – there was a struggle to act coherently and an absence of the kind of caregiving which can help individuals and organisations remain organised in the face of fear. This resulted in defensive attacks, directed at me and my paediatric colleagues especially. We came to be perceived as a threat to the well-being of any system or individual with whom we came into contact. The particular stigma attached to the women professionals at the heart of the crisis was such that my barrister's closing submission on my behalf was that it was not my fault that, through virtue of my job, I had met up with others 'all holding strong views about child abuse' (Butler-Sloss 1988, p.83). It is interesting that Butler-Sloss quoted this part of the submission in her report and denoted my and my colleagues' exploratory, interest-sharing behaviour as part of the problem.

Post-Cleveland, I could find no effective means of self-defence. The pre-vailing dynamics were based on dominance and submission and the only option presented to me by my employers was to submit. I was asked to agree not to work in my chosen field and to remain silent about the crisis. When I refused, redundancy was the only remaining option.

I was devastated by the loss of the work I loved. My equally traumatised peers could not attune to my needs. This left me with feelings of betrayal and my angry care-seeking put a strain on most of my relationships. My decision to undertake psychotherapy training provided some support, advocacy and caregiving but I felt like a refugee. I suffered a prolonged grief reaction for the loss of my former world, exacerbated by practical anxieties about earning a living.

I moved only slowly towards full recognition of what I had lost: loss of my professional identity and role; loss of relationships with colleagues; loss of the opportunity to contribute fully from my experience. I made constant efforts to retrieve the irretrievable. While this motivated me to write, speak and contribute to training events, I felt unassuaged, restless and frequently exhausted. A dilemma was that the only options open to me were private and individual whereas the problem was public and political. Being forced to resort to individual remedies also divided the colleague group and increased my isolation. Adult survivors of abuse became a significant focus of my work and of my support system. Through this affiliation, I could still find room for exploration and hope for renewal.

In 1991, the work of the Cleveland professionals was provided with powerful public affirmation by Roland Summit, an eminent American clinician, who led a standing ovation following a conference symposium presented by myself, Geoffrey Wyatt and Heather Bacon. Three experienced childcare professionals in the audience were prompted to disclose that they had been prevented by their employers from offering their help in 1987. This brought home to me that my sense of isolation and betrayal was based in reality. I released a lot of pent-up feelings of misery, recognised that I was suffering from secondary stress and felt a little stronger.

Throughout this time, I was actively supported and encouraged not to submit to the dynamics of fear and their destructive consequences by my immediate family and a few supportive companions with whom I could laugh, rage and tramp the hills. I also needed a lot of time and space of my own and wore out a pair of boots on frequent solitary walks. Holding on to and creating a personal supportive environment not only provided comfort, soothing and nurture, but also enabled my exploratory and interest-sharing systems to remain active rather than be entirely overridden by self-defence. I was able to sustain my professional interest in childhood trauma and to seek out new peers with whom I could explore this subject. Above all, I held on to what I believed was the importance of bearing witness to what we had learned from Cleveland's children and refused, despite the personal and professional cost, to be silenced.

In the longer term, sometimes I have still been misperceived by others as a potential threat to their well-being. This misperception has affected my role in the field of child protection. Despite finding a new role as a psychotherapist, I missed this field a lot. I wanted to find a place in it for my experience and my psychotherapeutic skills. I found it very difficult to find and to invest trust in another employer after my experiences in Cleveland. My tentative steps in this direction (see Tate, Chapter 1) led me to return to independent practice.

I find it sad to see the backlash against professional endeavour in the child protection field and the failure to integrate the learning from Cleveland about children in Group B who rely on an adult to advocate on their behalf. I have felt painfully excluded from the discourse on these difficult issues and have had to find creative ways of continuing to use my knowledge and skills. My experiences have increased my interest in ways in which supportive companionable relating can be maintained or restored, in organisations and elsewhere, whenever it starts to crumble under the pressure of fear. I still take heart from the human capacity to achieve this and hold on to my belief in everyone's potential for growth and healing.

The professional caregiver in Cleveland: Heather Bacon

As the only clinical psychologist working with children in Cleveland who became involved in cases of sexual abuse prior to and during the crisis, it was difficult to find interest-sharing peers. This led me to associate more with other professional disciplines in child protection, particularly social workers and paediatricians, with whom I developed close links and was able to explore and begin to understand about child sexual abuse, a new area of recognition for me in my work. I also sought training and expertise from reading and conferences outside the area (problem-solving and exploratory behaviour). Because psychologists are autonomous professionals, we can be independent and creative practitioners rather than organisationally minded, and that was the way I operated, enjoying new challenges in the clinical work. As Butler Sloss (1988, p.154) expressed it: 'The difficulties with … trying to establish sensible working arrangements with colleagues left Mrs Bacon not only independent as she chose to describe it but also isolated and unsupported in the complex work she undertook.' Clearly this departure held risks, but they were overridden by the excitement of learning how to do the work better in order to be a 'rescuer' of the children whose difficulties I was at last beginning to understand. As the Inquiry report put it: 'She had a strong commitment to help individual children through the use of professional skill and experience. She saw all her work in terms of the therapeutic value it had for the child and the family' (Butler-Sloss 1988, p.154).

As the crisis developed I became increasingly allied with a small group of social workers, relying on them as supportive caregivers when facing new and difficult issues that had to be processed at the individual and personal level as well as the professional level. This protected or prevented me from becoming aware of isolation from my employing health trust. During the inquiry I saw my position as sustained by the trust, and indeed they found no cause to discipline me. However, there was a conflict to be resolved about accommodating to the system in order, as the Trust's barrister put it, 'to fight again another day', or sticking my neck out to support my colleagues and my beliefs. I felt that my professional attachment system (the district health authority) was caretaking me in order to ensure my compliance, while at the same time making sure they did not 'see' me except to make sure I was not going to bring criticism on them. Unbelievably as I look back now, they did not acknowledge that my work required support, or provide me with any at a level that would have been useful. This was stressful.

During the Inquiry, I felt pressure to make me (a rebel) comply as an example to others. There were pressures to split the alliances I made with colleagues, and to combat this threat I stuck to them more closely in public, a defence which reduced my exploratory behaviour and ability to continue healthy debate with them about the real clinical problems in the work.

I coped by believing that in the end the Inquiry would see and acknowledge the truth (that we had been doing our best as a co-operative team to protect abused children). When it did not, I was quite devastated. I was criticised for not separating evaluative and therapeutic work on the grounds that 'basing my work with some of the children on the assumption that they had been sexually abused' had 'clouded my perception of the role of the psychologist' (Butler-Sloss 1988, p.154). Paradoxically, the report acknowledged 'the problem that arises when there is reason to believe there may be abuse and the child may need help to tell' (Butler-Sloss 1988, p.206). Since I accepted (and still accept) that the medical diagnosis of abuse is the only window of opportunity for some children, this left me in a double bind: I was criticised for not making my own independent assessment but this criticism appeared to me to negate the value of multidisciplinary work.

The most traumatising aspect of Cleveland for me was that I was made to abandon my work or, as I saw it, the children who had trusted me to help them. The guilt that this engendered was paralysing for a time. The next worst aspect was that my paediatric colleagues were banned from dealing with child abuse cases and Sue was unable to remain in her post. For this reason I saw the politics of the child protection system as persecutory and still perceive it as such.

Since that time I have made more efforts to ensure a secure base for my work, by moving to a different area, embedding the work in a supportive team, and seeking skilled supervision. None of these has come easily although they should be basic requirements for all professionals in this demanding field. After seven years I was lucky enough to start a small, specialist project, in a supportive companionable relationship with a trusted colleague. The work is still not adequately recognised or resourced, but some of the children are protected and we continue to develop our practice. This validates me enough to keep going despite pessimism about the lack of progress in the field as a whole. I am aware that the required secure base in the agency as a whole is still missing and that this makes me vulnerable. I have experienced re-traumatisation and have periods of crippling anxiety and confusion, particularly when I had to take on board the issues of a ritual abuse case. I am often frightened, but have learned to recognise this as a healthy warning signal. I still find it difficult to get angry although I know this would be protective, and at times probably achieve more: I recognise this as the legacy of being terrorised. I'm working on it!

The other vital component of work over the whole period since Cleveland has been the continuing contact, through thick and thin, with Sue Richardson and others who were there. This has been essential in helping me to process and develop my thinking, regardless of their departure from the field of action. The veterans of a war must feel the same. The recognition of shared experience and the mutual ability to support and trust, to disagree, argue with, and return over and over to the narrative, tussling with the contradictions and gaps until we began to make sense, has been the only way I could have constructed my own narrative and cleared the blanket of fog that persisted after the crisis and still threatens to descend at times.

Towards a collective narrative

One of the key effects of Cleveland is that the narratives of the children, their carers and the key professionals were lost. For this reason, we have encouraged all our contributors to construct their own narrative experience of Cleveland.

Several separate and competing narratives need to be brought together in order to overcome barriers to learning (Richardson 1991a) and undo the dissociative splits which are inherent in the field and which pose a real problem for many victims of child sexual abuse in our society. Some of this work has been undertaken from a radical feminist perspective (Itzin 2000). Itzin brings together a diverse collection of professional endeavour and reviews implications for policy and practice. We need to build on dialogues of this kind in order to create the 'storied community as secure base' (Papadopoulos 1999), formed from the collective narrative of child and adult survivors, protective parents, professionals and the community. This narrative must include an understanding of the issues facing children in Group B. It needs to be adequately supported and to be conducted in a supportive and companionable way. The sharing of the narratives in a supportive and companionable way would allow for a positive recognition and acceptance of uncertainty and differences in viewpoint, and for tolerance rather than avoidance of conflict when trying to achieve resolution. In short, the narrative should stimulate an open-minded and lively debate.

We are left with the following key questions for individuals and professional systems engaged in child protection:

- What is the minimum supportive environment needed to promote endeavour in this field?

- How can the effects of fear which give rise to dominating and submissive forms of relating best be managed?

- What is an acceptable system of personal defence for professionals to adopt without harming the interests of children?

- What should professionals do if their exploration risks prejudicing the interests of children in the short term?

- How can the damage done by the way in which professional exploration has been treated – i.e. its legacy of fear – be repaired?

- How can Cleveland be incorporated as part of the discourse of child protection in a way that includes the needs of children in Group B?

CHAPTER 3

Attachment, trauma and child sexual abuse

An exploration

Heather Bacon

Attachment has become the mainstay of my clinical practice and this chapter reflects my continuing search for ways to understand and help abused children. It explores the way in which attachment theory can contribute to our understanding of children's vulnerability to sexual abuse and how sexual abuse, particularly by attachment figures, might traumatise children. It proposes that working with their attachments can help children recover from child sexual abuse. It considers the vexed question of the 'cycle of abuse'. The particular difficulties facing sexually aggressive children in changing their behaviour are highlighted. A case example of positive intervention demonstrates the application of attachment theory to the intergenerational impact of abuse.

Attachment relationships

Attachment patterns formed in infancy can powerfully persist throughout life and influence how the child will behave as an adult, particularly in intimate relationships and as a parent (Ainsworth and Eichberg 1991; Crittenden and Ainsworth 1989; Rutter 1989). There is a growing body of evidence that neurobiological correlates of attachment patterns are laid down in the brain (see Glaser 2000 for an overview). These earliest, most intimate relationships are highly significant for later well-being and emotional development.

Attachments can be categorised as secure or insecure. Research has identified three main groupings of insecure attachment: anxious/ambivalent, avoidant/dismissive, disorganised/disoriented (Ainsworth *et al.* 1978; Crittenden 1988; Main and Solomon 1986).

Coping with distress

Attachment styles are evident in the way the young child copes with threat or distress. A securely attached child will approach the carer readily, confident in the carer's capacity for empathic attunement (Stern 1985) and will experience unconditional comfort and understanding. The internal representation of self that develops is 'I am valued, worthy of protection, love and nurturance, and I am capable and can develop'. This is the basis of trust in others and a secure attachment contributes to how well the child will deal with adverse events. Insecurely attached children may not experience empathic attunement, protection, comfort and validation, and the growing child and emerging adult is less flexible and adaptable. Their internal models of experiences in relationships (IMERs: Heard and Lake 1997) may not be based on a premise of trust, but on the need to accommodate to adult demands. The child may learn that the self is unworthy of nurturance and protection.

Attachment and child sexual abuse

There is little evidence about how different attachment styles might relate to the way in which children experience and cope with sexual abuse. Schneider-Rosen *et al.* (1985, p.204) found no clear relationship between quality of attachment and type of maltreatment. They make the point that:

> quality of attachment represents neither enduring nor transient influences alone but rather a multiplicity of factors that need to be considered in combination with one another in order to account for and adequately explain the process whereby a particular developmental outcome may be achieved. (Schneider-Rosen *et al.* 1985, p.210)

There are several discussions of maltreatment and attachment style in the literature (Cassidy and Shaver 1999), but none really provides unequivocal guidance for clinicians to rely on. At the same time it is clear that quality of attachment does act as a mediator in recovery from abuse (e.g. Egeland, Jacobvitz and Sroufe 1988). It is also clear that sexual abuse by attachment figures presents different, more complex problems for the child (James 1994; Ross 1997).

It is important to gender any discussion about attachment relationships and sexual abuse and much of the literature is inadequate in this respect. Most of the attachment literature is about mothers and children, rather than fathers. The weight of scrutiny can seem to rest on mothers and this is unfair. Alexander (1992) suggests that sexual abuse is more likely to occur where children are not securely attached to their caregivers. This may be simplistic, particularly as her analysis takes no account of the abuser's responsibility for sexual abuse.

Attachment styles

Children who develop avoidant attachment styles experience the parent as controlling, rejecting, interfering or agitating. Such children learn to keep a safe distance, denying or not showing their distress. They may eventually lose touch with feelings altogether, or only express emotion inappropriately with disturbed or aggressive behaviour in other settings. This might provide some explanation for the controlling, sexually aggressive behaviour of some children. Alexander (1992) identifies an avoidant/resistant attachment pattern with a theme of role reversal, where children adopt the roles and expectations of parents, perhaps becoming sexual partners to the parent or nurturing rather than being nurtured. Abusers manipulate children's attachments with their mothers so that the child believes that the mother will be non-protective (Wyre 2000). Children may comfort their mother while accommodating to ongoing sexual abuse by the father. The abuse remains undisclosed because the child fears that the non-abusing carer will be unable to cope. If a non-abusing mother or father does not recognise the child's emotional needs, the child is rendered more vulnerable to an abuser outside the family who offers the promise of attention. There is some evidence that parental distance and unavailability may also be associated with sibling incest (Smith and Israel 1987).

There is little research about children's attachment relationships with male primary caregivers who are sexual abusers. Coercive sexual behaviour, antisociality and aggression in adult life have been associated with insecure paternal avoidant attachment (Smallbone and Dadds 2000). Saradjian's (1996) work with women perpetrators illustrates the high incidence of insecure attachment histories in this minority of sexual offenders. The central problem of attachment to the perpetrator, and the resultant dilemmas for children abused in the family, are described by Ross (1997), who makes them a key part of therapeutic work.

Chaotic or disorganised attachment styles (Crittenden 1988; Lyons-Ruth and Jacobvitz 1999; Main and Solomon 1996) may mean that children who cannot find an effective strategy to achieve closeness resort to a mixture of behaviours such as avoidance, angry approach, hyperactivity and disorientation. In extreme instances, the child may withdraw completely or 'freeze' physically and psychologically. This can occur in response to a frightening, abusing caregiver. In the trauma-organised attachments (Bentovim 1992) characteristic of chaotic, abusive family environments and some institutional settings, there may be indiscriminate violence and sexual abuse of children. The perpetrator may use alcohol and substance abuse in order to dissociate from their own feelings of abandonment and memories of abuse. The non-abusive carer with a disorganised attachment history may become overwhelmed with a sense of history repeating itself. The child may have only siblings or peers to turn to in the face of chaotic caregivers.

Trauma and attachment

Psychological trauma means that the child's coping ability is overwhelmed by an actual or perceived threat. Children cannot cope as well as adults with trauma (Perry and Pollard 1998). Where the trauma is that of ongoing abuse, many factors in both child and circumstances affect the outcome, as does the meaning of the event for the child. Children process and remember events very differently at different stages of cognitive development. The intrusive process of traumatisation affects all realms of the child's mental organisation, memory, identity formation, emotional and spiritual development.

The post-traumatic stress disorder (PTSD) model, developed by clinicians to describe the problems of well-functioning individuals faced with one overwhelming event in the form of a 'critical incident' such as a fatality or kidnap, does not entirely fit the problems of children undergoing a long series of abusive events. Chronic abuse is not necessarily accompanied by obvious violence and danger (Finkelhor 1990; Finkelhor and Browne 1986). Herman (1992, p.119) addressed this in an alternative conceptualisation of 'complex PTSD' resulting from long-term abuse. James (1994, pp.55–56) makes a helpful distinction between attachment trauma (related to loss or unavailability of a primary attachment) and trauma-related attachment problems (arising from traumatising events that compromised the attachment relationship). Wieland (1997) describes very helpful clinical approaches for exploring how children themselves understand their abuse, making the point that the internal world of the traumatised child must be addressed, particularly the internal working models of themselves and others.

The trauma of long-term sexual abuse may be hidden, because the child develops coping mechanisms which ensure secrecy, and more obvious features of PTSD may be absent, delayed or obscured. The trauma may lie in the cognitive realm, in terms of distortions about sex, families and relationships, which are then applied indiscriminately to other situations as the child tries to deal with the world. The trauma of sexual abuse 'does not come from the abuse alone, but from the preceding conditioning process, and the aftermath' (Finkelhor 1990, p.329).

How young children react to trauma

Infants' and young children's brain processes and physiological defences are not yet sufficiently developed to cope with trauma, including the stressor of sexual abuse. Research indicates that stress alters the developing brain, so that the stress response becomes the template for brain organisation (Golier and Yehuda 1998; Perry and Pollard 1998). This is characterised by primitive protective responses to fear: fight, flight or freeze reactions. Young children cannot escape by moving away so will cry, dissociate or become unresponsive. These responses may become habitual, and the child will be constantly afraid and hypervigilant or irritable and hyperactive, and easily restimulated by reminders of the traumatising event. James (1994) describes various coping strategies: becoming a 'sitting duck', who is apparently dull, stupid and unaware, by lessening incoming information in order to reduce stress and eventually being unable to perceive actual threat; becoming a 'moving target' (hyperactive); becoming 'unseen', by attending to an internal world (dissociation). All these strategies are employed at the expense of exploration, creativity, play and the other tasks of childhood.

Children who cannot learn to regulate the intensity of feeling remain prone to states of fear, terror, excitement and elation; or shame, disgust and despair, depending on which aspect of the autonomic nervous system predominates. The discontinuities of thought, movement, expression and feeling observed in sexually abused children may be the result of sudden dissociative switches. These might occur when, threatened with an intrusive thought or feeling, the child's state of consciousness changes so that the child occupies an alternative reality.

Threats to attachment

Attachment relationships influence the ways in which sexual abuse trauma is resolved and healed in the longer term. Loss of the primary attachment figure represents a loss of everything to the child. Children experience their primary attachment figure as necessary for survival. Children's deepest fears can be alleviated only by attachment figures, whether safe or not. The child abused by a primary attachment figure suffers in multiple and complex ways. There is the pain, confusion and fear of the abuse itself; there is the extreme contradiction inherent in the source of danger and the source of protection residing in the one person. Perhaps most terrifying of all there is the fear of loss of the attachment relationship, which children often believe will happen if they try to protect themselves from being abused by a parent.

Traumatic sexualisation

It could be that children whose abuser is their primary attachment figure are especially vulnerable to becoming sexualised in the context of that relationship. Sexually abused children may learn that closeness equates with sexual behaviour, pain and confusion. Sexual behaviour with the caregiver may be one way that some sexually abused children achieve closeness: this does not imply that the child bears any responsibility for the abuse, but does mean that a sexualised attachment to the abuser may have to be addressed.

Traumatic sexualisation (Finkelhor and Browne 1986, p.181) is the result of children being taught by abusers how to behave in sexually inappropriate ways, by means of positive reinforcement and by controlling and frightening strategies. In addition to the social learning theories about the aetiology of sexual offending, a multifactorial model (Finkelhor 1984; Wolfe 1984) should encompass links between attachment, caregiving and abuse. Caregiving interactions with infants and children do involve intimate body contact, as does adult sexual behaviour. Bowlby (1969) points out that the three systems of parenting, sexuality and adult attachment are usually kept separate in our culture. However, Smallbone and Dadds (2000), in a study of male abusing behaviour, suggest that if distress (which normally activates the attachment system) instead activates the sexual arousal system, the result might be that the adult engages in sexually coercive behaviour because this produces relief from immediate anxiety. If proximity to a child, which normally activates the attachment system, is linked to distress (normally linked to the attachment system, but here linked to sexual arousal), then there may be activation of the sexual behaviour system. It may be that sexually traumatised children learn that sexual behaviour can bring relief from internal anxiety.

Wider problems with family relationships

Family difficulties arising in the wake of trauma can obscure the serious attachment problems that are generated by the traumatising event. Chronic and repeated abuse can result in a very disturbed relationship with the non-abusing parent, usually the mother. Children may believe they were not protected because they are unlovable, or that the non-abusing parent wants them to forgive the abuser. Serious attachment disturbances and traumatising experiences often coexist, and are interrelated, resulting in complex treatment needs.

Systemic approaches (e.g. Bentovim 1992) to family violence, including child sexual abuse, are criticised for their failure to address the gendered nature of power and responsibility (Itzin 2000). However, a systemic framework can be very helpful in addressing treatment dilemmas provided that the responsibility for the abuse is placed where it belongs: with the abuser. In each new generation, children can stimulate and challenge parents to update their own attachment models. This can provide forward direction and hope for parents who have themselves been hurt by abuse in their own childhood. A therapist can support change towards a more secure attachment style between parent and child. Working in this way is consistent with a systemic view.

Forgetting, remembering and healing

Many abused children deny their abuse or appear to resist intervention to protect them (Bacon and Richardson 2000). Such children may suffer from dissociative states. This phenomenon has been envisaged as one end of a continuum where 'normal' includes being able to perform two tasks at once, daydreaming or 'going on autopilot', and 'abnormal' consists of altered states of consciousness, trance-like states, disconnection, splitting and numbing (Putnam 1993). More recent evidence (Putnam 1997) points to the existence of a fundamentally different developmental trajectory resulting in 'pathological' rather than 'normal' dissociative states, childhood maltreatment being identified as the most likely source. Putnam (1997) identifies Bowlby's (1973) observations of 'profound detachment' in children who lose their primary carer as dissociative states. There is a clear gender difference: females are more likely to dissociate than males (Perry and Pollard 1998).

Disorganised attachment patterns are also seen as increasing vulnerability to developing a dissociative disorder (Liotti 1992; Putnam 1997) including dissociative identity disorder, formerly known as multiple personality disorder (Putnam 1993). The latter is frequently associated with severe forms of child sexual abuse such as multi-perpetrator, ritual or organised abuse (Gough 1996; Hudson 1994).

Helping children to process trauma

Up to the age of 3 or 4, children are unable to be 'meta-cognitive' (Main 1991), i.e. they cannot think about their own thinking or feelings. Symbolic interaction such as play accompanies the development of this capacity and the child can begin to take different perspectives, separating their own and other people's experiences and thoughts. Young, severely abused children, who have no opportunity to process and integrate the traumatic memories into the growing self, may go on to suffer the long-term effects of trauma so vividly described by survivors (Lindsay and Read 1994; Stein *et al.* 1988). Memories of trauma are laid down in an encapsulated form, inaccessible, separate from other events, and not in conscious awareness. The idea of 'false memory syndrome', useful to adults who wish to deny the reality of child sexual abuse, is a misrepresentation of how such memories may be accessed. In reality, children who 'forget' by dissociating can be helped to re-associate with their thoughts and feelings as part of good therapeutic practice (British Psychological Society (BPS) 1995). Memories of abuse can be recovered, explored and mastered in play, the normal way by which children make sense of stressful or confusing events. Re-enactment in play helps the child process the experience and think about it, moving it into a symbolic form. This is important because the child then connects and gains control of the feelings associated with the event. The monster can be beaten, and the child can become the hero.

Children without the time or safety in which to play are deprived of this process of internal healing. Instead, the child is left with a rigid set of responses, a limited repertoire for expressing feelings and thoughts, few coping skills, or chaotic fragmentation of the personality. The grief and healing work for abuse is remembering, not forgetting. This requires a safe, containing attachment relationship. The therapist who gives the child space and time to explore at a manageable pace can then acknowledge and witness the child's unspeakable truths and point out that the child has survived and can grow.

Without therapeutic intervention, dissociation may become habitual whenever the child is under stress, as this prevents the child being overwhelmed by feelings, thoughts or sensations. Thinking and feeling are avoided, or become disconnected. If an abuser tells the child, 'this isn't hurting you', while at the same time the child experiences pain, the only way the child can achieve coherence is to block out either the words or the bodily sensations. Children who cannot listen to what people say, or cannot allow feelings to register, cannot effectively solve problems. They may also resort to self-harming actions when emotionally distressed, because the anaesthetising effect will dull pain and reduce unbearably high arousal and anxiety.

Perry and Pollard (1998, p. 46) argue that 'understanding the persistence of fear-related emotional, behavioural, cognitive and physiologic patterns can lead to focused therapeutic experiences that modify those parts of the brain affected by trauma'. They argue for 'early identification and proactive interventions that will improve our ability to protect and heal … traumatized children.'

Attachment as a mediator in the long-term effects of sexual abuse

Even where children show no obvious problems, the dynamics of childhood sexual abuse might resurface in the area of interpersonal relationships. Main and Goldwyn (1984) suggest that a resistant or avoidant child may become a dismissive adult, idealising relationships, unable to recall childhood, uncomfortable with intimacy, and subsequently disappointed or even re-abused. An anxious or ambivalent child may become a confused and anxious adult: clinging, dependent and jealous, and overly emotionally expressive. A disorganised child might show a mixture of avoidant and preoccupied traits. This category has also been linked with more serious mental health problems.

On the other hand, many children recover from abuse and do not become abusers themselves. The most important factor for a positive resolution is a relationship with a safe, protective carer who can face the child's fears and help the child to think and feel his or her way to integration of the trauma, and to reorganise distorted thoughts and attributions. Securely attached children are more able to recover from adverse experiences: they have the capacity for self-repair (James 1994, p.145). As Ambridge (Chapter 10) describes, mothers whose children are securely attached do the best job for them. Where the relationship is less secure, they can still help provided they are given support.

Implications for treatment

Rather than the therapist working solely with the child, a combination of work on attachment relationships, therapy for the individual child, and joint sessions including the parents, can produce a more successful outcome. By creating a protective environment, new ways of relating may be found, and old patterns can be discarded. If insecure attachment problems predate and are compounded by the sexual abuse, the parent may need support to arrive at a more secure and nurturing relationship with the child. The therapist may helpfully take a 'grandparent' role to parent and child, providing a safe and nurturing new attachment in which patterns of relating may change.

Long-term sexual abuse distorts and impairs the child's sense of identity. Parents may have little idea how to go about putting this right. A model of a safe and nurturing attachment in therapy may be helpful in guiding child and parent to a better way of exploring and solving the trauma-related problems. Parents with their own history of abuse may need help to explore this, to set aside the effects, and to prioritise their own child. In this approach to treatment, the adult may need as much if not more time than the child.

The concept of a trauma bond (James 1994, p.24) describes children who are assaulted and in effect held hostage by their attachment figures. The relationship is based in terror rather than in love and separation is in itself traumatic. The child in a trauma bond with an abusing attachment figure is under constant stress, the response to which becomes the organising principle for behaviour. Any reminders of the traumatising event evoke a high degree of anxiety: the child may be overwhelmed by feelings of terror or panic, or be compelled to re-enact the traumatic event. This often occurs in therapy, when children let down their guard only to find that a flood of uncontrollable and frightening sensations or images may intrude. Such children are overactive and jumpy (hypervigilant) and may regress alarmingly. The therapist can use a gradual process of desensitisation to regulate the child's affect and help the child gain some sense of comfort without being emotionally overwhelmed. With patience, tolerance and low-key reactions, the child can gain trust and stop monitoring the adult's every move. Without help, trauma bonds can be a blueprint for avoidance and mistrust of self and others, or of abuse of the next generation of children (James 1994).

The vexed question of the 'cycle of abuse'

The 'cycle of abuse' is often used as a generic term to refer to three different cycles. First, the process whereby the child internalises the behaviour of the perpetrator and goes on to abuse others. Second, non-protective parenting, resulting from the impact of the parent's unresolved trauma. Third, what can be described as a cycle of pain in which the survivor's struggles with the long-term effects of abuse can contribute to the intergenerational transmission of insecure attachment. Those affected by the first cycle are primarily male. Those affected by the second and third are primarily female. None of these outcomes is a foregone conclusion for men or for women.

There are many factors that contribute to preventing the survivor of childhood abuse becoming caught up in any of the three cycles. Mediating factors are particularly related to the way that the growing child and the adult processes the childhood experiences (Main 1991). A crucial contribution is the survivor's capacity for reflective thinking (Fonagy *et al.* 1991). Adults who can recall and reflect on their own childhood can decide to do things differently when they become parents. Many parents, particularly mothers, will strive to protect their child when abuse comes to light and will be able to prevent further abuse. Many survivors, both male and female, become protective parents (Bacon, Chapter 4; Brooks, Chapter 5; Ambridge, Chapter 10). However, both mothers and fathers who were not given help or protection as children may be struggling to overcome the ongoing effects of their own childhood abuse. The tasks of repair and healing may involve a painful inner journey, continued into adult life. Even when children do receive adequate help at the time, there may be some parts of the healing process that are left until adult life (Ambridge, Henry and Richardson, Chapter 11).

Case example: intervening in the intergenerational impact of abuse

> Linda and her daughter Gemma, aged 8, were referred because Gemma was sexually abused by an older boy. In the background was a history of more serious abuse by Gemma's maternal grandfather, and by her cousin. Linda took immediate protective action when these events came to light: this meant cutting off from her own family. Gemma was able to deal with her feelings about the boy and then chose to finish therapy. After an interval, Linda felt Gemma needed more help: she was difficult and moody at home and could not talk about her grandfather. Gemma was ambivalent about attending, and although her mother tried to encourage her to talk, they often sat in silent tears together. Gemma adopted a com-

forting, parental role with her mother, wiping her eyes. Neither could easily talk about the family history, or the extended family's rejection when Linda told them she believed her daughter. Linda described a good relationship with her father, but knew that her sister had been abused.

Shortly afterwards, Gemma's great-grandmother died. Linda had never told her about the abuse, fearing 'it would have killed her'. Linda realised she might see her father at the funeral for the first time since Gemma's abuse came to light. Beforehand, Linda had a very distressing recurrent dream that her father was molesting her at a party, in front of the whole family. Nevertheless Linda decided to go to the funeral with her daughter. In the event her father did not attend. Linda came alone to the next appointment. She began to talk hesitantly about whether her father could have abused her, and to connect her poor physical health and constant pain with these feelings. She agreed to be put in touch with a survivor support group. In this way, the cycle of pain might begin to break.

Despite the efforts of victims to break free, abuse is perpetrated across and between generations. Some victims deal with their pain by taking a position of power in relationships, to reduce the risk of further hurt to themselves. Male victims do appear to be more at risk than female victims in this respect, and it is worryingly harder to recognise and help them as children. Childhood abuse (often undisclosed) underlies the behaviour of many adult perpetrators (Egeland *et al.* 1988; Wolfe 1984). One risk factor for becoming a perpetrator may be whether the abuse was normalised rather than experienced as traumatic or wrong (Briggs and Hawkins 1996; Finkelhor 1984). Abusers do create the next generation of victims and sexually aggressive children. Mechanisms by which male abusers do so include deliberate premature sexualisation and teaching children through social learning to arouse other children. Some abusive males may not be interested simply in deflecting the pain of past abuse via the victimisation of children. Child victims may be so cleverly groomed that they believe they are the abuser, for example when the perpetrator teaches the child to perform sexual acts on himself without touching the child's genitals. They may be sexualised to the point of seeking sexual contact with adults, thus feeding into the male abusers' view that children are provocative.

Problems for protective parenting

Non-abusing is not always equal to protective. This is not a condemnation, but needs to be understood in terms of attachment patterns through different life stages. Sufficient recovery for a single individual at one stage may not be enough at another to establish sustaining adult relationships or to screen out the ones that are destructive or abusive. For non-protective mothers, the relationship with the male perpetrator may be significant. They may be paralysed and split by a conflict of loyalties between partner and child, or fearful of the perpetrator. Some mothers believe, and at the same time deny, the reality of the abuse, 'wanting to hear it' both from the child and the perpetrator. This is difficult for professionals to acknowledge, but an understanding of the mother's attachment needs can be helpful in accepting these very real dilemmas in a non-judgemental way.

Adults (particularly women) abused as children may have coped by mini-mising the effects or by denying the reality of their own abuse, sometimes via the mechanism of dissociation. Survivors whose emotional energy as children was used to protect and defend themselves, rather than to develop and learn through play and exploration, may take longer to reach maturity. Many women survivors report that their own memories surface when they become parents. Some may find it hard to perceive the reality of what is happening to their child. Others burden themselves unnecessarily, looking ahead to problems that their child may not have to deal with. Some fathers report similar struggles.

Case example: father out of control

A male survivor of sadistic abuse described a fear of children almost amounting to a phobia, as the sight of a child could produce flashbacks to his own abuse. This man, who had two young children, indulged in rough and tumble play that verged on being fearful and physically risky for his daughters. He experienced very conflicting and highly aroused emotions during intimate contact with them, which led to perceiving them as an emotional threat. While stating vehemently that he would do anything to prevent harm to them and would kill anyone who abused them, he also denigrated their childishness, calling them 'monsters'. Both children were significantly failing to thrive. This ambivalent emotional state in a parent can make it very difficult to provide responsive, attuned parenting, and may increase the risk of abuse to a child.

Children who go on to abuse others

Recognition and intervention with this frequently ignored and misunderstood group of children and young people can contribute to breaking the cycle of abuse whereby some victims become perpetrators.

Children who sexually abuse others may say they see nothing wrong in it. In fact, it is usually obvious that they do know they are doing harm. They may find it difficult to stop unless their own abusive experiences can be accessed and the person responsible seen to be blamed or punished. Sexually aggressive children, almost all boys, seen in a specialist sexual abuse project (Bacon, Chapter 4), rarely present with their own victimisation disclosed. They are more likely to live in homes with a high level of domestic violence (81 per cent) or with an adult convicted of an offence against a child, and with one or more non-protective parents. The project found that a greater proportion of the children were eventually taken into care than in other groups (28 per cent) and one-third of the group remained unprotected. These children may go on to be vulnerable to further abuse in the care system (G. Hobbs, C. Hobbs and Wynne 1999).

The project's stance is that the children are primarily victims, even though they may not perceive themselves as such and we may not know the source of their sexually aggressive behaviour. Work with adult offenders rightly focuses on the adult taking responsibility for the abusing behaviour. With young (often pre-school) children, we cannot expect the child to take responsibility for the behaviour in the same way. This is a source of difficulty: in the district where I work, older children who commit sexual offences are not registered as victims under child protection procedures.

The work may involve parents in carrying some of the responsibility by imposing external control on the child or adolescent. In direct work with the child, in addition to encouraging the child to explore feelings of powerlessness and the resultant need to bully, it may be necessary to work directly towards changing internal scripts.

Changing perceptions

Children who become abusive have distorted perceptions about how to be close to others. Many children, particularly girls like K in our project, understand the need to change. K was able to address this herself, unlike her denying and abusive parents: 'I won't do the same, because I am doing work with B [therapist] and I don't want to become an abuser'. Other children, particularly boys like S, aged 9, with very low self-esteem, use aggression to promote contact with others, and are often excluded from school for bullying. Although unable to envisage the cycle of abuse at any level of sophistication, S was still able to decide that if he hurt people they wouldn't want to be his friends and that therefore he had 'better be nice'. Many children do want to take responsibility for their own abusing behaviour but can do so only if they are supported and accepted. Recognising one's own hurt inner child is probably the key to achieving true victim empathy. Therapy can be effective when a potential perpetrator is still a child, if the therapist is willing to hold on to the pain involved for a sexually aggressive child in facing their need to hurt others.

Sexualised children have particular difficulty with closeness and any activity that might equate with sexual arousal. Work may need to include more direct cognitive restructuring, including modelling and practice by the child. Other ways must be found to approach others, and to achieve proximity and friendship based on co-operation and respect for boundaries between self and others. This may prevent the victimisation of other children in a way that intervening to protect the victim cannot in itself accomplish.

Pathways to healing: breaking the cycle in the child's inner world

There are many pathways to healing. It is important that the experiences are actively processed and integrated at all levels – cognitive, emotional and social. For this to occur, the painful experiences must be somehow held in awareness long enough for processing.

Child victims can work in their own way on experiences of abuse, given a safe and holding relationship with a therapist. Children are not simply passive recipients of abusive behaviour by adults but strive to cope with the experience, and they can take an active part in recovering. It is most instructive and humbling to see children do this. Without even referring directly to the abuse experience but by reconnoitring and gradually approaching it in play, painting or other creative enactment, children can master overwhelmingly fearful material. This no longer remains in a raw form, ready to spring out as flashbacks or behavioural re-enactments. The child's healing will occur when the therapist trusts the process, gives it time, safety and space and bears witness to the child's work. While it may be impossible to deal effectively with the abuser, there is some comfort in knowing that such acknowledgement of the child's experiences and feelings, leading to integration of the child's sense of self, can be central to healing.

Conclusion

The potential impact of abuse on the next generation is broken by many children, adults, parents and families without effective intervention or therapeutic help (Kelly 2000). Attachment theory helps us to understand and support the healing process. It also allows for creative responses to the 'cycle of abuse' when it is harder to break. The best 'therapy' for abuse is the cessation of the abuse, and real healing is impossible where abuse continues. We have not yet begun to 'stop abusers abusing' (Itzin 2000). It is clear that without intervention, some child victims (mainly boys) may go on to abuse. They may become adults who fail to protect or repeat patterns of insecure attachment that render children vulnerable.

Protective support for the child and non-abusing parent can be of real assistance in the task of rebuilding lives when abuse comes to light. Survivors and parents have a vital contribution to making the child protection system take stock and work more effectively. Professionals must seek their views and include them in planning, and as direct participants, in therapeutic work with their children.

Professionals can draw on new perspectives in research about attachment and abuse, striving to bridge the gap between theory and practice. As always, we learn best from the children we work with. The unequivocal message they send us is that the 'dance of attachment' (James 1994, p.268) matters most in recovery from trauma.

CHAPTER 4

Telling the baby crocodile's story
Attachment and the continuum of disclosure

Heather Bacon

Last year 25,000 children called ChildLine about abuse. The likelihood of these problems ever coming to court or even reaching the Child Protection system is slim and even when they do, they are likely to be passive or unwilling recipients of the system. (Howarth 1999)

Cleveland and beyond

The majority of children I worked with as a child psychologist in Cleveland in 1987 were unable to disclose their abuse, despite in many cases having been subjected to serious sexual assault. Some were able to disclose after being afforded protection from further abuse, but many more remained silent. The concept of the 'continuum of disclosure' (Richardson 1991b, p.68) describes some of the dynamic factors that influenced their disclosure process. Since Cleveland, I have worked in a neighbouring area with children referred to a specialist child protection project that forms part of the child mental health service. This experience has confirmed and broadened the insights gained in Cleveland about the process of disclosure, and the challenges for achieving child-centred protection. This chapter moves away from a narrower band of cases that presented medically or through the child protection system, to a broader mental health perspective. It highlights the crucial importance of mothers, who have to deal with a crisis for themselves and for their children, often in a family context of male dominance which sometimes includes violence.

Classification of children in whom sexual abuse is suspected

When working with children who may have been sexually abused it is helpful to divide them into two groups (Wyatt and Higgs 1991, p.33):

Group A: those who present with a disclosure.

Group B: those who present without a disclosure but with other indications of sexual abuse such as medical findings or sexualised behaviour.

This classification has stood the test of time and is used in the description that follows. Children in Group B may be further divided into two subgroups:

Group B1: those who make a subsequent disclosure.

Group B2: those who make no disclosure.

Referrals to Brompton House Child Protection Project

The project is embedded in a locality child mental health team, which also includes a child psychiatrist, two community psychiatric nurses and a play therapist, any of whom may see the children involved. However, the majority are taken on by my colleague, Maggie Ambridge (see Ambridge, Chapter 10) and myself. We have received over 300 referrals in 5 years, comprising 285 children aged between 1 and 18 years (mean age 9 years), among whom are 34 sexually aggressive children, and 21 adult survivors who are parents. There are more than twice as many girls as boys. Referrals (Figure 4.1) come from primary health care teams more often than from child health doctors, paediatricians or social workers. This may be because sexual abuse distorts and interrupts normal development and causes emotional disturbance and distress, which usually present through health visitors and general practitioners (GPs). All the children we define as Group A or B1 have disclosed serious contact abuse, often penetrative, and many name the perpetrator. Many concerns about sexual abuse are first raised, not by a child making a spontaneous disclosure, but by a mother seeking help with a troubled child. Thus mental health services can be a way of accessing help.

Figure 4.2 shows the classification of the 285 children and 21 adult survivors referred to us. Over one-third, Group A, had been able to progress along the continuum of disclosure (Richardson 1991b). Many of their disclosures had led to a joint investigation that resulted in protection from further abuse. This group were more likely to have been referred by social services. However, the majority of children (52 per cent) were taken into the project from the general referrals to the child mental health team because there were

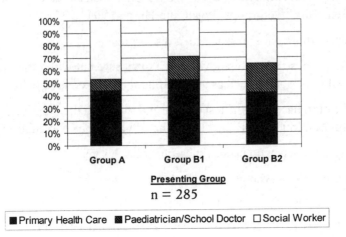

Figure 4.1 Brompton House Child Protection Project: referral sources

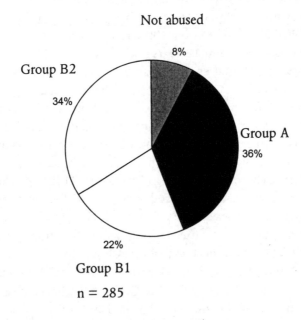

Figure 4.2 Brompton House Child Protection Project: presenting groups. For definitions of groups, see p.61.

concerns that sexual abuse might underlie their mental health problem. The accuracy of selection into the project can be gauged by the small number (7 per cent of all referrals) whose problems were shown to have a cause other than abuse.

Of the children who presented with a high index of suspicion of abuse but no initial disclosure (Group B), almost one-third made a disclosure during the course of our work with them, thus moving into Group B1. If it is accepted that children can be protected and helped only when the abuse is known about, it is clearly important to determine what it was that enabled children in this group to disclose.

However, as in Cleveland, many Group B children (61 per cent) who presented with significant concerns never made a disclosure, thus falling into Group B2. These remain troubled children who are puzzling to understand and difficult to help. Several of them had been referred to the child mental health service more than once, some as many as four times. Their dilemma was highlighted by Butler-Sloss (1988):

> The ideal would be to protect the child within his or her home and neigh-bourhood, preferably after identifying and excluding the abuser. However, if as is often the case, the perpetrator is unknown, or is suspected but denies the abuse, how can the child be protected? (Butler-Sloss 1988, p.7)

Presenting patterns

There were age differences between the groups. Children in Group A were on average two years older than those in Group B, while Group B2 were on average one year older than Group B1.

The commonest presenting problems across all groups, affecting 30 per cent of referrals, were sexualised and/or sexually aggressive behaviour. These are known effects of traumatic sexualisation (Finkelhor 1986, p.181). Many symptoms less obviously related to sexual abuse, such as behavioural and emotional disorders, were common among Groups A and B alike. However, there were differences in how the groups presented.

Children in Group A were more likely to present with post-traumatic stress disorder (PTSD) and its complex form (Herman 1992, pp.120–121), and with symptoms of externalising distress, such as acute behaviour disorder, acute separation anxiety and, in particular, conduct disorder. Expressed anxieties often related directly to the child's fears about the consequences of disclosure. There were far fewer sexually aggressive children in Group A (15 per cent). This may be because sexually aggressive children are more likely to be suffering from undisclosed abuse, and are not always perceived as victims themselves. Alternatively, it could be that protection from abuse helps the child to let go these behaviours.

Abuse may be suspected only through the presence of alerting signs or symptoms. During the assessment phase of the work, another cause for these symptoms sometimes emerged (22 children). Children whose parents have mental health problems, and who may be survivors of childhood trauma, may have disorganised attachment patterns or dissociative conditions (Egeland and Susman-Stillman 1996; Liotti 1992; Main and Hesse 1990; see also Chapter 3), and it may be difficult to disentangle whether or not the children have also been sexually abused. Despite continuing research (Lyons-Ruth and Jacobvitz 1999), no clear qualitative differences have yet been demonstrated between the disorganised attachment that results from physical or sexual abuse and that arising from other kinds of emotional trauma. This imprecision is exemplified by the finding that mothers of our Group B2 children were almost twice as likely as those of Group A children (43 per cent and 24 per cent) to have had mental health problems. Such uncertainty is uncomfortable, but in this clinical area it is necessary to live with some degree of doubt and anxiety – just as the child may have to.

Concerns that placed a child in Group B were often quite specific. One-third presented with sexualised or sexually aggressive behaviour. A small number (13 children, often siblings of others in the project) were referred because they had been in contact with a known abuser but had no other worrying symptoms. In one family where the youngest girl disclosed abuse, her two older sisters did not disclose despite the fact that their father admitted incest with all of them. Other indicators might be an internalised response to ongoing trauma, such as psychosomatic symptoms, self-harm, and dissociative states. We found a much stronger association of physical with sexual abuse in Group B2 (28 per cent, as compared with 15 per cent for all other groups).

Group B and the loss of the medical window

In Cleveland, many children did not disclose their abuse but came to light through the 'medical window' (Wyatt and Higgs 1991) when a medical diagnosis of child sexual abuse was made, thus falling into Group B. In our project, although a number of referrals came from paediatricians, this pattern was not apparent. Very few children had been fully examined. In those who were, it was nearly always as part of an investigation following disclosure.

Even among those who presented with a disclosure, only one-quarter had a medical examination that included the genitalia; 40 per cent of these examinations yielded positive findings, such as evidence of penetration, sexually transmitted disease or pregnancy.

The medical route to child protection in our district appears to have been almost lost (see also Wynne, Chapter 6). In only 1 of the 285 cases in the project had an initial referral to the child protection agencies been made as a direct result of medical examination. The girl in question had originally been referred at the age of 8 after concerns were raised by her mother about possible abuse by her father, from whom the mother had separated. Paediatric examination found 'scarring from penetrative abuse over a long period'. Unfortunately, the disclosure she then made in a video interview was not believed and she was returned home without protection. Four years later, she was referred again because of severely disturbed and sexually aggressive behaviour. She was included in the project but went on to develop a severe personality disorder.

The context of sexual abuse: mothers, fathers and perpetrators

The children we saw were far more likely to have been abused by a male than a female, and in their families rather than by an outsider (see Table 4.1). Only eight mothers were named as perpetrators. Children mostly named male relatives: fathers, stepfathers, partners, grandfathers, uncles and brothers accounted for 60 per cent of the identified perpetrators. A small group (3 per cent) were abused both by family members and by others. Of those who suffered extrafamilial abuse, half were abused by trusted males such as neighbours or babysitters. A significant number were abused by older children, mainly male.

In addition to the fathers named as perpetrators of the sexual abuse (27 per cent), a further proportion of fathers were said to be violent in the home (14 per cent). Girls were twice as likely as boys to have been abused by their fathers and to have fathers who were categorised as non-protective. For boy victims, there was a stronger association with domestic violence. There were 33 sexually aggressive children, mainly boys, with ages ranging from 4 to 15 years. Three were prosecuted for incest.

Most children were living with their mothers, through whom they came to our attention. Thus information about mothers was usually available and the work could include them, unless the children were already in long-term substitute care (23 per cent). Almost half the mothers, particularly in Group B1, were actively protective of their children and took steps to ensure that they would not suffer further abuse. In contrast, 22 per cent overall were classified as non-protective, usually because they had been unable to take effective action to stop ongoing abuse.

Table 4.1 Perpetrators of the abuse		
Intrafamilial	**178**	**74%**
Adult male relative	135	56%
Adult female relative	3	1%
Both male and female relative	15	6%
Older child in family	16	7%
Organised	9	4%
Extrafamilial	**56**	**23%**
Adult	36	15%
Child	12	5%
Organised	8	3%
Intra- and extrafamilial	**8**	**3%**

Note: N = 242 children for whom probable abuser could be identified

Mothers

Mothers usually have the main responsibility for rearing children and the main burden of dealing with disclosures. Many mothers were having to do this in the context of their own past abuse, 20 per cent having disclosed that they themselves had been sexually abused as children. Many (34 per cent) were suffering from significant mental health problems, often linked to intergenerational abuse that had not been dealt with by outside intervention. Despite these very difficult problems, time and time again we saw how determined mothers could be to stop their children being abused.

Mothers who are temporarily overwhelmed by the enormity of what they face when sexual abuse in the family comes to light can appear to be non-protective. Often their ability to protect the child is judged and found wanting in the spotlight of investigation and protection planning. Since two-thirds of cases in our project never got beyond the all too common category of JINFA (joint investigation no further action), mothers were often abandoned by the agencies just at the point where they were facing up to the reality of what the disclosure meant for their lives. By contrast, we found that the co-operation of the mother, provided she was adequately supported in her responsibility, was the single most significant factor in the outcome for the child. Unless a parent is willing to believe them and put their interests first, children may end up separated from the family. Where there was a successful prosecution in Group A children, the mother was more likely to be classed as protective and to have supported her child in disclosing. The mothers of children in Groups B1 and B2 also differed. Those in Group B2 were more likely than those in Group B1 to be survivors themselves (24 per cent and 11 per cent), to have adult mental health problems (48 per cent and 38 per cent) and a family history of domestic violence (18 per cent and 3 per cent). They were also less actively protective (45 per cent and 55 per cent).

Fathers

By contrast, fathers were much less visible. We knew nothing about 30 per cent of them. They may simply not be involved in the care of the child, they may be non-protective, or, at worst, they may be the source of the harm. They are rarely the focus of intervention or investigation. As Wyre (2000, p.52) comments, these may be fathers 'who know more about their cars than about their children'. This is a loss for the child who, in the absence of a protective father, can be more easily targeted by a paedophile. As Trotter (1998) noted with regard to 'missing fathers', we found a marked contrast between the focus on mothers and victims and the lack of information about fathers and male abusers.

Although non-abusing fathers could sometimes be actively protective (14 per cent overall, mainly in Groups A and B1), on the whole they were much less available to work with, only 40 per cent living with their children. In Group A, the fathers were more likely to be either actively protective, or excluded from the child's life because they were the abuser. In Group B1, fathers were less often at either extreme, usually being either protective or non-abusing and non-protective. In Group B2, a greater proportion of fathers were the likely abusers (38 per cent), had already been convicted of an offence against a child (9 per cent) or were involved in domestic violence (17 per cent). It was difficult not to draw the conclusion that some of these children were being silenced by these powerful figures.

Importance of a protective parent

We found in our project that, in addition to the efficacy of intervention in stopping abuse, it was the presence of a protective parent that made the most difference to the child's recovery and well-being. No amount of therapy or substitute care can be as good. Children abused by attachment figures are plunged into a mêlée of conflicting loyalties and misperceptions about responsibility. These arise, partly from the distortions imposed by the abuser during grooming and silencing, partly from the abuse itself, and partly from the dynamics of attachment to the abuser (Ross 1997). One strand in changing the perceptions of abused children is to show them that in our society sexual abuse is viewed as harmful and wrong, and that intervention is necessary. If, in the child's eyes, the mother rather than the child protection system becomes the most powerful element of future protection, the bond between them will be strengthened and flourish anew despite damaging knock-on effects of the abuse. This can reverse the belief that abusers commonly try to implant in children, that their mother will not believe them, is unable to protect them and may reject them. As things now stand, many children are left with the impression that intervention is powerless. In the words of Cooklin (1999):

> A child who has been harmed by abuse needs to know with no equivoca-
> tion that what was done to him or her was wrong: any equivocation plugs
> into the child's belief that they were responsible. No child can understand
> why an adult has not been punished, unless they accept that the criminal
> justice system is a flop, or can understand many shades of grey.

Case example: a protective mother's response
The baby crocodile's story

> Emma, aged 7, was referred for repeatedly sexually assaulting her younger
> brother. Emma's mother had moved with the children to live with her
> father following domestic violence by Emma's father. An investigation,
> including a video interview, took place after Emma told her mother that
> her granddad 'had put a balloon on his willy' (shown her how to use a
> condom). No prosecution followed. They moved house and were referred
> together. At the end of Emma's therapy, during which she had developed
> her own metaphors for what had happened, she wrote the following story
> which we made into a booklet for her to take away.

The crocodile's revenge

Once upon a time there was a crocodile, and a little baby, and a nasty old Granddad … and the Granddad wanted the baby for his dinner: crocodile soup! He got his fishing rod and tried to catch the little baby. But the Mummy called out, 'baby it's dinner time', so the baby rushed in the house. But the Granddad thought, 'not for much longer' … the day after, the Mummy was tidying up the lake that was their house, and the nasty Granddad caught the baby … the Mummy rushed out of the house and snapped at him, and put him in the cooker, but he got out again and grabbed the baby … But the Mummy came back and she said 'leave my daughter alone, pick on me' … And she killed the Granddad and said, 'are you OK darling?'; and the baby was frightened but she was perfectly alright. And the mother was not very pleased because there was blood all over the place and she had just tidied up. She had to start all over again. And they even moved house to the other side of the lake. She told the baby to forget all of that and just to get on with their lives.

The Mummy crocodile's story

After reading Emma's story, Emma's mother in turn told Emma her parallel story, which the therapist added to the booklet.

The Mummy crocodile went shopping: big mistake, because she thought that Granpy would look after the baby crocodile safely until she came back. When she came back, the baby crocodile started to cry and the Mummy could see that she had a hurt between her legs. Granpy said the baby had been out playing and had fallen off her bike. The baby didn't want the Granpy to bath her that night but her Mummy didn't know why. About a week later, the baby crocodile went to visit her other nan. She told Supergran what Granpy had been doing. Nan crock told Mummy 'your baby has got something to tell you', and she told her Mummy all about it. Baby crocodile was very frightened because Granpy had said the fairies would come after her and kill her if she didn't do what he wanted. So the Mummy crocodile had to go and kill all the fairies with a big wooden spoon, loads and loads, splat, before the baby could feel safe and tell. She cried loads and loads.

The baby crocodile went to a special place to tell somebody on the video. Baby crocodile tried so hard to make them understand, and Mummy crocodile got told off for trying to help. Mummy crocodile snapped her teeth so hard she got a headache. She had no-one to help her and she stayed angry and sad inside. Sometimes the Mummy and baby crocodile argued because they felt so gutted. They felt their lives had been ruined because the Granddad had got away with it. But not for ever, because they told more people who believed them, loads and loads, and they are going to fight back. In the mean time, they are not going to let him spoil their lives any more. They are going to go sailing, and the Mummy crocodile went to join a club for other Mummy crocodiles where they could help each other because they all felt the same.

Case example: non-protective parent

Anna, aged 7, was taken into care after telling her teacher at school that she was a model. A friend of 20 years' standing had persuaded her mother, Theresa, to take part in a series of mother and daughter photographs for an 'artistic book'. The court made a finding that the photographs, found on the home computer, were indecent. They were of Anna and Theresa naked, Anna being taught to pose in a series of increasingly pornographic images. Theresa's partner Roy acted as a 'chaperone' and, along with the friend, took some of the video and film. In the course of investigation it transpired that Roy had had an incestuous relationship with his half-sister from the age of 7 to 14. Theresa saw no risk to Anna because she convinced herself that this had been a 'love' relationship, long over, and that Roy was not a paedophile. She described herself as vigilant towards any possible harm to her daughter. Her previous partners, including Anna's father, had been violent, whereas Roy was not. Theresa herself had been severely emotionally abused, and probably sexually abused, by her grandmother, who had brought her up. She seemed to have no way of putting herself in Anna's shoes. Theresa chose to stay in the relationship and Anna remained in care.

Mothers, fathers and the child protection system

Colclough, Parton and Anslow (1999) point out that the result of refocusing services towards family support (Department of Health 1995) has resulted in the family being seen as a 'good thing' and not dis-aggregated. When the interests of fathers, mothers and children are different, for example where there is intrafamilial abuse, the picture is much more complex, requiring attention to 'responsibility' as well as to 'support'. Seeing mothers and fathers as 'parents' and children as 'offspring' is quite inadequate (Colclough et al.

1999). This is a central flaw in Butler-Sloss's (1988) analysis of the problems in Cleveland. She rightly commented that children must be seen as children and not simply as 'objects of concern', but she failed to distinguish between those parents who were protective and those who were abusive. For abused children, parent and abuser may be synonymous, and an attempt to separate them from their abusive parent may produce intolerable conflict.

Creative responses to the internal dilemmas of mothers can do much to help the child and produce a protective end result. Potentially protective parents, particularly fathers, often become marginalised by the child protection system. Often the intervention, with its police-led focus on investigation, results in the child moving backwards along the continuum of disclosure while no action is taken against the perpetrator. A non-abusing, potentially protective parent can be pushed aside and left unsupported and angered by the failure of the investigation. A parent who is preoccupied and stressed at the crucial time of crisis for the child cannot, even with the best will in the world, deal so well with the child's feelings.

At present, the 'gaze of the child protection response is on the victim and his/her family' rather than on the causes of sexual violence (Parton and Wattam 1999, p.3). Perpetrators are less visible, rarely admit abusing, and effective work with them is difficult. However, it does seem that more family support may be a key factor in community prevention of sexual abuse. Vulnerable children are particularly likely to be targeted by abusers. Community networks, in particular support for lone parents, and money to alleviate child poverty may turn out to be as important in prevention as targeting abusers. This is borne out by our observation that many children in our project were the victims of male abusers who had groomed a single-parent family to get access to the children. Single mothers who find themselves in this position may well become dependent on the resources offered by a perpetrator who is happy to help care for their children.

If a mother's capacity to judge and select a non-abusing partner has not been developed by good parenting and relationships in her own childhood, she may not realise she is being targeted by a potentially abusive partner (see Chapter 3). Alternatively, mistrust of male carers may mean that some potentially safe and good fathers could be excluded from caring for their children. Children with an insecure base at home may gravitate to quasi-parental adults outside the family, for example in a youth club, where they may become vulnerable to grooming for abuse.

Table 4.2 shows the outcome in terms of child protection for each of our three groups. Over one-third of the children were placed on the child protection register, and nearly one-quarter were removed into care as a result of the investigation. The abuse was investigated in one-third of the cases, and there have been 41 successful prosecutions (19 per cent of all cases). However, the majority of child victims were not protected either by prosecution or by removal into care. Over one-quarter are protected by their mothers alone, for example mothers who have separated from the alleged perpetrator and who make sure there is no unsupervised contact. Nearly one-third (32 per cent) of children were thought to be still subject to significant risk but were not afforded any protection. This was often because the child had been unable to make a disclosure or because the parents had dropped out of the project.

Table 4.2 Child protection outcome								
	Group A		Group B1		Group B2		Total	
Total	103		63		97		263	
Protected by conditions	10	10%	2	3%	5	5%	17	6%
Protected by care proceedings	23	22%	22	35%	15	15%	60	23%
Protected by parent	24	23%	22	35%	20	21%	66	25%
Prosecution of perpetrator	21	20%	7	11%	3	3%	31	12%
Not protected	23	22%	9	14%	51	52%	83	31%
Not known	2		1		3		6	

Recognising the child's distress: is disclosure necessary?

Where there is a strong suspicion of sexual abuse but no disclosure (i.e. Group B2), the child may continue to be at risk. For such children, the task within the project might be to see whether they can be enabled to disclose. Even if they can, a formal investigation might not follow or might not result in further action. Ongoing or past abuse often has to be dealt with mainly by the family, sometimes with help from the social services.

Our project is unusual in recognising that Group B children need active help. This can create difficulties. Trying actively to help a child to disclose can place a subsequent investigation or court case in jeopardy. Such risks are reduced to an acceptable level if the work is supported by the agencies who have statutory responsibility for child protection. The problem of working with undisclosed abuse is that, if and when it comes to the surface and the child makes a disclosure, the work can be discredited along with the child's disclosure. So as not to prejudice investigations that might take place, the project has a protocol for keeping other agencies informed of the work, often agreeing its outline by a prior stategy meeting or consultation with police and social services. We are also careful to record the work, subject to consent of child and parents, using video whenever possible. The explanation given is that what the child says is important and we want to make sure we can remember it properly. In practice this consent is rarely refused.

Sometimes, we may have to explain and justify our work to the court. This may be difficult and stressful and the professional has to be able to do it well, recognising that court proceedings are infinitely more stressful and risky for the child and family.

Problems with secrecy

Strategies adopted to cope with ongoing abuse, especially decisions to maintain secrecy, represent children's adaptation to their circumstances without losing primary attachments. Whether disclosure of the underlying problem is the only way to assist the child towards healthy development is a vexed question. Abuse may not leave physical signs, but the loss of the medical window (Richardson and Bacon, Chapter 2; Wynne, Chapter 6) for children who are suffering penetrative abuse but unable or unwilling to talk, leaves them without this potential route to protection. Professional acceptance of the present situation may seem like accommodation to a system that is powerless to prevent abuse. The time-scale involved in leaving children to find their own way along the continuum may be difficult to live with. However, although professionals can be supportive and make conditions as conducive as possible, the disclosure process must go at the child's pace and should not be driven by adult agendas.

For the many children who keep the worst of their experiences hidden, there is still plenty that a parent or therapist can do to assist the process of inner healing. Children who have experienced real horror sometimes seem to want to protect their parents and therapists from unbearable truths. The therapist may experience a lot of uncomfortable uncertainty, and the child may only be gradually convinced that these truths can be contained and witnessed without disintegration of either child or therapist.

Children can become so dependent on the mechanisms, including secrecy, they have developed to adapt and cope with the abuse and its inherent family dilemmas, that they cannot discard such well-established defences. These may ultimately damage the adult personality. In this situation, it may be best to accept that the child cannot disclose everything, and that they will nevertheless benefit from ensuring protection on the basis of an intervention that is accepted by the protecting parent. Children may remain unable to talk about or make sense of the abuse for a long time, during which they can still pick up a better developmental trajectory. However, children and non-abusing carers may need and benefit from help to give up their previous ways of coping and to rebuild healthier attachments. Processing abusive experiences into symbolic form (Ambridge, Chapter 10; Bacon, Chapter 3) may be important in children overcoming fear and containing the harm. Once underway, this healing process may make it impossible to access the experience in its raw form, so any investigation is likely to encounter problems. Children who say, for example, 'a snake bit my bottom' or 'a monster spider crawls up under my bedclothes' do not get to be video interviewed.

Children rarely signal abuse by primary attachment figures, but professionals or supportive adults may recognise that some signs and symptoms are an indirect cry for help. Otherwise, there is a danger that treatment for symptoms will ignore their underlying function. Children trapped in secrecy are often desperate to maintain this, while at the same time half hoping that the therapist will seek out the meaning of their distress. Even so, they may respond with strenuous denials. How best to approach a child in whom abuse is suspected but not disclosed is a major challenge for all professionals.

The difficulty of getting the child's evidence safely into the protection system creates additional difficulty. Problems of children's evidence are addressed in McLouglin (Chapter 9) and elsewhere (e.g. Westcott and Jones 1997). *Memorandum* interviews (Home Office and Department of Health 1992) are very problematic. A single interview in which the child can be given no direction to the subject in question is puzzling for young children and stressful for older ones. Their anxieties cannot be allayed, a trusting relationship cannot be built: an essential preliminary for children feeling able to speak about what may be a long period of abuse by an attachment figure. The way that small children remember things means that they find it hard to tell a detailed story without pegs to hang it on. The child needs the interviewer to provide a 'scaffolding' (Hewitt 2000). *Memorandum* interviews can seem like asking a child to write a story with the wrong hand in answer to questions in a foreign language.

Attachment, secrecy and disclosure

A central difficulty for sexually abused children is overcoming their fear of rejection or abandonment by the parent when the abuse becomes known. Bowlby (1973) linked the activation of the attachment system with the effects of fear, one function of which is to motivate children to extricate themselves from dangerous situations. Fear is a normal part of the dependency of childhood, serving to ensure proximity to the primary attachment figure as a means of survival. Attachment comes top of the hierarchy of needs for young children. The child abused by an attachment figure must find some way of preserving trust and feeling safe within the relationship. One way may be by focusing on the needs of the abusing adult. The child may then become emotionally and cognitively constricted in a clinging and compliant relationship (James 1994, p.36). This becomes internally represented as a trauma bond (James 1994, p.34, citing Herman 1992, p.96) in which attention to the parent's needs causes permanent distortion of the child's personality. If the mother is afraid of the perpetrator, her children are likely to sense this and react accordingly.

It is hard to classify attachment patterns of sexually abused children (Bacon, Chapter 3). Adult survivors have also been shown to 'exhibit unresolved states of mind with respect to attachment' (Lyons-Ruth and Jacobvitz 1999, p.545). The attitude of children towards abuse and secrecy is determined by the dialogue they hold in their head with their attachment figures, as well as by what people around them actually say (Wieland 1997). To recognise and disclose abuse, children must have had some experience of responsive care, and must not be overwhelmed by trauma.

If 'protective' intervention threatens the child's attachment system it may be feared and avoided by the child. Abusers recognise this and set out to distort the child's perceptions, enforcing secrecy by compromising the primary attachments. Children may reject intervention unless the positive elements in their attachment to the perpetrator are recognised.

A child who is beginning to move along the continuum to a point of disclosure enters an unpredictable area. Children will not risk moving from Group B to Group A unless they are sure of the unconditional love and protection of their attachment figure. A child's most basic need is for nurture and care; some children cannot prioritise avoiding sexual abuse even when they recognise that abuse is harmful.

Some children have secure enough attachments to disclose even intrafamilial abuse. In our project, however, only 24 out of 281 children were classed as having two actively protective parents. Older children may choose to confide in someone outside the family, particularly a best friend. This can lead to problems. For example one 16-year-old girl recounted how she confided in her older cousin, who promptly offered a sexual relationship to comfort her: she said this was like 'bringing in the wolves to guard the sheep when the fox has taken the lambs'.

Group A: children who have disclosed

As with Group B, Group A is not a discrete group. Many are securely attached children who have been able to alert a protective adult before getting trapped in ongoing abuse. Such children may present initially with the symptoms of anxiety or of PTSD. Similar symptoms are shown by children who are stressed or traumatised from other causes, taking the form, for example, of concentration difficulties, sudden changes in behaviour, regression to an earlier stage of development, separation anxiety, night fears, sleep and eating difficulties, or acting out of character with behaviour problems such as aggression. However, children whose inner world can be accessed may reveal being troubled by specific reminders of abuse. Once they can express and ventilate their feelings, these problems may be relatively short-lived, depending on their resilience and on the support and protection they are given. Some children benefit from a lengthy period of play therapy or counselling to help them sort out and put away the intrusive memories in their inner 'filing cabinet'.

Other children may be resistant to anyone coming close. This avoidant pattern is difficult to manage and may sometimes be mistaken for a conduct disorder. If an investigation has not led to action against the perpetrator, the child will feel angry, betrayed and resentful. Older children, particularly if they have accommodated to ongoing abuse, may resort to self-harming behaviour, when their inner distress becomes entrenched and more difficult to treat.

Therapy can encourage meta-cognitive processes (Main 1991), for example by using metaphors to explore the abuse. This may help children and their mothers find a way of expressing and organising the confused aftermath of emotions. This can help develop reflective functioning (Fonagy et al. 1995). Shared acknowledgement of the child's inner experience strengthens the mother and child, facilitates sensitive caring, and may lessen the damaging effects of abuse.

Case example: securely attached children in Group A

James, aged 3 years, and his sister Caroline, aged 5 years, had allegedly been abused by their mother's partner, while she was at work. Caroline told her mother that M had touched her bottom and showed her a condom. James added that M had locked them in the bedroom. After some anxious delay, their mother reported this, and a medical examination of Caroline showed evidence of abuse. However, Caroline was unable to say anything during the *Memorandum* interview, and the police could not take action. With support from the social worker, the mother got M to leave, although he went on harassing and threatening them.

Both children had nightmares and acute separation anxiety. James, previously a compliant, easy boy, became increasingly angry, having breath-holding attacks and rages. All this was directed at his mother, who became worn out, but just managed to contain and discipline him. In the first appointment, James bashed the toy hammer pegs loudly, and was undirected and chaotic, with frequent confrontational outbursts. This reduced his mother to tears of frustration and embarrassment. His sister spent the time ignoring James, drawing and writing loving messages to their mother. After two sessions, James suddenly became more verbal. He put on a police hat and, using a magnetic fishing game, picked out a 'bad fish shark' that he caught and hammered, saying 'you're dead'. He placed the fish in a house with a police guard. His sister meanwhile caught other fish and cooked them for their dinner, tenderly looking after her mother; she also protected the remaining fish from the shark by covering them up. Both children then made a picture together of the 'baddie fish' in a cage, energetically scribbling on it. James seemed much happier when he left. The anger had been transformed into symbolic play that could then be expressed and dealt with by the children, although the perpetrator remains in the community, untroubled by any intervention. While difficult for their mother, this approach at least meant the children became free to move on.

Group B: children who do not initially disclose

Again, this is not a homogeneous group. Some children in Group B, particularly B2, with anxious attachment styles show protective parental behaviour towards their mother at their own expense. Other Group B children with chaotic attachment styles receive both internal and external messages that create anxiety and confusion about whether what they have experienced is abusive and whether it is safe to disclose. Some children with dissociative conditions can look as though they have attention deficit hyperactivity disorder (ADHD) (Howes, Richardson and Robinson-Fell 2000). In fact, this mechanism may have the effect of protecting them by turning them into 'moving targets'. Where mothers have mental health problems, they may be unavailable or not close enough for the child's disclosure or alerting comments to register.

Where children have accommodated to ongoing abuse the picture is bound to be complex. In order to offer the best help it is often important to understand intergenerational attachment patterns in the family. Parents without a history of secure attachment relationships themselves may be more able to cope with the child's disclosure if given support. Some may have accommodated to the child's abuse by a partner out of their own fear of abandonment. There may be an impossible conflict of loyalties if the abuser is an older sibling, or a powerful grandparent who also abused them as a child. It is difficult for some parents to dismantle their own coping mechanisms such as dissociation or denial, even when they want to respond effectively to their child's needs. They can help the child better if the intervention is not blaming of their failure to protect.

Case example: moving into Group B1

> Marianne's mother, Claire, went to her health visitor worried about her 7-year-old daughter's disruptive behaviour at school, which included touching other children in a sexual manner. Claire had been depressed for a long period, following a protracted separation from her husband, eventually moving nearer her own family. Marianne and her older sister Rebecca went regularly to visit their father at weekends. After a few appointments, Marianne's behaviour deteriorated. She was cheeky, non-compliant and horrible to Claire, who admitted losing her temper and smacking Marianne. We asked both children: is there anything Mum ought to be worried about that was making Marianne so angry and upset? Becky immediately became silent and uncomfortable. Marianne seemed disturbed, but eventually said that she had a yucky secret with Dad. A strategy meeting decided that we should keep on working with Marianne. After anxious weeks, during which Marianne continued to be disturbed

and agitated, this secret finally emerged. In the end, a character called 'Mr Secrets' (see Figure 4.3) helped Marianne to tell. Marianne's initial response to Mr. Secrets' dilemma was to say that 'he should keep the secrets in more', but gradually she let out different parts of the secret, saying 'I hate you, you're not my friend, I am sad'. Eventually, Marianne disclosed oral sexual abuse by her father. 'Mr Secrets' went with Marianne to a *Memorandum* interview, along with a teddy bear for support, and managed to tell the 'real police lady' about the problem. Marianne also told how her dad had done the same to her sister. Although the police took no action, Claire, with support from the project, social services and her own therapist, took a private law action to stop unsupervised contact for the children. The evidence from the therapist's report and the *Memorandum* interview allowed the court to make a finding that the father had abused Marianne.

Becky remained unable to acknowledge any abuse to herself, so remained in Group B2, but both girls decided that they did not want to see Daddy at his house any more. In a contact visit, Marianne told him that he was a pig. This seemed to help a lot in reducing her anger towards Claire.

Group B2: children trapped in silence

Many children unable to disclose may be suffering from dissociation (Bacon and Richardson 2000; Putnam 1997; Silberg 1998; see also Bacon, Chapter 3). Working with a dissociated child can be a puzzling experience, often producing a kind of reciprocal blankness in the clinician. When children experience confusion or terror, the processes of memory and recall are distorted and disrupted. Feelings become disconnected from thoughts and words. This applies especially to very young children and where children are abused in organised or ritual settings. Children with disorganised attachment patterns may also become dissociated (Liotti 1992, 1995); the mechanism for this is possibly linked with trauma (Fonagy *et al.* 1995; also see Bacon, Chapter 3).

These fragmentations can be addressed provided the child is afforded a safe space. A non-directive and reflective therapist can help the child's own capacity for inner healing come into play. A lot of confidence is needed on the part of the therapist, and not many children are given the necessary time. Provided the child is protected, the therapy is the focus regardless of whether the network of adult abusers is dealt with. Unless the clinician can accept this, unnecessary emotional energy will be expended, sometimes at the cost of meeting the child's real needs. Disclosure of organised abuse rarely leads to successful investigation or prosecution.

Figure 4.3 Mr. Secrets

Case example: dissociative state in a Group B2 child

Debbie, aged 9 years, is also described in Bacon, Chapter 8. She was taken into care because of physical abuse and neglect. During initial assessment the therapist asks: 'Can you do me a drawing of a whole person?' Debbie: 'A mermaid?' Therapist: 'Not a mermaid, a whole person.' Debbie draws a head. Therapist: 'Not just a head, but a whole person.' Debbie: 'This is a person who goes to our school, but not in this dress that I've just drawn, it's another little girl whose mummy might smack her, so she can't tell, and nothing rude happened to her because she always stayed with me, and when they do that they always come back and tell me and then I sort them out, but they don't often tell me ... then I sort them out, but they don't often tell me ... girls shouldn't see a widgey [penis] because I don't like to touch them.'

In a further interview, Debbie speaks to herself using a baby doll: 'The baby needs D to help her not to be always telling lies, she doesn't know why she tells lies it just happens, the baby has a lot of boyfriends and is too young to have them. Her mum is jealous, they like to kiss her on her lips and [Debbie points to her genitals], and they mustn't interfere.'

Later on, using worry dolls in which to confide, Debbie says: 'There are two children that have been taken into care because of bad things, naughty things, and they don't want to talk about it because they think their mum and dad will be in trouble. That's the real problem, she's just too worried about going home and she is worried about what mum will say if she says she doesn't want to come home.'

It seemed that Debbie used the third person to distance herself from abuse and fear. It also seems that she viewed the victim of the abuse, her little sister (self), as bad. Debbie used the sessions to explore her fragmented and unprocessed memories, to name her fears, to regress, and eventually to tell a more coherent story.

Eventually she told her foster mother a catalogue of sexual abuse by both parents and other adults, which included her older brothers. This often occurred on significant occasions such as her birthday and Christmas day, and involved restraint such as tying her to the wall. Her father, holding her head under water at the beach, had said this is what he would do if she told anyone. Debbie's abuse was re-enacted in nightmares, but in therapy she never referred directly to her experiences. She suffered numbing, rarely felt pain, and expressed a brittle and unreal persona in the therapy.

Particular problems in organised and ritual abuse

The few children seen in the project where organised abuse was suspected or discovered have usually presented in Group B. Experience of ritual abuse (McFadyen, Hanks and James 1993) suggests that it silences its victims by systematic terrorisation that attacks the young child's inner world, belief system and attachment bonds. A power-driven substitute attachment is superimposed on the child by means of bribery, reward, complicity, pain, helplessness and ultimately loss of control. Children have told us of intimidation by separation from their attachment figures and of being instilled with fear of abandonment, for example by being hung up and left alone in a frightening place. Their inner conscience may be deliberately distorted. For example, they may be told they are wicked, or they may be made to lie to attachment figures. They are shamed and degraded, for example by being made to take part in unspeakable rituals. They may be disoriented and confused, by being drugged, by being told that things are not what they seem (for example that their parents are not their real parents), or by being taken to forbidden places. A context is created that will cause disbelief and incredulity about anything the child says, for example, 'I was made to watch people being killed'.

Case example: ritual abuse

The work with Sean, aged 8 years, is also described by Ambridge (Chapter 10). While his mother was ill in hospital, over a school holiday he had been systematically groomed by an older boy, who had entrapped a group of younger children into sexual activities with each other, the boy's father, and other adults, including bestiality and pornography. Eventually, Sean described being involved in ritual abuse ceremonies where blood and urine were drunk, operations were performed, and Sean believed he had seen adults and children hung up and tortured. He was told that the adults involved were now his 'real' parents. He was told that evil was more powerful than good, and that if he disclosed, an insect implanted near his heart would sting him to death. He suffered from extreme night terrors and his behaviour became disturbed and aggressive. He involved his younger sister in the sexualised games he had been taught, and he tried to tie himself up and hang himself.

At the start of his therapy, Sean was able to draw a picture of himself divided into good and bad, recognising that the bad things were only one part. By accepting his mother's support, by recovering his 'good' core personality, and by drawing on the safe foundation of his early childhood, after more than a year in therapy Sean began to try and make sense of what he had experienced. His therapist helped Sean to re-create and master many of the objects and symbols of terror. Much of his work expressed anger towards his abusers. He enacted investigation, trial and imprisonment of the boy and his father. He made strong symbolic figures such as the Angel of the North (a large sculpture outside Newcastle upon Tyne) to guard the therapy room where he worked. Sean reported a gradual diminution of the need to stay up and watch all night over his family, and he became re-attached to his parents. He talked with his therapist about the meaning of good and evil. He insisted that his mother should read him the story of the return of the prodigal son over and over again.

During this process, the therapists and Sean's mother were going through a frightening and frustrating attempt to get the child protection system to recognise and deal with the case. The alleged abuser had been named and his address was known, as were those of many of the other victims. However, the local police child protection team could not investigate events that had occurred abroad. Within weeks, the site had been altered to remove all signs of a hut, tunnels and other places that Sean had described. During the initial investigation Sean (then aged 6) had given a nonsensical story, which he subsequently revealed had been fed to him by the abusers. When he felt safe enough to tell his parents more of the truth, there was a cursory further investigation that got nowhere. Thankfully, Sean was protected by his parents. The cycle of abuse, in which he was undoubtedly being prepared to abuse others, may have been broken for him, but may well have continued for the other children involved, particularly the older boy who had co-opted him into abuse.

Conclusion

In general, the difficulties we found in Cleveland of matching intervention to the needs of children at different points on the continuum of disclosure have not lessened over time. Despite the benefits of increased awareness and acceptance of the incidence and prevalence of child sexual abuse, the political and societal reaction to Cleveland has resulted in the balance being tilted more towards the rights of adults, including abusers, than towards the rights of children (Speight and Wynne 1999). As a result, professionals who attempt to engage with abused children still have a difficult task.

This chapter has considered some of the dilemmas for intervening at the point when the child is victimised. Responsibility at the point of disclosure is still invested mainly in the child. In our project, we have seen that children and protective parents or carers frequently wish to initiate change. Sometimes they are successful, but often they do not receive sufficient help from the child protection system to enable them to overcome the great difficulties that beset them.

Therapeutic dilemmas, already complex, become impossible in an inadequately resourced child protection system. Despite this, professionals who are in a position to listen to children should endeavour to view this as an active task. This means conveying a message to the child that we know there is something to hear. In our own project, we try to be available to children at all stages of the disclosure process, not just at the end of the investigation. We hope that, by listening and trying to make sense of what children tell us, we can reach some who are trapped in secrecy and silence. In the words of Lisbet Smeyers: 'The child's experience is the point of departure. The professional has to give words or language to the observed signals, so that professionals can take responsibility from the child' (Smeyers 1999).

CHAPTER 5

Multi-perpetrator abuse of children
Mothers of the victims tell their story

Isabel Brooks

Origins of LASA

In 1994, five women met each other for the inaugural meeting of the League Against Sadistic Abuse (LASA), a support group which was about to share experiences of a most complex, painful and shocking nature. Our common experience was that our children had made disclosures of multi-perpetrator sexual abuse. Despite the fact that the mothers came from all over the UK and we had not previously known each other, there were striking similarities in our stories, both in terms of the bizarre methods used to abuse our children and also in how the authorities dealt with our cases. This chapter is based on narratives from mothers in the group.

My own adult daughter revealed, after my divorce, that she had been sadistically abused by her father and his associates throughout her childhood. I was devastated and was also appalled that I had been unaware of what was going on in my own family. But my reactions were overshadowed by the despair and powerlessness felt by the other women. They asked the authorities to help protect their very young children, and to understand the unbelievable things they were hearing. Instead they found themselves discredited. The tables were turned on them and they were accused of emotionally abusing their children. Somehow, the authorities decided they had managed to tutor their children to make false statements about the abuse. Some of the children were removed from their care and were placed with their allegedly abusive fathers.

Since 1994, the numbers in the support group have grown to 25 parents (21 mothers and 4 fathers) with 43 children in total; 36 of the children have alleged abuse. Their siblings have also been affected by the distressing events that followed. As each new member told an extraordinarily similar story, a pattern emerged which will be demonstrated in the case studies in this chapter. These case studies have been selected because they represent LASA group's experiences. Names and identifying features have been altered.

Our 36 children were usually pre-school when the abuse commenced. The abusers were people who regularly come into contact with small children – parents, grandparents, nursery staff, babysitters. Mostly male and middle class, they presented as decent reputable people, but were described by the group as plausible and devious, cruel bullies and breathtakingly audacious.

The parents in LASA fall into three main groups. First, those who had their children removed from them by the authorities (8 parents and 11 children). Second, those who still have their children at home (8 parents and 15 children). Third, those whose children were adults when they first felt able to speak about the abuse (9 parents and 10 children) and thus the issue of removing the child from home does not arise.

Although all of our 36 children have made similar allegations, I will suggest reasons why some mothers have lost their children, while others have not.

Group 1: parents whose children have been removed

Case example: Cath and her daughter Chloe

> Our story begins over ten years ago when Chloe was 6. We lived near her father, from whom I had separated, but with whom she had very generous contact.

> Once she started school, Chloe began to resist her father picking her up from school. This became increasingly unmanageable, and eventually I was under an injunction not to be present for the handover.

> A hearing took place, and a local social worker was asked to assess our situation. Although he did not think Chloe should be medically examined, he recommended that we needed therapy.

> When therapy started, Chloe began to talk about the frightening things that happened when she visited her father. At bedtime she would say, 'Mummy can I tell you a story about Daddy's hurting parties'. She needed reassurance that her father would not kill me if she told me what took place. When I told her that this would not happen she described a series of

'nasties'. Her father dressed up in face paints and masks and unusual clothes; sometimes he was addressed as 'she' by other members of his family who were present. She talked of places where she was watched and touched by people in strange clothes. She demonstrated sex with sound effects and talked of killing animals. Eventually she described an eye-contact, fingers-waving procedure called 'spiders' which she would try not to notice and to escape from, as this was a prelude to the worst of her ordeal, during which she was tied up and gagged.

Chloe spoke of some of these issues to the therapist, who remained cynical. The police took statements and made videos with Chloe, who told me that she had demonstrated some of the things that frightened her. After liaising with the hospital therapists they told me that they believed Chloe's father, who had protested his innocence throughout. Eventually, supervised access to her father was recommended with an injunction forbidding my presence.

Soon Chloe's father, a prominent business man, asked for care and control of his daughter and on the eve of the hearing my solicitor warned me on the phone that the courts might well find in his favour. Within an hour Chloe and I had left our home with a change of clothes in a couple of carrier bags. We lived in the women's refuge system, moving around the country for 18 months, taking a new name after each move, which Chloe never had trouble remembering. She was wonderful during those months, very brave, mature and loving because she knew it was hard for me – I lost my home and all but what we stood in. During our absence my husband – for the divorce had not yet been finalised – obtained a court order returning my house to his ownership, rendering me effectively destitute.

He hired private investigators who found us and revealed our whereabouts to the police. Chloe was taken from me and into care. She had three foster homes. It seemed that when she spoke about the abuse to each foster family she was moved on, and social workers who became concerned at these disclosures were taken off the case.

During this period a different police department, psychiatrist and social services department was involved, and Chloe had a guardian ad litem. She was told that she must see her father again and could not see me until she did. We did not see each other for ten weeks while she was being reintroduced to him. A psychiatrist was in charge of this punishing regime. I then heard from the social services that she had broken down shortly after writing a letter saying that she had made it all up. I was told that I suffered from schizophrenia and a psychological condition known as 'Othello's syndrome'. (I have never received treatment for mental illness or depression.)

After a full hearing of the case, Chloe was told that she must never live with me again, and that she was to be rehabilitated with her father. This happened swiftly. Her father enrolled her immediately into a private school. The social workers left her to cope, visiting her twice in six months.

The judge's statement described me as complex and imaginative, feeding off my daughter's fantasies – despite testimonies in court from a social worker and educationalist that they believed Chloe. Apparently my deep-rooted delusions would remain with me throughout her childhood and adolescence and would be damaging to her.

She now lives with her father and is pale and heavy-eyed.

It is impossible to assess her feelings. Our supervised contacts were closely monitored for several years. I could not talk about or explain relevant matters. When I told her that I loved her I was told not to be emotional or access would be curtailed.

She is aware that I do not mention the past during our brief and precious meetings. She bestows on me a silent, bemused, deep gaze, which I understand. Her perception of right and wrong must be affected by this. She disclosed details of harrowing abuse to seven adults and none of us improved her situation. In fact, we made it worse.

As for my feelings, I am very shocked at the professional treatment received by my child. I cannot describe the horror at the loss of my child, or my anxious, powerless feelings.

No one can give my child back what has been taken from her. No one can restore our relationship to its original state. Few appear to care.

I have managed to rebuild my life. I have learned that others have tried to protect their children from this sort of situation.

Case example: Moira and her daughter Sheena

Moira had received counselling from the women's refuge, which helped her to end an abusive relationship with her violent partner. She felt relief, and wasn't too concerned about her 3-year-old daughter Sheena's visits to her father, because his mother was there to look after her granddaughter.

However, within weeks Sheena began to make very serious allegations concerning her father's behaviour when she stayed with him, since apparently her grandmother was not always present. Sheena became hysterical whenever preparations were in progress for a visit to her father and finally she disclosed to her mother that 'daddy hurts my bum'.

Social services agreed that a Rape Crisis worker who had met Sheena previously would interview the frightened child, but without her mother present. Until they presented their case notes to the judge at the hearing, Moira had no idea what her daughter had disclosed. She listened to a catalogue of abuses, which included knives and snakes, and threats that her mother would die if she spoke about their 'secret'. The father had tried to trick his child, telling her that he knew the worker from Rape Crisis was listening from inside a cupboard and approved of what he was doing.

The father issued a writ for care and control of his daughter on the grounds that Moira was mentally unstable and therefore unfit to be her mother. We have become familiar with this defence, often used by husbands in child abuse cases. No one has yet managed to explain how a mother is supposed to make a very young child repeat a complicated story in her absence and with evident fear.

In Moira's case, the court based their decision on the fact that Moira had suffered postnatal depression for which she had been treated. Her infant daughter had remained with her throughout the six weeks spent as an in-patient, and at no time had anyone suggested that the child was at risk. None the less, the court decided in favour of Sheena's father, with whom she now lives.

Postnatal depression is fairly common and here it was used to brand a mother as unfit to care for her child. One can speculate on the legal vulnerability of mothers if this case were to create a precedent.

We see a pattern where labelling the mother as mentally unstable enables the authorities to discount the allegations of abuse made by the child, on the basis that these are false allegations originating in the mother's delusional state. This appears to enable the authorities to conclude that the mother is emotionally abusive: the child must be removed from her care and placed with the father, regardless of whether or not he is the alleged perpetrator.

When mothers seek to deny ex-partners contact with their children, their genuine concerns are often set aside. An assumption is made that they do so out of vindictiveness and will falsely accuse the father. In fact, mothers in

LASA had been willing to allow contact and it was only when their children disclosed abuse by their fathers that they sought to stop the contact.

Group 2: mothers who regain or retain the care of their children

Case example: Alice and her daughters

> Alice's children had been sexually abused and tortured by their father, an upper-middle-class academic, and his friends. The marriage had ended because of the father's abusive behaviour towards his wife, and it was some months later that the children, aged 3 and 5, spoke about parties in their father's village. The little girls said that they were given sweeties that made them feel like they were flying, and others that they described as magic because they went to sleep in one place and awoke in another. The children described being placed in a circle, with the adults in the outer ring choosing which child they would abuse. They described holes in the ground, into which they were put for what seemed like hours, and being made to eat excrement, which their father fished out of the loo at his house.
>
> The alleged abuser was questioned but denied everything. Despite the eldest child having a sexually transmitted vaginal infection, the extreme youth of his victims mitigated against a criminal prosecution. He was released and, shortly after, left the country. The girls were offered therapy when they were counselled for their *fantasies*. The mother likewise was told that her *delusions* were not helping her girls.
>
> Five years later the family was struggling. Alice took a college course – at which she achieved a gold medal – enabling her to find employment, but her daughters were chronically anxious and unable to cope with the idea that their mother was not at home. The youngest child kept running away to look for her mummy and was placed in foster care. The previous history of allegations of bizarre sexual abuse of the children was a factor in deciding that the mother was mentally unstable. Depressed and missing her sister, the eldest girl attempted suicide months later, age 11. She too was placed in care. Alice had a breakdown.

The family are now reunited. One can only wonder what might have happened if the children's father had been around at the time the family fell apart. Would social services have approached him to parent his daughters on the grounds that the children's fantasies originated in their mother's delusions and not reality?

The picture emerging from the collective experiences of the mothers in the group is that mental illness is a smokescreen for the real issue. Before the mothers approached social services for help no one had questioned their competence as mothers. The women see themselves as scapegoats, their children left unprotected because the authorities are reluctant to investigate allegations of sadistic multi-perpetrator abuse in middle-class families. Alleged perpetrators need only to protest their innocence, while credibility is denied to mothers.

Cath was accused of being dangerously mad, Moira had suffered a bout of postnatal depression and Alice had a nervous breakdown. By blaming the mothers, social services could be said to avoid accusations of neglect of duty to protect children under the Children Act 1989: they can turn round and say they are protecting the children – from their mad mothers.

Case example: Clare and her son David

> Clare describes her childhood as 'like the Wests' (a well-publicised case of a couple prosecuted after abusing and murdering their own and other children). Her parents were violent towards each other and to their two daughters. Clare has a permanent disability from the daily beatings she received; police visited the house for sex with her mother, but worst of all were the trips to the moors where she and her sister Helen were sexually abused by many people.

> Following her parents' divorce when Clare was in her late teens, her mother confessed one day that 'we did a child murder when you and Helen were little'. Four years later, Clare was to tell psychiatric staff in the hospital where she was receiving treatment for severe depression about her life, with its bizarre abuse by groups of men and women 'witches'. Her allegations were noted but she was told that 'women don't do that'. In her twenties she became a busy mother with two children. The marriage did not last and the children's father left the scene.

> But 3-year-old David disclosed abuse by 'people and grandma'. Although Clare subsequently curtailed all contact, Clare's mother was working for a charity at the time that assisted her in going to court for contact with David and his sister. Clare gave evidence in court about her childhood including cannibalism, pornography and ritual abuse. Clare's mother's

case did not succeed: the judge placed an injunction forbidding her to approach her grandchildren.

Clare alleged bizarre, multi-perpetrator ritual abuse, in its most extreme manifestation, and her young son did the same. She pestered the police to investigate her mother and was stigmatised as a 'psychiatric case'. She is a needy resident on a poor housing estate; her son is frequently excluded from school. Yet she has not lost her children. We feel that the reason Clare's children were not removed from her was that, despite her history of depression and bizarre allegations, she had no ex-husband anxious to take over the children.

Other children of mothers in LASA have disclosed broadly similar abuse which included multi-perpetrator bizarre practices and torture. There are key differences in the outcomes. Significant factors in instances where the children were not removed from their mother include: the father was working class; he did not pursue custody; he left the country; the abuser was not the father and had no legal rights over the allegedly abused child. The authorities could have used the mental health label in these cases in order to justify removing the child, but somehow it was less of an issue. Was this because the equation lacked the component of pressure from a powerful father? Although this is a small sample, we think it is telling.

Group 3: children who cannot disclose until they are adults
Case example: Isabel and her daughter Patricia

> Our story has some of the elements that crop up again and again in the histories of the parents in the support group, but Patricia is the oldest of our children and can accurately be called a survivor. She was not removed from my care and, however blighted by abuse, her childhood was at one level normal. It remains to be seen if other children in the group will fare as well.
>
> When she was 21, my daughter told me that her father, from whom I had recently separated, had abused her throughout her childhood and that, although this abuse had mostly taken place at home, on other occasions she had been taken by him to a building some few miles away where a group of his associates were gathered. There he had undressed her and taken pleasure in watching her many abusers rape and humiliate her. There were other children present, and during the several years that Patricia suffered in this way she believed some had a much worse fate – she witnessed two child murders. When I asked her if the victims' parents were

present when this happened she responded that they came from children's homes.

Patricia made a statement to a child protection officer in the local police. The woman police officer warned her that it could set in motion an investigation leading to a trial where she would be torn apart by a defence barrister – since there was no proof, it would be her word against her father's.

My daughter did not sign her statement. She went back to university and buried herself in studies, which culminated in a first-class honours degree and the start of a successful career.

But, despite this, her life and mine were traumatic. Patricia and I felt let down by the police system that did not seem to take her seriously. On top of this devastating disappointment, Patricia's brothers denied that what she was saying was possible and accused me of putting her up to it. Overnight she had become a liar and I a malicious ex-wife. Contact with them became infrequent and strained.

In 1993 my ex-husband joined the newly formed British False Memory Society and sent my daughter various tracts purporting to show that she had imagined the events she had described. Our mother-daughter relationship was very painful; she was angry with me, convinced that the abuse could not have happened without me somehow, at some level, being aware of what was going on. I was sad and lonely – deprived of my sons because I supported my daughter, and deprived of her because I had not prevented her abuse.

But at the same time she spoke of how the physical and sexual abuse was not the worst thing that the perpetrators had done – 'it's what they did to my head'. She was told that I did not love her, in fact that I hated her; she was introduced to a woman who pretended to be her real mother and came to our house at dead of night to drive father and daughter to the place of torture. This woman, who said she loved Patricia, abused her. My daughter was told that she and I would be killed if she spoke about what her father was doing and yet she was also convinced that I knew about everything and did not care. Wrong is right and right is wrong, a topsy-turvy world that 'does your head in' when you're 8 or 12 and have been given something to drink that makes it hard to stay upright and concentrate.

Several years later, in 1997, I heard on the news that an inquiry had been held into how Fred and Rosemary West had managed to pick up some of their victims from outside the local children's home in Gloucester without anyone blowing the whistle. The girls simply disappeared without trace, were put down to having done a bunk when in fact they had been tortured and put to death.

I remembered my daughter's words and next day travelled to the Family Protection Unit where years earlier she had made her statement. Across the bottom of her file someone had written 'False Memory Syndrome'. From the police sergeant I learned that the director of a children's home in that city where the abuse had taken place had recently been convicted of sexual assault on the children in his care over an extended period. For a moment I wondered if I might have found the place from where the two murder victims of my daughter's abusers had been selected. 'Will you be looking through the files for any missing children?' After a slight pause, 'When I've got the odd ten minutes'.

Many years have passed since my daughter confided in me, in that time she has not gone back on her story and has been strengthened by talking to me and to others who have believed her. She is compassionate, energetic, bright and blooming with health. Despite a busy career, she is a kind and gentle partner and mother.

Munchausen's-by-proxy: a common thread

Sufferers of Munchausen's disease inflict injuries on themselves to gain medical attention. A variation is to injure someone else – usually their own child – to achieve the longed-for objective of receiving care for themselves – hence the 'proxy' part of the label. The afflicted family present as concerned parent and sick infant, but behind the facade is a terrifying malignancy. Covert surveillance techniques have exposed such a parent deliberately asphyxiating its own struggling offspring. At the point of death the parent pulls back and comforts the gasping infant with coos and kisses. The child must not die because the parent has to go on and on perpetrating this abomination, driven by some unspeakable pathological urge.

Munchausen's-by-proxy and familial sexual abuse have common elements. Assault by close family members is secret and hidden, with the tiny victim bound in both cases by the accident of birth to the perpetrator who is governed by a compulsion to abuse. The victim may be beguiled and rewarded in some way before or after the assault. Both kinds of abuse are hard to detect, particularly in the case of Munchausen's-by-proxy. In fact, sexual abuse can be investigated successfully by experienced and committed professionals even in the absence of forensic evidence. But in the case of Munchausen's, it is extremely difficult to prove or disprove. If mothers are in every way functioning and stable and won't go away and shut up because they want justice and protection for their children, then Munchausen's-by-proxy is a very handy label with which to discredit them. Several of the mothers have been told they suffer from Munchausen's-by-proxy.

In many cases in LASA the authorities have reversed the facts by labelling the mother as the perpetrator. The problem is that this interpretation ignores the allegations of the child. A cynical assertion might be made that the Munchausen's-by-proxy label is useful to the authorities confronted by a crime that they don't want to investigate. It is notoriously difficult to prosecute incestuous parents successfully. If incest cases are difficult to prosecute, how much more difficult are cases of incestuous torturers who take their own children out to a club for other adults to hurt and humiliate. Most juries would have difficulty contemplating this crime and that is where the label of Munchausen's-by-proxy can come in. If the children's assertions are ignored, the mother is unlikely to be able to contest such a diagnosis. It becomes like the old test for a witch: throw her in the pond; if she drowns she's innocent, if she floats she's a witch and she gets burnt at the stake. Either way she loses.

As will be seen from the above cases, the issue of going away and forgetting about the abuse is not an option if the father is persistent.

Summary and implications for the welfare of children

Our experience shows that children cannot be protected or escape from sadistic abuse if the father is persistent and demands unsupervised contact with his children. If the child refuses to go to these contacts, expressing a clear desire to stay with the mother and manifesting terror in the presence of the father or even at the mention of his name, the issue is turned on its head. The mother is accused, both of sabotaging the access right of the father, and of emotional abuse of her child by preventing a relationship with the father – a topsy-turvy world.

Why don't social services want to investigate these cases of sadistic multi-perpetrator sexual abuse? There have been successful prosecutions – the Wests, the Pembroke, West Country and Ealing cases. The significant difference in the LASA cases is the social class of the fathers. But what about the nice middle-class mothers in LASA, in professional occupations in the public and private sectors? They are not afforded the same indulgence or credibility – quite the reverse. In the case of adult survivors reporting childhood abuse, they are accused of weak mindedness and false memory.

There are a variety of reasons for the general reluctance to deal with sexual abuse cases. These relate to resources, outcomes and denial. Social services departments are under-funded and investigations are costly. The government has not encouraged focusing resources on investigations. There are too many agency staff and inexperienced social workers who do not have the skills for this work. A minority of cases reach prosecution stage and only a fraction of alleged abusers are convicted. This acts as a disincentive to take on cases. It is also likely that even seasoned professionals don't want to believe the atrocities that the LASA mothers report, or that middle-class fathers could be involved.

Listening to the experiences of 23 mothers in their battles over years to gain justice and protection for their children, deeply disturbing patterns emerge, not only in the rituals used by the abusers, but also in the methods employed by the authorities to justify their reluctance to investigate these cases. In particular, mental health is used as a smokescreen to discredit competent, productive members of society – mothers in LASA.

Since social services departments across the UK appear to have adopted remarkably similar formulae for dealing with these cases, it is difficult not to regard this as a conspiracy. Is it likely that officials get together and consciously plot? Possibly we are seeing an organic process of trial and error in finding the best way to silence these mothers. This is compounded by overworked or inexperienced staff, apathy, collusion, a certain amount of misogyny and the issue of social class. It is also often the case that professionals who believe the children get transferred.

Labelling and disbelieving are not the only strategies. LASA members have frequently reported intimidation of themselves and their children; draconian restrictions on the mothers' conduct during supervised contact forbidding expressions of normal loving behaviour; isolating the child, not only from the mother, but also from other relatives who believe the child; persuading the child their experiences are fantasies; threatening mothers that unless they take anti-psychotic drugs or engage in therapy to 'cure' them of their delusions they may lose their children. These are some of the methods that are very familiar to these women.

MULTI-PERPETRATOR ABUSE OF CHILDREN

The specific nature and circumstances of the LASA cases seem to have exposed the mothers and children to actions by the authorities that defy logic and common humanity. There is a cavalier attitude shown towards the spirit of the Children Act 1989 and the civil rights of the mothers and children. The paramount importance of a child's testimony appears to have been woefully ignored. By disbelieving these children, by depriving them of their mothers and by failing to protect them, the authorities can be said to be guilty of causing significant harm. It is known that to believe and protect children sets them well on the road to recovery. Nothing is more damaging to a child than to be disbelieved, to know that adults are not stopping the abuse, and to experience their own total powerlessness and that of their mothers. These children will have lost trust and faith in the adult world and have been persuaded to distrust their own experiences. What kind of future can be built on this damaging start in life?

Creative responses: how LASA has helped its members

Has LASA achieved something worthwhile and positive? To answer this question, I have turned again to the words of the parents themselves:

> I understand now that the treatment I have received from the authorities is not personal to me but was being meted out ten years ago to other mothers in LASA, often by the same expert court witnesses and social workers. This was a huge relief. At the time, the attacks against me were so personal that they sabotaged me and undermined my integrity. In black and white on court papers, all this character assassination and value judgment looks very real. Meeting others who had been through identical experiences from various parts of the UK was liberating. It allowed me to focus my anger and frustration instead of being self-destructive.

> I sit in the meetings and there are all these 'together' men and women and so I know that this situation didn't happen because I'm stupid; it allowed me to crawl out of the woodwork.

> It was fascinating, and more wonderful than I am able to articulate, to see how everyone who had been living this ghastly experience for ten years had got on with their lives; they were still able to laugh.

> I had been isolated for so long – and I wouldn't say this to any of the doctors involved in my case – but frequently there seemed no point in

going on living, this was the end, it couldn't get any worse. It was amazing to be part of this group, it was like coming back into society.

It was interesting sitting in the group, seeing how different people had dealt with their situation – it gave me options.

The handling of the case pushed my life out of alignment, everything I took for granted had been shaken and uprooted. Where I had been raving mad to myself, the pieces slotted into place once more.

I had been bewildered for so long it was as though a veil in my brain prevented me from understanding. When I came into the group I was able to comprehend the bigger picture. I became whole where before I was like Swiss cheese.

I could say what I felt and hear the same story coming from the other parents in the room, it relieved a lot of the confusion.

It was fascinating to see what company I was sitting among. I don't know what preconceived notions I had about the sort of families who would find themselves in this situation, but certainly I had assimilated the idea that I was a stupid person to get myself in this position. Here I was in a room, surrounded by attractive and intelligent men and women.

Having the words put to my own feelings, hearing my thoughts in another member's voice.

I was actually disempowered by the process which culminated in the removal of my child – threatened that if I spoke to anyone about the case I risked losing the meagre contact of one hour a week with my children which the courts allowed me. I felt powerless, emotionally paralysed, I couldn't make decisions. Joining the group has helped me to deal with things, to write letters, see myself as a person with rights rather than a sub-human who cannot even be allowed to have contact with her own children unless supervised.

I had been fighting three police forces and at last I knew it wasn't just me. If you put someone in a blue room and tell them it's red and go on telling them it's red and you are in a position of power, then lies will triumph over truth. Coming to LASA meetings was restoring the truth to me and me to the truth – from the first meeting I went up two or three rungs on the ladder.

When I know what my daughter went through I wonder how she survived. In joining LASA, I hoped that we might be able to stop other children going through this trauma.

I looked at a new member who was in a state of devastation and I could see how I must have been – how disordered were my thoughts and emotional well-being – and I realised I had travelled a long way and was going to be all right.

I sat in the group and looked at women who must be incredible mothers – I looked at Cath and thought how, if I was a child, I would go to her and she would be loving and cuddle me.

Before I joined the support group I was isolated – if you talk about, say, cancer to your friends, they would have their own experiences. But no one had a comparable experience to what had happened in my family; they were embarrassed and couldn't find the words to empathise. Most stopped contacting me.

My first visit to the group was my child's eighth birthday; I fell apart and it was perfectly okay. No one looked at me as though I had overstepped the mark. I didn't feel as though I was infringing everyone's sense of well-being by being needy.

I was believed – there wasn't shock, there wasn't horror, there was acceptance, which meant, of course, that I could accept more fully what had happened and deal with it more appropriately.

The main gain for me in belonging to the support group was that I learned to cope and to go forward. Initially, it seemed an impossible task to have contact with my daughter that was not coloured with the abuse. We were not permitted to speak about it but it was there, permeating everything. Mundane conversations would resonate with it because I would imagine that really she was using a code to tell a deeper, more stark truth. After a while, I realised that I should try to move on and that I had to do this for her; that if I had friends and interests and she could see me laugh and be successful, instead of falling apart, then that would be a positive role model. I trusted her to intuit that the knowledge of what had happened to her was the most significant factor in my life. She needed to see that I wasn't destroyed by it and then she, in turn, could see that it was possible to recover and have a happy, successful life.

CHAPTER 6

Flamingos or sparrows?

Paediatricians and the recognition of child sexual abuse

Jane Wynne

Child sexual abuse is common but many paediatricians avoid seeing sparrows (the obvious diagnosis) in favour of pursuing flamingos (exotic, non-provable rarities) and children remain unprotected. This chapter is based on my experience as a paediatrician in a large northern city. It discusses some of the difficulties that paediatricians may encounter in dealing with probable sexual abuse, such as working with uncertainty, risk and working with professionals from other disciplines.

The report of the Inquiry into Child Abuse in Cleveland (Butler-Sloss 1988) should have been the starting point for paediatricians to take up the challenge of child sexual abuse. The report dealt with all aspects of this issue, including approaches to management. The medical assessor to the Inquiry, Professor David Hull (later President of the British Paediatric Association, forerunner to the Royal College of Paediatrics and Child Health), acknowledged that child abuse was 'difficult for all concerned' (Hull, personal communication, 1987). At the same time, he recognised that it was part of mainstream paediatrics and that consultant paediatricians should be able to manage all but the most complex situations. However, many paediatricians have denied their responsibility towards abused children in general and sexually abused children in particular, usually on the grounds that they are not trained for it or that it is too time consuming. Most have avoided the protean challenges that flow from the recognition of child sexual abuse; and resources have not been adequately established for the initial recognition of abuse and the provision of therapy for children and support for their carers. As a result of current practice, as many as half of the children are abused again within six months of presentation (Jones and Ramachandani 1999).

The recognition of child sexual abuse prior to Cleveland

Kempe and Kempe (1978) have pointed out how the recognition of child sexual abuse in North America and Europe follows that of other forms of abuse. Table 6.1 gives a chronology of the official response to child abuse in the UK. Child sexual abuse was not recognised as a category of abuse on child protection registers until 1986 and no official advice was available from the Department of Health (DH) or professional bodies until after the Cleveland crisis in 1987.

Table 6.1 Chronology of the official response to child abuse in the UK	
1970	The term ' battered baby syndrome' generally used
1974	The term 'non-accidental injury' (NAI) introduced Child abuse registers and inter-agency procedures established
1980	Different categories of abuse recognised: NAI, severe neglect, emotional abuse, failure to thrive
1986	Guidelines *Working Together* issued (DH) Child sexual abuse added as category for registration
1989	The Children Act 'Grave concern' added as a category for registration Concept of 'significant harm' introduced
1991	Guidelines *Working Together under the Children Act* issued (DH) Publication of first Royal College of Physicians (RCP) report on physical signs in child sexual abuse
1992	*Memorandum of Good Practice* published (Home Office and DH)
1995	*Messages from Research* issued (DH)
1997	Publication of second RCP report on physical signs in child sexual abuse

Source: after Birchall and Hallet 1995

Before 1986 most paediatricians accepted the need for a service for abused children, dealing mainly with physical abuse, but also with neglect and non-organic failure to thrive. As paediatricians became more skilled at detecting physical abuse, the threshold for referral went down and less serious injuries were more likely to be detected. Children were removed from abusive situations, often being admitted to hospital while further investigation was carried out. Doctors talked to the families, who were usually socially disadvantaged, and, as long as the injuries were not too severe, would empathise and do what they could to help.

Examinations were carried out in paediatric units in accident and emergency departments or police stations. The latter were less satisfactory because the doctors were not paediatricians and the ambience was often inappropriate. Facilities are better now, where larger hospitals have an emergency department designated for children staffed by paediatric specialists. Examination in police stations was rarely satisfactory and was threatening for the child, who might well think she had been taken there for doing something wrong. The investigation frequently rested on the outcome of medical examination, the police preferring 'certainty' rather than findings 'consistent with' abuse or 'no signs of recent penetrative abuse'. Most police surgeons in Leeds were general practitioners and had inadequate training and did not see enough children to gain expertise. In addition many of the children had ongoing medical problems, for example in their growth or development, so that 'one-off' examinations were inappropriate. In Leeds the majority of abused children are now seen at clinics, held every afternoon at both the major hospitals by community paediatricians. However, in some places the examination of children may sometimes still be performed by inadequately trained doctors in non-child-friendly settings.

There were case conferences with the social services, but no parents were present and they were over within an hour. The paediatrician was treated with respect, a parking place being reserved and disagreement, if any, being courteous. Legal proceedings were uncommon, usually being before magistrates in the juvenile court, and often over in less than a day. Doctors were given priority as witnesses and afforded due gravitas as experts.

A persistent difficulty is the requirement for all agencies to work together, and despite training together all professionals inevitably have different perspectives (Department of Health 1988). From the outset, inter-agency training was recognised as a priority and each district general hospital nominated a consultant paediatrician (hospital and/or community-based) as a member of the Area Child Protection Committee and later Designated Doctors (Child Protection) were appointed.

Early recognition of child sexual abuse

By 1986 it was apparent that child sexual abuse was being managed in Leeds in a different way from physical abuse. In cases of physical abuse immediate protection was seen as the priority, whereas sexually abused children were often left at home while the investigation proceeded. In any event the large number of children where sexual abuse was suspected precluded hospital admission. Although foster homes were sometimes used, professionals often accepted a compromise, and risks were taken – and continue to be taken – with the child's welfare (Cleaver, Wattam and Cawson 1998).

The research we carried out in Leeds between 1986 and 1990 and the resultant publications (Hobbs and Wynne 1986, 1987a, 1990) proved very useful when our clinical work was challenged. We gained confidence in our clinical work as increasing numbers of children went through the child protection process. We had time to manage the cases with a proper multi-agency approach.

However, as paediatricians we found the work difficult and there was no advice forthcoming from our own organisation, the British Paediatric Association (BPA). In August 1986 Chris Hobbs and I, thinking it important to start a debate about this, submitted a paper entitled 'CSA (Child Sexual Abuse), Where to Start: A discussion paper' to the BPA. The paper found its way to the Academic Board, who 'received it' – that is, put it on a shelf. At Easter 1987 there was an embargo on child abuse papers at the annual meeting of the BPA. Child sexual abuse, a subject in which we were all on a steep learning curve, was not open for formal discussion by the profession's leading organisation. Meanwhile, at the Easter AGM Chris Hobbs and I arranged an 'alternative meeting' at which, together with other colleagues, we presented 5 or 6 papers on abuse to an audience of around 150 paediatricians, including 5 professors. The Child Protection Interest Group (CPIG) was established at the AGM to give a forum for paediatricians to discuss problems, report research and support colleagues. Our paper was resurrected and published by the *Archives of Disease in Childhood* in the autumn (Hobbs and Wynne 1987b). The BPA, however, continued to recognise only its own separate standing committee on child protection. It was not until 1995 that a room was made available for CPIG as a matter of course at the BPA meeting. There was tacit agreement that CPIG was here to stay, and it became an official subgroup of the more kindly disposed British Association of Community Child Health.

The impact of Cleveland

The media initially directed their criticism at the paediatricians and social workers in Middlesbrough. An assault on Leeds paediatricians followed. At this stage we all felt beleaguered. Reading how colleagues in the USA tackled criticism by self and peer review, we looked at our clinical practice, ensured we read the literature, listened to patients and their families, checked out our research ... but tried to remain child focused. In Leeds we were partially protected by the lecturing we had done at the behest of our wise and experienced social worker Jill McMurray and by Dr M.F.G. Buchanan who offered his wealth of experience (we had a monthly sex-abuse interest group from 1980), bolstered by smoked salmon and cream cakes. We spoke to MPs at Westminster; Leeds Education and Social Services Departments; with the elected members at Leeds Civic Hall; at a fringe meeting at the Labour Conference in Brighton; at conferences for GPs; to hospital doctors, nurses, midwives, health visitors; at numerous local meetings (e.g. Women's Institute, Young Wives, The Rotarians).

The paediatricians in Middlesbrough did not have time to establish their credibility in the management of child abuse but they were well liked and respected. Colleagues, patients, families and professionals alike spoke well of them and their commitment.

As a Leeds team we had not understood until presenting our evidence in Cleveland that, while the objective of the Inquiry was to understand how medical practice had unravelled, the imperative of the media was that we were to be stopped – we were to be presented as anti-family, antisocial and wrong.

This was a very difficult time. Presenting our data to the Inquiry, including a videotape of reflex anal dilatation, was interesting: being assaulted by the stepmother of one of my patients in the toilet at the Inquiry was not. The cross-examination by counsel for the inquiry was less daunting than it might have been had Professor Hull been asking the questions. Many of the difficult medical issues were not addressed.

In general the media proved to be dishonest and intrusive. We had been advised to talk to journalists and explain the issues and to begin with that seemed like good advice. However, their genuine interest did not last – newspapers have to be sold. Meanwhile, our clinical work, giving evidence in court, had to go on as usual.

Despite the conclusion of the Inquiry that 'an honest attempt was made' to address 'new and particularly difficult problems' (Butler-Sloss 1988, p.243), social workers and paediatricians in Middlesbrough were scapegoated and disbelieved. Management of cases, which was based on the existing protocol for non-accidental injury, was made very difficult by the attitude of the police, who were encouraged by their senior police surgeon to dismiss the paediatricians' diagnoses as mistaken (Butler-Sloss 1988, pp.103–104). However, an independent panel, set up by the Northern Regional Health Authority to provide second opinions, in the main confirmed the findings of abuse (Kolvin 1988) and the Inquiry preferred the evidence of Leeds paediatricians to that of police surgeons (Butler-Sloss 1988, pp.198–200). Yet the police surgeons whose evidence was disregarded by the Inquiry have been allowed to continue their work. Ultimately many of the children were not protected. This outcome has been repeated in the child protection field many times since, realising the fear expressed in the report: 'We hope that the professionals will not as a result of the Cleveland experience stand back and hesitate to act to protect children' (Butler-Sloss 1988, p.244).

The post-Cleveland climate

As recently as 1996 a professor of paediatrics asked, in all seriousness: 'Don't you think that sexual abuse is a Leeds disease?' In fact, child sexual abuse continues unabated throughout the UK, although there is no national audit and the numbers on child protection registers do not reflect its scale. In Leeds, disclosure remains the most common route to professional intervention (55 per cent). How do we give children the confidence to say and professionals the courage to listen? Children tell when they feel safe: this may take months or even years, by which time children's circumstances may have changed, and no one may be asking. The disclosure may be piecemeal and may not make sense for some time. If children feel that they are disbelieved they will readily retract or, more seriously, suffer a breakdown, especially if they were initially vulnerable (Sinason 1992b). The rate of diagnosis depends on the child's ability to say, the family's ability to hear and say, and the professionals' ability to hear, say and investigate. The *Memorandum of Good Practice* (Home Office and Department of Health 1992) sets an unrealistic standard for interviewing and consequently invalidates the disclosures of many children who are young, have disabilities or who are frightened or anxious. Research into the use of interviews videotaped according to the *Memorandum's* recommendations (Davies 1995) shows that most never see the light of day. Of 15,000 tapes, 5000 were sent to the Crown Prosecution Service but only 100 cases went to court, 79 supported by the videotape. After a long, emotionally damaging delay before the trial, it is very traumatic for children when abusers are

acquitted; less than 5% of cases of child sexual abuse end in successful prosecution. (Frothingham *et al.* 1993)

Features of child sexual abuse seen in a paediatric setting

In the early days of our work with child sexual abuse we had expected to see
older girls from poorer families who had been sexually assaulted by relatives
or family friends. The reality was different (Hobbs and Wynne 1987a). We
found that child sexual abuse occurs across the social spectrum, but recognition is greater among poorer families because articulate middle-class adults
are more likely to be believed. Abusers come in all guises. Some are uncouth
bullies with poor social skills, others are intelligent and charming – but at the
same time manipulative and ruthless. More than two-thirds of abusers are
male family members, one-third of these being natural fathers. There are
fewer stepfathers than we expected. One-quarter of abusers are teenagers or
younger. Women may also be abusers, whether as instigators or as coerced
partners, and their participation tends to make cases more tangled and
difficult to understand. Abuse by strangers or within paedophile rings,
although much talked about, is a less common presentation. However, child
sexual abuse may occur in all types of institutions, such as schools, residential
units, sports clubs, choirs, youth clubs, temples, churches, synagogues and
mosques. No racial, cultural or ethnic group is exempt.

Boys are abused almost as often as girls, the ratio in Leeds being 2: 3. Adolescent boys are at greater risk than we realised: a local pizza palace near a
children's home ran a brothel on the first floor serviced by boys as young as
10. The peak age for diagnosis is 7 years, though victims may be much
younger: I have seen attempted rape of a girl of 6 weeks and sodomy of a girl
of 15 months. The abuse is rarely limited to fondling: oral, vaginal or anal
penetration is attempted in the majority of cases we have seen (for further data,
see Butler-Sloss 1988, Appendix pp.313–319).

The physical examination

The report of the Cleveland Inquiry (Butler-Sloss 1988) highlighted the need
to apply the usual clinical method to the diagnosis of child sexual abuse, to
reach consensus on the physical signs and to agree a vocabulary. The notion of
a jigsaw of pieces of information from the various assessments by each agency
was used to counter the media allegations about snap diagnosis. Good
progress has since been made. The examination of children who may have
been sexually abused is now well described (Hobbs *et al.* 1993; Royal College

of Physicians 1997) and there is better agreement on the significance of various physical signs. However, there is still confusion about reflex anal dilatation: Cleveland seems to have left some people with the impression that it is of no significance, an opinion that is manifestly erroneous but still sometimes repeated (Bedingfield 1998). In fact, the report stated: 'The sign of anal dilatation is abnormal and suspicious and requires further investigation. It is not in itself evidence of abuse' (Butler-Sloss 1988, p.193).

An important advance in paediatric practice has been the use of the colposcope (an instrument with a light and a camera), which provides good illumination and magnification of the ano-genital region, and a distance between examiner and child. In pre-pubertal girls and boys it is not an invasive examination. Once a girl goes into puberty, the hymen grows larger and thicker under the influence of oestrogen. External inspection of the genitalia is no longer adequate because abundant hymenal tissue may obscure tears or dilatation in the hymen itself or in the vagina. Differences in methods of examination may account for discrepancies in reported findings in girls known to have been sexually abused. Since the prevalence of sexually transmitted disease in adolescent victims of child sexual abuse is now more than 25 per cent and brings the risk of subsequent infertility, it is in the best interest of older girls to be screened for sexually transmitted disease (STD) with the use of a speculum, subject to their consent. In pre-pubertal girls, however, the prevalence of STD is less than 5 per cent and routine screening is not recommended.

Photography is the best form of recording, and the colposcope has an integral camera. Photographs of good quality will obviate the need for the child to be re-examined for forensic purposes (an examination to look for evidence of child sexual abuse), and are also useful for peer review and for teaching. However, a competent examination can be made without a colposcope, and photographs can be taken with a suitable hand-held camera. Before taking photographs the examiner must always consider whether the child may have been involved in pornography. Forensic tests (swabs to collect evidence of the assault and assailant, ie saliva, blood, semen) are rarely helpful, but are recommended if there is a history of vaginal intercourse in the last five days (three days if the girl is pre-pubertal, and less if penetration was oral or anal).

Any examination, investigations or photography must always be subject to the consent of the child and the parent. Older children who understand the position and are considered 'Gillick competent'[1] may give their own consent if informed and freely given. In any event unless the child/teenager is cooperative no physical examination may take place – physical restraint may be considered further assault. Once court proceedings have started the consent of the court is also required. The examining doctor should always be accompanied by a chaperone, who should not be the child's carer and preferably is a nursery nurse or a children's trained nurse. The General Medical Council (2000) is explicit on this point.

It is important for the diagnosis to be based, not on the examination alone, but on a complete jigsaw of all available pieces of information (Hobbs 1991). Pieces of the jigsaw may include: the history given by the child, with due allowance for the child's age and emotional state; the history given by the carer; the child's behaviour; evidence of previous abuse, including emotional abuse and neglect; abuse of friends or siblings; worrying physical symptoms; physical signs; pregnancy, or sexually transmitted infection; results of any forensic tests; outcome of police investigation and of social work assessment. This approach is particularly useful in care proceedings, but less valuable in the criminal court with its stricter rules of evidence.

In any event the evidence including the child and carer's statements must be tested, although it is very uncommon for a child to tell lies even when there is repeat abuse with further allegations. Teenagers are more likely to manufacture or exaggerate allegations, but in an individual case ask, why? It is also uncommon in my experience for adults to lie but women are often severely maligned especially in the matrimonial courts.

Non-accidental injury and child sexual abuse

A study in Leeds showed that one out of every six physically abused children had been sexually abused, while one out of seven sexually abused children had been physically abused (Hobbs and Wynne 1990). Some of the injuries seen in sexual abused children were typical of those seen in non-accidental injury, such as bruising to the face, ears, back, buttocks and backs of the thighs. Other injuries were particularly associated with child sexual abuse, for

1   Gillick (1986) judgement established that children under 16 years can give legally effective consent to surgical or medical treatment independent of their parents' wishes provided they have sufficient understanding of their condition and what is proposed (BACCH 1995).

example grip marks on the inner aspect of the upper arms, knees and thighs; signs of attempted suffocation or strangulation; bruises on the lower abdomen and particularly over the mons pubis; love-bites; injuries to the genitalia – it is evident that previous teaching that boys' genitalia are rarely injured is wrong.

Case example: physical and sexual abuse in a young girl

> A mother went out one evening to have a fitting for her wedding dress leaving her fiancé looking after her 3-year-old daughter. When she returned the child was asleep in bed and the man seemed 'in a bit of a hurry to leave'. She found that her daughter's face was badly bruised by a hand slap and her back had multiple bruises from fingertips. Although the subsequent ano-genital examination was normal, the child, whose language development was good, described being hit after Daddy had squashed her and gone up and down. She said he was rude and tried to put his willy in her mouth, and it tasted horrible. The man was cautioned by the police.

Burns and scalds may be indicative of sadistic injury and particularly unpleasant abuse. Although the existence of satanic abuse is officially denied (La Fontaine 1994), we have seen elements that correspond to this and in Leeds we have no doubt that satanic abuse does occur. However, its ramifications may be very sophisticated; it is always carefully concealed and may occur on a spectrum like other forms of child sexual abuse (Gallagher 2000).

There have been cases in Leeds in which murdered children had signs of sexual abuse and it is now clear that this is not uncommon – though doctors may not look for or reveal it for fear of causing more distress.

Case examples: fatal injuries to young children

> A boy of 4 years was shaken to death by his mother's boyfriend while his mother was out shopping. He had an anal tear, compatible with recent anal penetration; there was no bowel disease.

> A boy of 2 years died from a head injury inflicted by his foster father. There were also signs of recent child sexual abuse, and his older brother later disclosed oral and anal abuse.

Domestic violence and child sexual abuse

There is a correlation between physical and sexual abuse of children and violence to their mothers. It has been shown that in families where there is violence to the mother, all children are affected emotionally to a greater or lesser degree; physical abuse occurs in up to 70 per cent of cases (Bowker 1988); sexual abuse occurs in 45 per cent (Stark and Flittcraft 1988). Drugs and alcohol are often implicated.

Case example: child sexual abuse ending in 3 deaths

> A girl of 14 years had been abused by her stepfather from the age of 6. She disclosed the abuse and her mother arranged for her to stay with a school friend over the weekend. Social services and the police planned that the stepfather would be arrested on the Monday, but meanwhile he raped, buggered and strangled his wife and the child and then hanged himself. It is clear with hindsight that a misjudgement was made about the mother, whose articulate and educated presentation masked her inability to protect. She had known that her daughter had been sexually abused for the last eight years, so why would she be able to protect her for that last weekend?

Violence may sometimes be extreme. There may be abuse of the fetus as a result of stabs, blows or kicks directed at the mother's abdomen. The mother may miscarry while the fetus may be injured or killed.

Case example: fetal abuse as part of domestic violence

> A 22-year-old woman who was 24 weeks pregnant was admitted with multiple stab wounds to her abdomen inflicted by her boyfriend 'in a temper'. The baby was born two weeks later and he too had stab wounds in the abdomen. He died at the age of 3 weeks.

Violence may occur in any relationship including gay families, and in any ethnic group. While the majority of violence is committed by males, women have been increasingly recognised as perpetrators of all forms of child abuse (Hanks and Wynne 2000).

Young abusers

The paper Hobbs and Wynne 1987, noted the importance of recognising young abusers and that whilst these children have needs of their own which need addressing the first priority is to stop their abusing behaviour before it escalates and becomes addictive (Hobbs and Wynne 1987b). Juveniles perpetrate at least 25 per cent of child sexual abuse, the abuser sometimes being as young as 5 years. The younger the abusing boy, the more likely it is that he himself has been abused. Almost all abusing girls have themselves been victims (Johnson 1989).

Case example: rape by a teenage boy

A mother went out with a friend leaving her husband to look after her 3-year-old daughter. The father then wanted to go to the chemist, and got the neighbour's 16-year-old son to babysit. Meanwhile the mother came home and on impulse looked through the letterbox. She saw the teenager get up from the child and pull up his jeans. The girl was taken for a medical examination, which showed that the hymen was bruised and swollen and the posterior fourchette (entrance to the vagina) abraded and bleeding. Forensic tests were negative but the boy admitted attempted rape, which was consistent with the story told by the child. It was later revealed that the boy was already on a diversion order for the sexual assault of a 5-year-old female cousin. He was an intelligent boy, the son of a teacher, but he was socially isolated and had no friends in his peer group.

It is important to address the needs of the abusing child as well as his behaviour. The murder of 2-year-old James Bulger, for which two 10-year-olds were subjected to a criminal trial which the European Court of Human Rights subsequently ruled had violated their human rights, illustrates the harsh and punitive attitudes in the U.K. towards children who abuse, and the low priority given to rehabilitation. The damaging effects of child sexual abuse are shown in Table 6.2. It is well known that child sexual abuse gives rise to severe emotional and behavioural problems that are often very difficult to ameliorate. Children suffering such problems are often angry and disagreeable, and tend to lash out at everybody they come across, especially those who try to care for them.

Disability and child sexual abuse

It has been difficult for paediatricians working with children who have disabilities to acknowledge that they are at increased risk of all types of abuse, particularly sexual abuse. Staff in child development centres and in special schools become very fond of the children and their families, which makes them less likely to suspect abuse. In addition, adults who choose to work with such children have often been accorded an unquestioning admiration.

Table 6.2 Follow-up study of sexually abused children in Leeds

Outcome	Index group N = 148	Control group N = 148
Surname change	29%	2%
Legal status change	3.1%	1%
Average no. of schools	3.5 (range 1–11)	2.2 (range 1–6)
Average no. of addresses	3.0 (range 1–13)	1.4 (range 1–5)
Further abuse		
• at home	38%	0%
• in foster care	14%	0%
Adverse behaviour		
• total	58%	16%
• angry, aggressive, violent	22%	1%
• sexualised	19%	1%
Education problems	26%	5%
Statement of educational needs	17%	1%
Growth problem	21%	6%
Wetting	19%	6%
Soiling	9%	1%
Referral to mental health services	29%	1%

Subjects were 148 children diagnosed with child sexual abuse when aged 7 years or less, followed up for eight years.

This study was designed to look at the longer term outlook for sexually abused children. Follow-up of the children was difficult and the information concerning each child was collected from the School Health Records and Hospital records: no information was available from Education Authority or SSD. Any information on the child was recorded; many of the abused children were known to the Community Paediatric or the Mental Health Services. The Controls were the next child on the School Register. The conclusions make a depressing message of failure for the child socially and educationally.

Source: after Frothingham *et al.* 1993

Case examples: children abused by respected adults

A deputy head teacher at a school for children with learning difficulties in Leeds is currently serving a very long prison sentence for sexually abusing children over a period of 20 years. It is likely that the abuse would have been identified and stopped much earlier if other professionals, including teaching colleagues, a psychiatrist, a psychologist and police officers, had followed the proper procedures.

The abuse of a 14-year-old boy and his 10-year-old brother, who was severely handicapped, came to light when a friend deciphered a list of sexual acts and their cost from an imprint on a note pad. It transpired that the boys had been sexually abused by their adoptive father for many years. Medical examination of both boys confirmed evidence of chronic anal abuse. The adoptive father, who was a youth worker, had a limp from polio in childhood, and had himself been abused by an uncle. He admitted the abuse and was sent to prison for three years.

Abuse of children in care

Unfortunately, taking children into care by no means guarantees their protection against further abuse. A study of 133 children in children's homes or foster care in Leeds showed that they were at least six times more likely to be referred for assessment of possible abuse than children in the general population (G. Hobbs, C. Hobbs and Wynne *et al.*, 1999). The abuse was sometimes severe, with 1 death, 18 cases of vaginal penetration and 34 cases of anal penetration. Half the children had already had more than one previous placement, and many had had four or more. Awareness of this problem may partly account for reluctance to use the care system. If a child is a previous victim of abuse the investigation is always more difficult, especially if an experienced carer is a possible perpetrator of re-abuse. If a previously abused child makes repeated allegations of re-abuse they should be taken seriously.

The legal system

In dealing with child abuse the legal system is slow, expensive and self-congratulatory but overwhelmingly inefficient. The outsider sees a judge who must be appeased, barristers who must appease or be appeased in turn, court procedures ruled by decorum and respect except to witnesses, and children who are viewed as fanciful, unreliable and dishonest. One study showed that in cross-examination 25 per cent of the questions were not age appropriate, and 17 per cent of barristers 'consistently used inappropriate language' (Davies and Noon 1991). Giving evidence is very stressful, sometimes boring. The judge on one occasion said to the parents' QC: 'Dr Wynne has answered that question fifteen times, I don't think she will change her view on the sixteenth'. I am quite clear that I would not want a child of mine to be in court as a witness. Few children seem to benefit from their 'day in court' – many feel re-victimised. Of course there are examples of excellent practice, but there is an urgent need for a radical reappraisal of children appearing in civil and criminal courts. Adult witnesses are bullied too; not everyone is a 'robust' witness and it is humiliating and cruel to have, for example, nursery nurses, foster mothers and teachers crying in the witness box. Why should bullied witnesses be seen as more credible? Any reappraisal must involve consultation, on equal terms, with all relevant disciplines taking part. The present appalling cost of court proceedings would be better used in funding therapy for abused children.

However, courts do have a very important role in the management of severe abuse. Table 6.3 shows some of the apparent changes in outcome that have come about since Cleveland – though it has to be asked whether the children are better protected as a result. There are now fewer child protection conferences, and the number of children on child protection registers in England fell by 2000 in the three years from 1997.

Of 160,000 referrals of possible abuse to social services, 75 per cent have a home visit by a social worker, 25 per cent have a child protection case conference, 15 per cent are put on the child protection register, 2 per cent are taken into care and 1 per cent are still in care six months later (DH 1995). The courts are seeing the tip of the iceberg.

Any delay in starting court proceedings affects children adversely. In 1996 the average wait for the high court was 64 weeks, 50 weeks for the county court and 38 weeks for the family court. Delays have got worse, and are said to result from poor court management, lack of court time, complex cases (or simple cases made complex by the legal profession) and conflicting expert evidence. Care proceedings have become increasingly adversarial, with aggressive and hostile cross-examination that prolongs the hearing and discourages potential witnesses. It is clear that the judiciary and the legal profession need more training in child abuse so that they do not add to the damage it does to its victims.

Table 6.3 Outcome of suspected child sexual abuse cases in Leeds before and after 1987

	1985–1986 N = 337	1989 N = 237	Significance expressed as p-value
Mean age	8.0 yrs	6.9 yrs	
<5 yrs	38%	41%	
Boys	28%	28%	
Girls	72%	72%	
Disclosure by child	39%	40%	
Disclosure by other	11%	11%	
Physical abuse	10%	2%	0.001
Worrying symptoms	19%	18%	
Physical signs Genital			
• total	42%	58%	0.001
• boys	2%	8%	0.018
• girls	58%	78%	0.001
Anal			
• total	42%	58%	0.001
• boys	83%		
• girls	25%		
Child protection conference	67%	67%	
Registered as CSA	86%	62%	0.001
Taken into care	36%	24%	0.003
Criminal conviction	17%	5%	0.001

This study was designed to see if there was a significant change in the management of child sexual abuse post-Cleveland. Table 6.3 shows that although the medical practice was much the same, the Social Services' response changed and was probably more sensitive to perceived societal demands.
Source: after Frothingham *et al.* 1993

Why do paediatricians find child sexual abuse so difficult?

GPs do not in general feel comfortable working in the field of child abuse; they have a commitment to all members of the family, which may include the alleged abuser, and later on they may be involved in any rehabilitation plan. Paediatricians too like to work closely with families and do not like conflict, complaints and negative media attention. Paediatricians say that child sexual abuse causes them more anxiety than any other part of their work apart from parental complaints. There are a number of reasons why they might feel so uncomfortable:

- They do not feel at ease discussing anything to do with sex.

- They perceive themselves as not trained to examine children who may have been sexually abused. That this is a specious argument is shown by the fact that where agency doctors are employed by the police for child sexual abuse work, they receive just one day's training on the subject before they are regarded as experts. Paediatricians already have 15 years of training and simply require extra advice.

- They regard it as too time-consuming. Yet a glance at Table 6.2 will show how needy these children can be. What is more important for any general or community paediatrician? (I acknowledge that a system specialist such as a paediatric cardiologist cannot realistically be expected to do more than make an appropriate referral.)

- They themselves may have been victims of child sexual abuse. Social class and a boarding school education are not protective – indeed the reverse may be true of the latter.

- They themselves may be abusers.

- They are wary of suffering the same fate as did the professionals in Cleveland.

- They find child sexual abuse too painful an aspect of human behaviour to contemplate.

Cresswell (2000) cites the following additional reasons:

- The NHS as an organisation does not understand the nature of the work.

- The work is stressful and can lead to personal or professional dysfunction.

- The courts are adversarial.

- The media are blaming.

- Society dislikes uncertainty.

Conclusion

The clinical picture is changing in the direction Kempe (1978) predicted. Eventually, when society comes to regard children as individuals and not as chattels to be owned, it will be accepted that children have rights and parents have responsibilities. As Butler-Sloss (1988, p.245) stated: 'A child is a person not an object of concern'. In 1991 the UK signed the United Nations Convention on the Rights of the Child: Article 19 deals with the protection of children from abuse and neglect. It is of concern that the UN committee which monitors the convention in 1994 made over 20 recommendations that have not properly been heeded. In consequence, children are still abused in care, or in secure accommodation, and further abused by the legal system. It seems that the English on the whole do not really like their children, and there is a need for a Children's Commissioner or Ombudsman. The responsibilities of health practitioners under the UN Convention are well described in *Child Health Rights* (British Association of Community Child Health (BACCH) 1995). In the words of Nelson Mandela, spoken during a visit to an inner city school in London, 'the civilisation of a country may be measured by the treatment of its children' (Mary Marsh, personal communication).

CHAPTER 7

Advocacy for the sexually abused child
The role of the guardian ad litem[1]

Pat McLoughlin

> The crucial importance of the guardian's role is that it stands at the
> interface between the conflicting rights and powers of the courts, local
> authorities and natural and substitute parents in relation to the child – the
> guardian ad litem has to safeguard the child's interests ... to make a
> judgement between the potentially conflicting demands of children's
> rights, children's rescue, the autonomy of the family and the duty of the
> state. Children now move centre stage and guardians ad litem move with
> them, to occupy a pivotal role in the successful implementation of the Act.
> (Timms 1992, p.3)

This chapter is about intervention on behalf of the child during the legal
process of child protection, and how this can contribute effectively to
planning for the child's future. It looks at the particular difficulties in the
post-Cleveland era for sexually abused children in getting the court to listen
to their experiences, wishes and feelings. It considers how the courts regard
children in public law proceedings and what occurs at the interface between
children and their advocates and the courts. The impact of split hearings
(factual hearings) is examined in the context of their differential impacts on
the children and their parents. Reference is made to the limitations of the
Memorandum of Good Practice (Home Office and Department of Health 1992),

1   Guardians ad litem are now incorporated into the Child and Family Court Advisory and
     Support Service (from 1 April, 2001).

which lays down guidelines for the interviewing of children on video for the purpose of criminal proceedings, because such video evidence can also be used in the civil court. Evidence presented by children must satisfy strict legal requirements. Since 1992, the interviewing of children has been limited by guidelines contained within the *Memorandum*. Police and social workers are trained to comply with this guidance.

Reflections on Cleveland

At the time of the Cleveland crisis I was working as a social worker with sexually abused children. The post-Cleveland lesson for practice in Leeds was the jigsaw theory (Hobbs, Hanks and Wynne 1993; see also Wynne, Chapter 6), where a medical diagnosis of sexual abuse could not be considered conclusive. Making a case depended on building up a picture of evidence from different sources. The jigsaw theory has since been employed as the correct approach to investigation, although it presents difficulties for children who are a symptomatic apart from medical findings.

From my present perspective as a guardian ad litem advocate for children, I frequently feel the tension between the cold scrutiny of the law and the struggle that children experience in conveying their wishes and feelings and being listened to in the legal forum.

The task of the guardian ad litem

The Children Act 1989 provides for care proceedings in which legal decisions are made to protect and safeguard children who may be at risk of harm. The start of legal intervention for a child who may be suffering significant harm is an application by a local authority to a Family Proceedings Court for an order under the Children Act 1989. Under Section 41 of the Children Act 1989, the court appoints a guardian ad litem, who is an independent social worker acting for the child, so that the voice of the child can be heard distinct from that of other parties in the proceedings.

The guardian ad litem appoints a solicitor to act for the child, forming a team frequently termed the 'tandem model of representation'. This model provides 'a neat and effective working synthesis of rights and welfare, which ensures that courts are given the maximum information and opportunity to make proper and wise decisions in respect of children' (Timms 1995, pp.81–82). Theoretically, this puts the child on an equal footing with other parties in the proceedings. The child certainly enjoys the same privileges as other parties, such as entitlement to expert opinion, full disclosure of documents, and the right to make certain applications on the child's behalf on questions such as contact. However, there are particular problems for those representing children in civil proceedings not encountered by those representing adult parties.

The appointment of an expert witness on the child's behalf

The guardian has the important task of gathering evidence to present the child's case to the court. This may include commissioning expert independent opinion on behalf of the child. Such experts are commissioned if possible by the guardian ad litem with all parties contributing to a joint letter of instruction. This practice is promoted by the court to reduce the number of experts giving evidence in proceedings, to safeguard the impartiality of expert witnesses and, not surprisingly, to limit costs on the public purse (Care Proceedings: Case Conduct 1998).

A common example in cases of child sexual abuse is the appointment of a child psychologist with specialist knowledge of assessing and treating child victims. Acting upon the letter of instruction, the role of the psychologist is to assist the court by providing an expert opinion about the issues for the child and an assessment of the child's needs. Where the child has made allegations of sexual abuse, the psychological expert is commonly asked to comment on disclosures made by the child, and to give an assessment of their coherence and credibility.

Problems of children's evidence

In our society, until very recently, children have traditionally been regarded as deficient in their understanding of right and wrong and lacking in their comprehension of the value of the truth. Gradually, as the status of childhood has been recognised through a process of development culminating in the UN Convention for the Rights of the Child 1992, understanding has slowly burgeoned that children are separate human beings with rights conferred on them by virtue of their birth, rather than their position in society or their responsibilities.

The UN Convention is now formally integrated into the British legal code through developments such as the Children Act 1989, in which the child's welfare is paramount, and the Family Law Act (S. 64 1996), which provides for separate representation in private law cases (it should be noted however that S. 64 has not yet been enacted). However, children still have major difficulties in getting their voices heard with the same strength and volume as an adult in our courts, and in presenting themselves and their unfolding development and understanding of the world.

Those who represent children are charged with the particular duty of speaking with the child's voice. At times, in conveying the fledgling person to the courts with all their complexities and intricate family relationships, guardians ad litem and solicitors attract some of the perplexity and lack of comprehension that the children themselves encounter in the adult world. In cases involving children's disclosures of sexual abuse, this problem becomes acute. Research by Masson (1999, p.156) into children's perceptions of the care proceedings highlights the fact that 'the system appeared to exist for adults, not for them', and that overall, children were 'out of hearing of the legal process'.

Particular problems with child sexual abuse

The way in which very young children disclose abuse is often problematic for the courts. If an adult victim of rape or violence decides to make a complaint, they do so out of a consciously thought out process: they need to tell someone about a criminal act of abuse they have suffered. They can seek out the most appropriate person and once embarked on that path, can usually deliver a complete or near complete narrative that describes their experiences, including the degree of pain and damage and how, when and where events occurred. The process for children who are abused by people known to them is vastly different. While there are a few children in Group A (Richardson and Bacon 1991a) who seek out and alert an appropriate adult, who they have identified as safe to tell, and reveal to them abuse they have suffered, a larger number of abused children are in Group B (Richardson and Bacon 1991a) and come to attention via the investigation of other concerns. An investigation can be triggered by concern about behaviour at home or school, inappropriate language or concerns that often, though not always, go hand in hand with abuse, such as neglect, emotional disturbance, physical abuse or dysfunctional family relationships. Once the child is recognised as in need of protection, the assessment then begins to piece the picture together and gather information that, with professional interpretation, can come together as evidence.

The child in foster care during the proceedings

When children are removed into foster care in order to protect them, the psychological and emotional issues are legion. They are faced with a series of adjustments and new relationships that test their resources to breaking point. There is psychological and emotional pressure from separation from parents and sometimes brothers and sisters, adjustments to a strange house with new rules, discovery and evaluation about their safety and relocation in a new environment. Forming new relationships with foster carers, perhaps moving to a different school or nursery, add to the child's tasks. Underlying all this is the awareness that foster carers, social workers, teachers and guardians ad litem all know or suspect that someone has hurt them physically, emotionally and sexually. For the child who is the unwilling custodian of intimate secrets, this changing world can be a terrifying place.

The cast-list of new people – social workers, guardian ad litem, solicitors, police, etc., who are charged with the responsibilities of investigation, representation and protection – all wish to speak to the child. Unsurprisingly, children can easily feel pressurised and overwhelmed. Their story may be told in small fragments. Tiny details, sometimes just a phrase or two, emerge, sometimes as sparse but revealing as 'Trevor touched my ha'penny', the phrase used by a 2-year-old to tell someone at her nursery that sparked off a child abuse investigation. Another example is a 4-year-old who said, 'Daddy touched my bottom'. Further detail was added over a period of weeks. When set alongside other pieces of evidence, such as medical and other information from statements and interviews, a picture of the context of her abuse and clues to possible perpetrators slowly unfolded.

The interface between the child and the court

How does the court then respond to this messy and inchoate picture? In care proceedings, where findings of fact are sought by the local authority as to the perpetrators of child abuse, the immediate task is to present the evidence as fully and clearly as possible. The child's allegations are clearly an important part of that evidence and need to be presented in as vigorous a manner as possible. A child who has been interviewed according to the guidelines and standards laid down by the *Memorandum of Good Practice* (Home Office and DH 1992) clearly has a better chance of his or her evidence being given weight by the court, though that in itself offers no assurances that the court is truly listening to the child's story.

The process that occurs at the interface between child and court is of great interest and concern. The court will scrutinise the child's utterances with its own cold logic, exposing and scrutinising each word and action of the allegation to an evidential test. The experience of abuse and the child's ability to give an account is expressed through:

1. the child's ability to use expressive language

2. the child's age and developmental stage

3. the child's psychological state

4. expert evidence, which assists the court to understand the child.

The court must be willing to overcome the first three obstacles in its efforts to assimilate what the child has said, and take each of them into account when deciding what weight to attribute to a child's words. Children's interests are placed centre-stage by the Children Act 1989 and become the paramount consideration of the court. The court has a clear duty placed upon it to exert its powers and abilities to serve the child's best interests. For the court to discharge this duty, obstacles 1–3 need special attention.

The guidelines contained in the *Memorandum of Good Practice* (Home Office and DH 1992) mould a child's evidence into shape to fit into the requirement of the rules of evidence demanded by the court. This imposes limitations upon the child (see also Wynne, Chapter 6; Palmer, Chapter 9). Many children who try to tell their story, and many a social worker or police officer who attempts to help them, fall foul of those rules in the course of *Memorandum* interviews and the endeavour to bring the child's story into the full evidential glare of the court's gaze aborts at an early stage.

The child's language, any prompts used by the interviewer, any inability to recount events in context or clearly identify them in time and space, these all work against the child's story being heard. Many professionals working to represent children's interests in the courts view the *Memorandum* as an adult-centred approach to children's evidence (O'Neill 1997).

Unlike other jurisdictions, notably those of the Netherlands, Norway and South Africa, there is no interlocutor or forensic investigator working alongside the child to help them give their story (Spencer *et al.* 1989). The child's evidence arrives before the judge in its raw state, which, especially when imparted by a very young child, can seem sparse and almost devoid of meaning. If the court can put the evidence in the context of the child's language ability, social context, the circumstances in which the child was cared for, the stage of their development and psychological state, and the events that alerted concerns for the child, children's evidence can then communicate a real depth of meaning.

The example of the small girl who said 'Trevor touched my ha'penny' illustrates this point. On its own, the phrase conveys relatively little until one enquires what is meant by 'ha'penny'. In Yorkshire parlance it means the vulva, along with a lot of other words, such as 'tuppence', 'fairy', 'tuppy' and 'fanny'. Even when one has identified that meaning, the ambiguity persists about what 'touched' means: was Trevor changing her nappy, or was he touching her for sexual gratification?

Without the assistance and full participation of the guardian ad litem, the solicitor and others who represent the child's interests, it is difficult for the court to reach a clear understanding of the child's story and decide what weight to attribute to a child's allegations. Similarly, because the child's story rarely comes in the neat wrappings that would conform to the provisions of the *Memorandum*, that evidence often needs to be interpreted and clarified by an expert.

The expert instructed by the guardian ad litem on behalf of the child often faces similar difficulties in giving their evidence to those who advocate for the child. For example, a psychologist who tries to explain and interpret to the court the language structure and idiom used by a 4-year-old child and the limitations imposed by the child's stage of development. The expert of whatever discipline is bound by the guidelines clearly enunciated by Mr Justice Wall in Re B (2 FLR 211 1998). The expert and the guardian ad litem must confine themselves to interpretation and opinion: the question of truthfulness is a matter to be decided by the court.

The challenge for the court is to take the child's limitations into account without allowing them to diminish the child's story. However, in my experience as a practitioner, the court may take as much notice of an expert who is seeking to discredit the child's evidence on behalf of the child's parent.

Courts do commonly accept, as a model of abuse investigations, the 'jigsaw' theory (Hobbs 1991), where a picture is gradually built up within an overall context. However, many guardians ad litem, practitioners and children's solicitors find it hard to avoid the conclusion that the child's contribution to that picture – telling their own story – seems to carry less weight.

Standard of proof

A judgement by the past President of the Family Division laid down guidelines for the courts in cases where findings of fact are sought and established the principle of cogency of evidence:

The required standard of proof for an allegation of sexual abuse is the balance of probabilities, taking account of the fact that the more improbable the event, the stronger must be the evidence that it did occur, before the balance of probability of its occurrence will be established (Re H and R Child Sexual Abuse: Standard of Proof: Sir Stephen Brown, 1996).

These guidelines have been instrumental in determining the success or failure of child sexual abuse cases. While no one could argue that the court should not test evidence to its own satisfaction before making findings that attribute responsibility for abuse, this does seem to discriminate against those children who have suffered the most serious forms of sexual abuse. The efforts required meeting the standards of proof in the most serious of cases, where children have made allegations that adults find hard to believe, are much greater, and have a lesser chance of success, than those who suffer less serious forms of abuse.

The raised standard of proof seems to militate against the child more than against any other party in the proceedings, particularly when children have a more bizarre or incredible story to tell (see also Brooks, Chapter 5). There is less likelihood of a factual determination being made against abusers because the onus for providing the case falls upon the local authority, pushed hard from behind by the guardian ad litem. In some cases of course, where the local authority is willing to lead the way, the alliance between the child's advocates and the local authority on behalf of the child can be empowering, but this is not always the case.

The scenario is akin to a trial where the alleged perpetrator (if a party to the proceedings) has to defend themselves against the child's allegations, with the odds weighted against the child because of the need to meet a high standard of proof. Recent judicial utterances have cast disapproval on to care proceedings developing into a trial, with all the implications of adversarial conduct and costs. While a less adversarial style of hearing is to be welcomed, the alternative of Orders of Findings made by consent has some disadvantages. This is where the Schedule of Findings is basically the result of negotiation, agreed by all parties. This avoids the evidence being heard, and the agreed schedule is presented to the court for approval. This 'compromise' can sometimes appear to abrogate the rights of the child to a proper hearing. In the more serious cases, the court should hear all the evidence in order to understand the full significance of physical, sexual and emotional harm. The case for a full hearing of the facts of serious child sexual abuse becomes more cogent when considering the very small number of criminal prosecutions. Care proceedings are the only forum in which some children can be heard and make their own case with proper, full legal representation.

The problem of split hearings

Care proceedings may be divided into two stages. At the first hearing, either called a factual, causation or threshold hearing, evidence is heard in order to decide the factual basis of the case: for example, whether or not the injuries caused to a child are non-accidental or whether or not a child has been sexually abused, and if possible to determine who may be responsible. The practice of split hearings was established in a judgment of Mrs Justice Bracewell. This recommended that courts consider whether

> questions of fact in a particular case, such as an allegation of physical or sexual abuse, might need to be determined at a preliminary stage and in such a case the early resolution of those issues would then enable the substantive hearing to proceed more speedily and to focus on the child's welfare with greater clarity (Re S (minor) (Care Order: Split Hearing) 1996).

Split hearings are now usual practice in courts where such questions arise. Good practice suggests that if the facts of the case are established at an early stage, this provides a good basis for decisions about what assessments, if any, should follow.

An example is the scenario where a child is thought to have been sexually abused while living in the care of his or her parents. Often in such cases there are no disclosures from the child that could amount to sufficient evidence to put before the court. Despite this lack of evidence, the court is often asked to make a factual determination, or 'finding of fact'. For example, a typical finding may be that a child has been sexually abused and the abuse occurred while the child was in the care of a parent or other carer. Such findings can be extremely helpful in planning for the future safety of the child (and possibly that of other children) and in settling such issues as contact and type of placement. Additionally, there may be findings that one or other parent or carer failed to protect the child from sexual abuse. A schedule of the findings being sought from the court is filed at court in advance of the hearing, and all parties have an opportunity to consider this, and to decide to what degree they support or disagree with them.

In this way, Schedules of Findings are subjected to intense negotiation, which results in shaving down through horse-trading between the parties. This can render the findings less and less meaningful and send ambiguous messages to parents or carers and child alike.

Case example: limitations in fact finding in family proceedings

Four children are subject to care proceedings. Three of them have medical signs of sexual abuse. The three older children have made allegations that a maternal uncle, aged 13, has abused them. The parents deny all knowledge initially that the children had alerted them to the uncle's sexualised behaviour. The youngest child, aged 2, had medical signs of sexual abuse of far greater severity than the older children. It appeared unlikely that the adolescent uncle had caused these. The local authority sought findings that sexual abuse had occurred in the care of the parents, and that the parents had failed to protect the children from that abuse. While the finding expressed in this way sets the responsibility for the abuse in a broad context, it fails to take the question of responsibility as far as it might.

However, this is still problematic as the term 'failure to protect' implies some degree of knowledge on the part of the parents or carers of the children at that time. Degree of knowledge is of course an extremely elastic concept, ranging from harbouring a suspicion, to deliberate collusion or complicity.

In this instance, in order to reflect the accounts given by two of the children that were highly suggestive that the parents knew of the abuse, the guardian ad litem made efforts to include the element of a degree of knowledge on the part of the parents. This effort failed. The parents' legal representatives convinced the court that lengthy and expensive litigation would ensue if the court chose to test the evidence of the children, and the court decided not to hear the children's accounts on that issue. The parents agreed to a finding of 'failure to protect' from a perpetrator likely to have come from the wider maternal family. The findings were agreed by consent, and the parents walked away without accepting any responsibility for the abuse that had occurred in their care.

When an agreed Schedule of Facts is not investigated by the court but is subject to negotiation between the parties, it becomes grey and indistinct and

represents a lesser force than the findings upon which the court has adjudi-
cated. No assertions have been tested, and the outcome can be that little is
achieved in terms of new levels of awareness and responsibility. Hunt and
MacLeod (1997) consider the advantages of negotiation over litigation:

> It may produce better outcomes for all the parties, particularly where it
> allows for flexible solutions which could not easily be formalised by the
> Orders set out in the Children Act, outcomes which have the strong
> support of the parties, or real co-operation to make arrangements work.
> However, negotiation may provide inadequate protection for weaker
> parties, produce coerced agreements, which fail because they are not
> accepted, or lead to outcomes which compromise the child's welfare.
> Whatever the impact in individual cases, negotiation leads to a
> marginalisation of the court. (quoted in Masson 1999, p.43)

I would argue that, rather than leading to the marginalisation of the court,
negotiations over Schedules of Findings can lead to the marginalisation of the
child. I suggest that there is a qualitative difference between negotiating on
matters such as contact, where the argument is one of final details, and negotiations on findings where a parent may be impugned. As we have seen, findings
can provide the basis for future plans and assessments and assist in decisions
on issues such as future contact between the child and other parties.

Detailed judicial observations on the evidence brought at factual hearings
can clarify what is needed in the next stage of planning for the child's welfare.
It gives the parents new and substantial material that promotes the 'period of
reflection' recommended by Mrs Justice Bracewell (Re S (minor) (Care Order:
Split Hearing) 1996). Robustly exercising this function in this way can contribute significantly to a child's understanding that their account has been
tested and authenticated by the court. A finding of fact of abuse wrung dry of
real meaning can appear to a child to be avoidant of the truth and collusive to
parents.

The impact of the court's findings upon the children

What is the impact of findings on the children themselves? What is their view
of that part of the court process? Direct work with children by the social
worker or therapist usually has several commonly accepted aims. One is to
encourage the child to talk about their experiences, both positive and abusive,
and the relationships that are important to them. Over time, and with the

commitment of the foster carer and social worker, the child can build up trust and confidence in the professionals caring for them. The child often starts to reframe experiences against new values and standards of behaviour. For example, the child may learn that bath-time in this new foster family does not signify an opportunity for someone to abuse him or her, or that what they thought may be sexual overtures are actually an innocent show of affection.

As this kind of learning experience accrues within the context of a new attachment, the child may start the process of learning that those past sexual behaviours, of their parent, carer or relative, were in fact wrong, and judged by the professionals and society in general to be wrong.

The child also learns that the guardian ad litem and social worker go to court and tell a judge that the child has been hurt and abused and the judge will want to know, if possible, who is responsible for that and how the child can be protected in the future. At its best, the learning process therefore tells the child that abuse is criminally and morally wrong and is considered unjust.

How does the child's view of the process compare with the reality of how the courts and the legal system actually operate? In other words, do children receive justice; do they see their abusers brought to account for their actions? The sad reality for many children is no.

Do we believe children have the same interest in pursuing the truth as adults? Not perhaps in the same way engaged in by professional adults during legal proceedings, by searching investigation and establishment of the facts. At the same time, children are as committed as any adult to obtaining open acknowledgement of their reality. Does the social worker, guardian ad litem or judge believe the account of abuse given by the child? Is the attachment they are developing with the new foster carers one that can be relied on, and does it afford security? Acceptance by new carers of a truthful account of abuse is one of the first steps in overcoming the trauma of abuse. It ends the isolation of living with memories of abuse and the psychological and emotional harm that flows from that.

If the court makes a Finding of Fact that abuse has occurred and is able to attribute some degree of responsibility, it is extremely important that this message be given clearly and unequivocally to the child. Children need to know that their contribution was taken into account and valued by the judge.

Children who have undertaken *Memorandum* interviews often have a heightened awareness of the court process and are conscious that a crime has been committed. The involvement of the police and the experience of talking to a police officer inevitably emphasises the fact that the authorities are taking their account of events extremely seriously. Yet all too often, children's accounts of their experiences, as relayed to the court within the framework of a *Memorandum* interview, fall under the intense scrutiny of lawyers and are judged insufficiently reliable to stand as cogent evidence. All childcare professionals are only too familiar with the kind of cross-examination that seeks to devalue and undermine children's accounts, in the pursuit of protecting adult clients' interests.

Dismissing children's accounts of abuse as unreliable has damaging consequences that may reach into the children's future. The lingering sense of injustice often proves a barrier to moving on to other development tasks and future relationships. The failure to draw a line under the experience of forensic investigation, and the failure to establish trust by ascertaining the truth, can lead to unresolved anger. This can surface later in further attempts to pursue and clarify the truth.

The most powerful players in court during care proceedings are frequently those who exercise the greatest degree of scepticism. Representatives and advocates of children need to 'ensure that the child is fully visible in the proceedings which requires that they must make themselves fully visible, in their role as an independent advocate for the child, as well as an officer of the court' (O'Neill 1997, p.42).

In my experience, all too often the outcome is that paedophiles walk away from court, unsullied and unscathed with little or no blame or responsibility adhering to them. The consequence of this, as many childcare professionals know, is that many abusers appear and reappear in other families, other proceedings, and other child abuse investigations in other parts of the country.

Finally, I would like to open or perhaps inflame a debate that simmers quietly. In many cases, findings are made in the civil courts in care proceedings, and attribution of blame and responsibility has been established through forensic examination and thorough testing of the evidence. Those conclusions are clearly crucial for the future planning of those particular children. However, even where there is a known history of a particular abuser targeting families and vulnerable children, that information remains closed in the individual files of those children. The important question is: should that information be made available to other professionals investigating child abuse?

If a system were available to alert social workers and others to the presence of a proven dangerous person in a family where the safety of children is of significance, such awareness would generate a genuinely raised level of concern and contribute in a substantial way to the protection of the children. Armed with such knowledge, both social workers and parents would be in a position to make informed choices about the named abuser, in much the same way that they could when confronted with knowledge of a convicted sex offender.

At present, reliance is still placed on the scrutiny of suspected persons' offending history to alert professionals and parents to convicted offenders. That reliance is becoming even more eroded as fewer and fewer convictions for offences again children are successfully prosecuted.

The promotion and dissemination of such information is clearly not straightforward. Lady Justice Butler-Sloss, President of the Family Division, ruled in 1998 against information about a sexual abuser being passed from one local authority to another (Re L and W (minors) and V (minors) 1998).

The public debate about the register of convicted sex offenders also raised similar questions about civil rights and the physical safety of the people named on the register. However, the arguments about civil rights and public safety could be applied with equal force to children. In cases where individual families and children are perceived to be at risk because of the presence of a known sexual abuser, failure to apply and act on that information could amount to an abrogation of the child's civil rights and physical safety. In the balancing exercise that occurs in consideration of civil rights, adults' rights weigh far heavier than children's.

Conclusion

Children are relatively powerless in the largely male, powerful and over-whelmingly middle- and upper-class legal system. Those who advocate for the child at the interface of the legal and child protection process must have a clear understanding of their own position in it and be prepared to challenge the establishment orthodoxy, which, however unwittingly, can and does diminish the child's voice. Courts are prepared to take account of other adult interests in civil proceedings. This means that advocates for the child must continually strive to make the child's voice heard.

Children who have suffered sexual abuse deserve the best and the most humane regard that society can offer them. This is especially true of their treatment within our legal system. At present, while our civil laws are designed to offer protection and to consider their welfare as of 'paramount' importance, in many respects children are still second-class players within the very framework we invoke to help them. Our intentions are good, but we continue to fail. Society has a responsibility to advocate for our children and the law must be no exception. Children are not at present centre stage in civil law, we must advocate to make them so.

Cases

Re B (minors) (Care Proceedings: Case Conduct) 1998

Re L and W (minors) and V (minors)

Re H and R (Child Sexual Abuse: Standard of Proof) 1996

Re S (minor) (Care Order: Split Hearing) 1996

Re B (2 FLR 211 1998)

Re L and W (minors) and V (minors) 1998

CHAPTER 8

A zebra among horses

Sexually abused children in the care system

Heather Bacon

This chapter is about children who cannot return to their family of origin after coming into the care system. It is based on clinical work in child mental health settings. It deals with children who remained in care in Cleveland after the 1987 crisis and with children subsequently taken into care in North Yorkshire and referred to a specialist child protection project (see Bacon, Chapter 4). While I examine some of the particular problems associated with Cleveland, I argue that all children who come into the care system as a result of sexual abuse have complex needs for which the services are largely inadequate. To emphasise their needs for care, the term 'children in care' will be used in this chapter rather than the more recently introduced phrase 'looked after children'.

Sexually abused children entering the care system, often with the extent of their abuse unrecognised, face enormous tasks in adapting to new and unfamiliar environments and putting down new roots. The children carry histories of abuse, violence, rejection and victimisation and legacies of loss, insecurity, grief and confusion. These issues may be further compounded by protective coping strategies the child has adopted to deflect intimacy. We are particularly aware of the devastating fears, invasion of the inner self and loss of trust in others that result from organised abuse (Bibby 1996) and ritual abuse (Sinason 1994). Children who have endured these forms of abuse and who have no safe base within their families may end up in the care system following protective intervention.

Children referred for psychological assessment or support frequently present complex behavioural and emotional difficulties, compounded by months or years of being moved from place to place. Their capacity to settle and to form relationships may be severely impaired. Often their behaviour may be abusive and aggressive, and sometimes sexualised, leading to rejection by others. Their new carers are often ill equipped to take on the long, complex task of helping and taking care of them.

Attachment theory can help clarify the tasks and dilemmas facing children who must remain separated from their families. Sexually abused children and their new carers have to overcome the child's distorted inner models of family relations in order to arrive at healthier forms of intimacy. The carer's ability to communicate with the child's inner world is a crucial element in making placements work. While protected from the original abuse, children in the care system remain vulnerable: safe caring is their primary need (Rose and Savage 1999) and re-abuse is the ultimate betrayal.

Children often arrive in the care system confused about the adults who abused them and those who failed to protect them. They must attempt to adapt and interact with many new adults. The skill and confidence required would challenge many well-adjusted adults. If those caring for the child are unsupported or untrained, the child's problems can provoke responses that are unwittingly judgemental and punitive.

The context of Cleveland

Children who came into care in Cleveland were particularly unfortunate in that like the children themselves, the agencies responsible for their care were traumatised and fragmented by the crisis. Unlike the children returned home in 1987, who were the focus of intense public debate, those who remained in care as a result of protective intervention had no public prominence. The court hearings in the Cleveland crisis were perceived as divisive rather than being the result of successful interventions, and those who were not returned home were lost to view. The polarisation of opinion at the time distanced professionals from the community. This affected the new carers, who, while living in a general climate of disbelief, were listening to – and usually came to believe – the children's accounts of their experiences.

Despite this difficult context, in the longer term, follow-up of some of the children showed that they were able to make new attachments and some have done well. This may be because sexual abuse was diagnosed medically at a relatively young age, the diagnosis was accepted, and the children were offered protection and received therapeutic help at an early stage.

Case example: outcome for children of different ages in Cleveland

> Michael, the eldest of four children, was placed with his aunt at the age of 9 years. He is now 21, and his whereabouts unknown. His brother Peter came into care at the age of 6 years as a result of a medical finding of penetrative abuse; he eventually disclosed that he had been abused in an organised setting by several adults, and probably by Michael. Very disturbed, he went through a series of foster placements where his acting-out behaviour included self-harm, arson, locking himself up and running away. At the age of 18 he already had two children, both of whom are in care. The youngest brother, David, was taken into care when 5 and already very disturbed; he was moved at 8 to a long-term foster placement, and at 17 was doing well. Their sister Caroline, aged 4 years at the time of intervention, made no disclosure of abuse but was protected on the basis of medical findings and what her brothers had said. At age 14, she had been in a successful adoptive placement for eight years. The two younger children were able to form stable new attachments and received therapeutic help.

The best chance for children unable to return home is in adoption or long-term foster placement. It is known that such placements are more successful when new carers are given full information about children's backgrounds (Farmer and Pollock 1999). The label of being a 'Cleveland child' may still have resonance, carrying echoes of unresolved issues from that time. A significant factor for the long term may have been the dearth of information that accompanied many of the children into their placements. This was the result of the political and organisational pressures to close over the past and wipe the slate clean (see Tate, Chapter 1; Richardson, Chapter 12). A process of active forgetting led in practice to a loss of records. The disorganisation and confusion in the system was mirrored in unplanned moves for which troubled children were ill prepared. Cleveland was an extreme example of how children moving in the care system may part company from their history, so that it becomes impossible to put together a complete story to help them make sense of their lives.

Case example: loss of information

A positive outcome has been achieved for one Cleveland child who at age 17 is studying for A-levels in her adoptive placement. This is despite the fact that the after-effects of the sexual abuse she suffered until the age of 4 were compounded by moves of placement prior to adoption. Her adoptive parents, while realising that she needed to know what had happened to her, had very little reliable information, and were in any case reluctant for her to know her early history because they felt it would be harmful for her to know she had 'come from Cleveland'. She received no therapeutic help until age 15, when her parents became desperate to understand why she still showed insecurity and ambivalence in the family and had a serious eating disorder. It transpired that her social worker became ill with stress during the crisis and had been able to write to them only once about the girl's background.

Case example: successful outcome despite being returned home unprotected

The young daughter of a mother who was caught up in the Cleveland crisis as a child has been referred. The mother had been returned home during the crisis. She subsequently asked to be taken into care again, and lived in a foster home for most of her adolescence. This re-parenting has proved its worth in that she now has a good partner and has made an attachment to his family. However, she still has a confused and ambivalent relationship with her birth family, and this places her little daughter at risk. This daughter was placed on the Child Protection Register because of contact with abusive adults in the family, in particular her maternal uncle who had also been abused as a Cleveland child and returned home. He now lives in a secure setting.

Although many children received good care from committed foster parents, few specialist services were available to support them, and many of the older age group seem to have ended up in children's homes as a result of placement disruption. Sadly, some were re-abused in a residential care setting and at least one committed suicide. These difficulties were not peculiar to Cleveland but have also been seen in children from elsewhere.

Patterns of presentation on coming into care

Children who have disclosed (Group A) are differentiated from those where the sexual abuse is undisclosed but suspected on other grounds (Group B).

Once the child begins to feel safe, often with the care and support of a foster carer, disclosure becomes a possibility and a Group B child may move along the continuum of disclosure (Richardson and Bacon 1991a); a Group A child may reveal more than was previously known. The child may become more disturbed during this process, but in the longer term a better outcome is possible as help can be informed and targeted. On the other hand, some children may be able to process and integrate their experiences through being re-parented. Rather than making direct disclosures they may need to forget, perhaps until a point of psychological transition such as adolescence or parenthood when they may once again become preoccupied with the past.

Relatively few sexually abused children now come into care through the 'medical window' (Bacon, Chapter 4); the extent and nature of sexual abuse can remain one of the child's most closely guarded secrets. In practice, there are still many sexually abused children within the care system whose abuse has not been understood or fully investigated. The problems of proving sexual abuse in court are discussed in McLoughlin (Chapter 7). In the author's experience, Cleveland resulted in local authorities becoming reluctant to seek a care order on the basis of sexual abuse when it might be more easily obtained on other grounds. While this approach might have been expedient in the post-Cleveland climate, it means that undisclosed abuse may act like a time bomb for which new carers are unprepared, and which may lead to breakdown of the placement. A finding in court that sexual abuse has occurred can strengthen a care plan for the child and guide future decisions about contact. The reluctance of professionals to focus on possible sexual abuse or to seek a medical opinion about it can condemn the child to a longer period of abuse. If the sexual abuse is left out as a factor that might contribute to the need for a care order, the child's underlying problems may not have emerged and therapeutic needs may not be fully appreciated.

Initial assessment of the child

The importance of understanding attachment patterns

Patterns of relating have their roots in early attachments (see Bacon, Chapter 3). For abused children, these patterns are learned from distorted family roles. It is crucial to understand the child's internal world, because distorted patterns create problems if replayed in foster care. Attachment behaviour can be assessed directly by observing the child with the parents during supervised contact, and the internal attributions of an older child can be explored by structured interview. Other indirect approaches, such as family doll play, can add to the picture of the child's internal working model of attachment figures and patterns. The importance of this assessment, particularly the implications for understanding and changing the child's behaviour with new carers, cannot be overestimated. Wieland (1997) has developed an internalisation model to assist therapists working with sexually abused children:

> It is the child's internalisations resulting from the abuse, and not the symp-tomatic behaviours, that need to be addressed and changed if the abuse is to be something that happened to the child, rather than a determinant that shapes the child's life. (Wieland 1997, p.xii)

Most children with disrupted primary attachments are able to form secondary attachments with their new caregivers. They inevitably approach this task 'primed by the history of their experiences in their primary attachments' (Heard and Lake 1997, p.84). These are overlaid or enhanced by the new internal models of experiences in other relationships (IMERs: Heard and Lake 1997) formed in the care system. If the care system does not provide children with a secure base to compensate for losses, especially if there are further moves and losses, the problems of abuse will be compounded.

Case example: distorted relationships

> Jemima, an adolescent with learning disability, had a model of attach-ments based on sex with all male members of her family, including her brother with whom she was initially placed in a children's home. She expected the same of her new foster family. Once she grasped that sexualised approaches to them were unacceptable she did not know how else she could be close. She became demanding and sometimes aggressive with her foster mother, desperately seeking reassurance that her new family would like her and not send her away. At the same time, she began targeting younger children of neighbours and at her special school in sexualised play. Ongoing therapeutic help in a specialised project (see also Ambridge, Chapter 10) has enabled Jemima to unlock and express some of her deep anger and her fears of being sent away. Her foster mother has needed a great deal of support in coping with such difficult issues, such as Jemima's constant complaint: 'When I first came here you didn't want me and I don't think you'll keep me for ever, but I need to be here for ever'.

The importance of the child's history

Careful mapping of the history can yield valuable insights into patterns of attachment. It can also highlight areas where important information may be missing and might be retrieved. By definition, sexually abused children who are made the subject of a care order have sustained significant harm, which may also have included physical and emotional abuse. They may present with an array of behavioural and social problems, depending on their age and personality. It is important to track backwards in the child's life, looking for clues of particular times of trauma or disruption, or stages where the child may have been less resilient to stress. Older children in particular may present with a 'hard front', but records may describe anxiety or emotional disturbance in the past. As a jigsaw is assembled, previously unrecognised symptoms can sometimes be linked to the timing and duration of abuse. 'Thick file syndrome' can make this a daunting task and may sometimes result in important details being overlooked.

Neglect and poor parenting can cause developmental delay and underachievement at school. There may be a pattern of multiple carers. One child recently assessed during care proceedings had had 24 moves of house, 6 changes of main carer and 3 changes of school in her first 7 years. It is hardly surprising that she was described as 'a child of limited ability with shallow affections'.

Seriously traumatised children can split off or dissociate from their experiences and feelings almost completely. Intervention must then have an approach that enables them to reconnect their experiences before they can alter their disturbed behaviour (Putnam 1997; Silberg 1998).

Initial responses to protective intervention and reception into care

For many children, being in a family equates with being abused. A first experience of being safe in care can help children to make disclosures about abuse. Young children may do this by re-enacting learned patterns of sexualised behaviour in the context of intimate care in the foster home. This should be explored, if necessary through a specialist referral, and the child's needs for therapeutic help and re-parenting evaluated to inform future carers. If the abuse is known about but the child remains unable to talk about it, some evaluation should be made as to why this might be the case and what might bring change. The child may need help to understand and accept that being in care should bring safety.

Children who have not told of the sexual abuse (Group B) may be very puzzling for their new carers: they may resist rescue, say that nothing has happened, and want to return home. Those who have disclosed (Group A) may be agonised by their perceived disloyalty to their natural family, including the perpetrator; they may retract disclosures and appear angry or rejecting of care, while desperately seeking attention in other ways. Others may be so disturbed by ongoing contact that their foster parents reach breaking point even before the care hearing. Disturbed children's behaviour and communication are easily misunderstood, and attention may be directed to the behaviour itself rather than to its meaning and adaptive function. Expectations that the child should quickly change patterns that were previously adaptive may simply teach the child that conforming is more important than expressing distress. Because of worries about prejudicing the outcome of a court case, temporary carers are often instructed not to talk to children about their past experiences or their worries about the future – the very things that would most help the children begin to make sense of their experiences and regain a measure of internal control.

Reception into care can be the first step in being placed in a number of foster and institutional settings, a process that can vary from overnight stays to placements of months or years. Placements are often provided initially on an emergency basis, according to availability of beds rather than suitability. Short-term carers are inevitably ignorant of important facts. At the point of the final hearing, children who have already been in a number of placements may already believe that everything is their fault because they are unlovable. Transient placements can produce or increase disorganisation in the child's attachment system. This will discourage emotional commitment, and the child will resort to shallow relationships that give proximity without attachment. Children can become emotionally or sexually 'promiscuous' in this way through insecurity and being unsure of themselves as lovable individuals. The receipt of love may have been associated in the past with painful feelings and sensations in a 'trauma organised system of sexual abuse' (Bentovim 1992), in which the basis for mutual relationships is impaired or non-existent and the child is vulnerable to exploitation. New carers quickly become aware of this but may not understand it and may become almost fearful of the child's approaches. If supported in coping with the child's disturbance and in talking about their own feelings, they can provide valuable information about the sort of parenting the child needs. A careful evaluation of these factors in the initial weeks should inform long-term planning; otherwise decisions about placement may be wrongly based on factors external to the child.

In some respects, these transient placements are bound to be difficult for children and carers alike. However, if carers are supported in encouraging children to express their feelings and voice their worries, it can help them make a start in the re-creation of trust.

Good practice in planning for permanence: therapeutic and task-centred placements

Children who are very troubled may benefit from a specialist placement early on. Only too often they undergo a series of moves, during which unmet needs intensify and problems become entrenched. More intensive early support, for example in the form of counselling or play therapy in tandem with sensitive planning and focused re-parenting, may establish foundations upon which they can become less confused, grieve for their losses, and develop receptiveness to safe parenting. This will reduce the risk of breakdown in subsequent placement.

It is often believed that very disturbed children cannot benefit from therapy until they are settled in a permanent placement. However, while this may be true of long-term treatment for problems of attachment, in practice many children have to wait a long time for permanence and some may end up in limbo. There are interventions that can help at an earlier stage; for example, children can be helped to relinquish patterns of behaviour that stem from past abuse and to express the pain of removal from home and family. To enable the child to retain some links with the family of origin, once the care order is in place contact can sometimes be re-established, so long as it brings no risk of undermining permanent placement. The child should also be helped to understand some of the reasons for the intervention. Many children retain a dream of returning to their birth family. Support in grieving can pave the way for re-parenting and the possibility of accepting new carers.

Unless carers and children are supported in the struggle to replace damaging patterns of relating with new IMERs, further problems can arise. If the child will not accept safe parenting and appropriate control, the foster carers may feel that it is they who are being rejected. It is often difficult in practice to disentangle these strands. Unresolved issues of loss, grief, anger and abandonment, or distorted ways of relating, can impact profoundly on psychological and emotional development, particularly the child's ability and willingness to form new, healthier attachments.

Regaining the capacity to trust, of paramount importance in healing, is particularly difficult for older children and adolescents. In the extreme, this can show itself as an attachment disorder – yet another label for the troubled child (Fahlberg 1991). Children who experience a series of placement break-downs may appear deliberately to invite and precipitate rejection, but their behaviour can be understood as a profound fear of *being* rejected, which the child desperately wards off by becoming proactive, thus creating at least an illusion of control. To break this repeated sequence, carers must gain insight into the thinking that underlies the child's responses and seek creative ways to change their own reactions so that the child experiences a different caregiving pattern. This in turn may eventually promote new responses in the child. Prior to a move to permanency, or after a series of breakdowns, children benefit from a task-centred placement where specialist foster carers do not expect attachment in return for care. This enables some children to let go the fears that otherwise might act as barriers to putting down roots.

Case example: complex problems for a Group B child

When Gillian was taken into care at the age of 5, sexual abuse had been suspected but not proven. Over a period of nine months, in three succes-sive short-term placements, her behaviour was considered unexceptional. Generally very passive, she sometimes showed flashes of aggression, expressed verbally or by lashing out. She was watchful and reluctant to allow herself to be touched or held.

At the conclusion of the care proceedings she was moved into a fourth, longer term placement, during which the foster carers were to undertake an assessment of her needs in order to identify an appropriate adoptive placement. They soon found her behaviour unmanageable; in particular her increasingly violent outbursts, with no obvious external trigger, posed a threat to their own small daughter and to other foster children in their care. Gillian would often attack the face of another child while her own face would go blank. The foster carers were concerned at her wandering stealthily through the house at night, and they sometimes found her in their daughter's bedroom, silently gazing at her. They felt that whatever had occurred in the past, of which they knew little, had profoundly damaged her, and they were fearful of the consequences for their own family. Gillian also began to exhibit sexualised behaviour at school, removing her underwear and attempting to pull down the pants of boys and girls in her class. She would try to touch their genitals and persuade them to do the same to her. School exclusion was discussed.

Concern for Gillian's well-being was increasingly superseded by anxieties about the welfare of children with whom she had contact. Although it was recognised that she had suffered serious abuse, she came to be seen as a threat to other children around her.

Such problems require specialist intervention and cannot be dealt with in a placement where other children are at risk. Unpredictable changes in behaviour suggest that Gillian was having dissociative episodes, and that everyday occurrences somehow triggered re-enactments of the trauma, leading to blanking off and to attacks on others. The unresolved trauma Gillian had suffered had perhaps become inaccessible, the extreme defence of the traumatised child where 'compartmentalisation or separation of areas of knowledge and experience from each other shape the behaviour in ways that are largely out of awareness' (Putnam 1997). In her first placements, Gillian appears to have protected herself in avoidant attachment behaviour, perhaps based on fear of re-abuse. It could be predicted that this might develop into the apparently detached 'dismissing' style, where affective content of experiences is denied or minimised (Crittenden 1995). This would present a very puzzling picture to prospective carers.

The new carers' hopes and expectations

New carers naturally want to rescue the child victim from the abusive past. They may have to deal with horrifying accounts of abuse, revealed to them once the child feels safe. They may feel angry with professionals because information was not given them at the beginning. Their feelings about the perpetrator may not mirror those of the child. The fact that children may still be attached to abusive parents and profoundly ambivalent about coming into care can be difficult for foster families to accept. Yet children in care often defend their birth family, however abusive, against all criticism, and say they would like to return to them as soon as possible.

Case example: retaining hope of return home

Louise, aged 8, expressed this in play therapy, using wild animals to represent her natural family and farm animals her foster family: 'There's this fence between the animals. Me and S [sister] are here [two baby zebras], with the horses to look after us [foster family]. We have to have the fence between us and just look at each other through the fence [touching noses with the mother zebra on the other side], but I'll be able to jump over it when I'm old enough.'

The child's internal conflict can muddle agencies who have to decide the extent and nature of the child's ongoing contact with abusive parents. Foster carers need support in coping with their feelings about this.

Case example: attachment dilemmas for children in the care system

Debbie, aged 10, had been in foster care for three years. Although there were concerns about possible sexual abuse, this issue was not addressed in the proceedings, and a care order was made on the grounds of physical and emotional abuse and neglect. Debbie then began to disclose a catalogue of serious sexual assault by her parents, her two older brothers, and other adults. This included rape, buggery, being tied up, and threats of drowning and murder of her mother if she told. Her father had a previous conviction for manslaughter. Although Debbie eventually managed to tell of the abuse in some detail, no action was taken to prosecute the parents. The therapist thought that ongoing contact with her parents was emotionally damaging and should be terminated, but social services disagreed because Debbie's older brothers both enjoyed visits, and the policy was to preserve family relationships if possible.

During an assessment session the following exchange was recorded:

Father: I'm innocent, that child has been brainwashed by you people. You people are frightened of the truth coming out. I want her to tell the truth, and before I die she will, because it's killing me. I lie in bed worrying about it. I'm prepared to go to a psychiatrist to prove it, or any court. It's hurt me that she's made these allegations.

Debbie (to therapist): It isn't their fault they abused me because they were abused as well, it happened to him when he was a child, and he didn't have any parenting skills.

Mother: If I believed you, I would split up with him.

Debbie: I don't want you to split up with my dad because that would be my fault, I'll lose my dad, for telling. What I'm trying to do is bring our family back together, not like it was before, but better. If you believe me then you're going to split up with my dad, and my dad is too scared that he's going to get sent to prison again. If he goes on fibbing then I don't want to tell any secrets, if my dad goes to prison then I'll never forgive myself. He's my dad, so I'll decide whether he goes to prison or not.

Eventually, Debbie's brothers began absconding from their placements, returning home at intervals. The children received mobile phones for Christmas and parents could speak to them unsupervised. Debbie's specialist foster placement was due to end, but at 12 years she had still not been matched with a 'forever family'. She broke down completely, to the point of psychological disintegration. In a state of great distress she begged her therapist to accept that she had not been abused.

'My life's in turmoil because I don't know where I'm going. I need a mum and a dad, I need to be a baby. I'm back to six months. I need my birth mum, and my baby brothers. I want to be somewhere forever. Dad can't rest until I've said he didn't abuse me, and my brothers are going to see the judge and provided they say the same, they can go home. You've got to write it down, that I haven't been abused'.

The therapist reflected back that Debbie wanted to end the hurting by saying it hadn't happened, but that she couldn't tell the judge this because she believed that Debbie still needed to be kept safe. Debbie ran out of the room. Care staff at her temporary placement reported that she began talking nonsense, rocking, and refusing to co-operate with the most basic requests. Debbie moved to a secure 52-week therapeutic placement, which has eventually given her stability, but her parents then applied to the court to have the care order revoked. The solicitor acting for the local authority recently commented that 'with hindsight, we should have terminated the contact years ago'.

Unless confusion about responsibility for abuse and reception into care are addressed, the child may remain emotionally frozen and dissociated. Highly vulnerable and damaged children can then end up in situations where they have to rely on their own resources in finding some way of coming to terms with their past abuse and separation from all that is familiar.

Problems in caring for sexually abused children

There are difficult behaviours and problems specific to sexual abuse. Some children will be passive, over-compliant and clingy, while others may be angry and 'acting out', and these patterns can change or switch. Children may exhibit sexualised behaviour, such as compulsive masturbation, self-display and inappropriate touching of other children. Older children may be provocative and flirtatious with adults, while smaller children will create unease when overly physically intrusive. Where the child has learning difficulties or disability, such behaviour can be more difficult to change. It is important that carers are trained to expect these problems, and to monitor, share and deal with their own reactions. Behaviour may vary according to the gender of the child, the previous abusers and the caretaker. Carers can become very disturbed by sexualised children. Sometimes the child may target an adult to try and re-create a special relationship, mirroring the dynamics of past abuse. This is damaging to the new family. Once the realisation hits home, the child is likely to be precipitately rejected. Anticipating and discussing these potential difficulties creates a climate of openness and makes them less difficult to resolve. However, it demands a certain robustness to talk about what 'willies, fairies, bums and boobies' are for, and to talk at the child's level about why children can't have sex (e.g. 'babies are too heavy to carry about when you're 7, and how would you manage to change their nappy when you're at school?').

Sexually inappropriate, aggressive or disturbed behaviour should be addressed in depth so that the child can achieve the desired closeness in more appropriate ways. Cognitive behaviour therapy has been shown to be particularly helpful (Cohen, Berliner and Mannerino 2000). Difficult behaviour can be a great saboteur of placements where there are other children. It is important that the carer's reactions and feelings should be addressed in parallel. A joint approach to these problems can prevent feelings of helplessness and labelling of the child. Many practical ways can be found of helping carers address children's inappropriate behaviours and replace them with ways of feeling close in non-sexual ways. For example, children can be shown how to sit next to an adult while watching TV and have a cuddle, and how to give kisses that are non-sexual. Reducing any fears of a sexual approach may be needed. For example, one little boy who had night terrors following repeated sexual abuse by an older brother, was helped when his foster mother gave him a sleeping bag and told him that as long as he had hold of the zipper tag, no one would be able to get him. Sexually aggressive or acting out children may need a task-centred placement with sufficient supervision to minimise risk to others while a programme of work is undertaken to help the child gain control. Sometimes sibling groups may need to be separated to protect younger children. Focused work at this stage can sometimes widen the options for the permanent placement.

Approaching such issues in a direct but non-punitive manner can prevent a child who is primarily still a victim being perceived as a potential threat. Otherwise a child may be labelled as a perpetrator, with all its negative connotations. Very subtle changes in attribution can obscure the child's needs as a victim. Boys are more likely to externalise their disturbance in aggressive behaviour, and their underlying feelings of powerlessness may remain hidden. Girls may present rather differently, often as compliant and passive or promiscuous and provocative, or sometimes a mixture of both. Inappropriate 'parental' behaviour towards younger siblings and even towards foster parents is a frequent pattern.

Residential settings

At present, residential care is not seen as the preferred option for children in care. Children who come into residential units have often experienced a series of placement breakdowns ending in rejection. They are the most damaged and vulnerable of all children in the care system. Their long list of problems may include: school refusal, sexualised behaviour, alcohol abuse and other self-harming behaviour, mood swings, mental health problems, inability to integrate in school, family or other social settings, delinquent behaviours and criminal acts. Carers may be ill equipped to understand the meaning of these symptoms and instead may focus on managing behaviour. Children are hesitant about making yet another attachment because they are fearful of further rejection, choosing to protect themselves by becoming actively rejecting and hostile. This defence against pain is often interpreted as attack.

Case example: contradictory messages

Michelle, aged 15 years, had five placements in five years. She was referred for aggressive, out-of-control behaviour. She refused to attend school and frequently absconded from the children's home. Staff said that she was 'working as a prostitute', failing to see that this was really re-abuse of a very vulnerable sexualised girl. Michelle frequently got into fights with other girls, where she was verbally and physically very aggressive. Her demeanour at other times was passive and sullen. She disconcerted peers because her approaches switched rapidly between the seductive and the quarrelsome, and rather than perceiving this as her only effective means of communication, people came to ignore her loud extremes. Her threats of leaving, used to control other people's availability, and her restlessness and attention seeking are typical of a child with an anxious/ambivalent pattern, designed to keep other people actively involved at all times (Crittenden 1995).

Children in the care system who have been sexually abused are vulnerable to further abuse and to abusing other children in turn (McFadden and Ryan 1992; Farmer and Pollock 1999.) There are greater risks of both for children in the care system (G. Hobbs *et al.* 1999). Those in children's homes and in day care are more likely to be targeted by paedophiles or to become involved in organised abuse, and older children may be exploited by entering prostitution (Faller 1998). The inadequacy of staff training and support also adds to the risks for children in institutions (Utting 1997). Of course, it is important to identify staff who abuse children in residential settings, but it is also necessary to make sufficient therapeutic resources available if children are to be kept safe and past trauma healed (Lindsay 1999). In our experience, shortage of placements means that abused and abusive children are placed together, increasing the risk to both.

There is an enormous challenge for the carer in understanding and meeting the needs of these children. There are particular problems where children must accept staff shift systems. Without consistency of care, challenging behaviour is likely to be addressed by superficial behavioural interventions which take no account of the children's deeper emotional needs. Children in institutions are more likely than those in families to learn problematic or potentially damaging ways of surviving. Although children's homes are recognised as the least satisfactory form of care, it is often difficult to place siblings together in a foster home. Imaginative measures can be helpful. For example, one local authority has recently been able to avoid splitting a sibling group of four by renting a council house and staffing it as a family group home with a relatively small number of carers.

Some children end up in residential placement following an allegation that a foster carer or adoptive parent has abused them. It must be recognised that foster carers can be abusive and are less easy to monitor than residential homes. However, this situation can also arise when a child misperceives intimate care and family life as grooming and preparation for further sexual abuse, or is hypervigilant about any signals that might suggest this. Whether the allegation is true or false, skilled and neutral intervention is needed for the sake of both carers and child (Calder 1999). If the allegation is not well handled, the child may end up in residential care so that other foster parents are not exposed to risk.

Case example: possible abuse in care

Martin came into care aged 4 because his mother, a single parent, had been unable to look after for him. Following his allegation that his adoptive father had abused him when he was 6, Martin suffered three foster placement breakdowns. He was eventually moved to a special setting for attachment-disordered children, but by age 15 had still not been able to join a family. Placements broke down when Martin placed intolerable demands on the foster mother and then acted out violently towards her when she could not meet them. At the same time he was unable to accept parenting from the father-figure. It proved very difficult for the system to contemplate or accept that he might have been abused in his adoptive placement. Abandonment by his mother was compounded by abuse in the 'rescue' setting, leaving Martin with a legacy of anger and inability to trust, coupled with a longing for closeness to an idealised non-existent mother figure. His insecure or ambivalent attachment pattern meant that he could not tolerate any separations or changes of plan. Promises about the 'forever family soon' were in effect lies, leading to loss of trust. His only recourse was to anger and acting out: his relationships ran on an emotional rather than a cognitive agenda (Howe *et al.* 1999). Intensive work with Martin in the clinic proved inadequate and the best that the therapist could do was to provide some continuity of support during changes of placement.

In play therapy Martin expressed his situation as follows: 'The train is going too fast for the coaches and they are derailed, but the train says to the coaches, "you have got to be braver than I am".'

The need for change in the system

A radical review and overhaul of the care system is long overdue. The British Agencies for Adoption and Fostering (BAAF) *Action Plan to Improve Adoption Services* (Collier 1998) recommends new legislation as a matter of urgency, in order to reduce delay for children awaiting placement, to give greater clarity to planning, and to strengthen the duties of local authorities to provide post-adoption support. A BAAF survey (Collier 1998) showed that 16 per cent of children who have been freed for adoption remain unplaced after two years. The assessment of potential adopters is a lengthy process and many have to wait far too long before a child is placed with them. The use of adoption for children in care is declining (Ivaldi 1998), partly because it is not seen as an option for the many children who are already suffering insecurity as the result of too many moves and are at risk of further breakdowns in placement.

There are enormous political issues about funding. Some children require so much support that caring for them becomes the equivalent of a professional task, placing great demands on the carer's time. In this situation there should be provision to pay carers so they do not need to work. Destructive, hyperactive or disturbed children are expensive to care for, and periods of respite are needed. Foster care, particularly the provision of task-centred or specialised placements, allows for such arrangements, but until very recently less support has been given to adoptive parents, who are implicitly expected to cope. For the most troubled children, a more flexible range of placement options is needed. In practice, this would mean that carers of children in both adoptive and long-term foster placements would be offered the appropriate level of support. Over the years, changes in practice in adoption and fostering seem to have been a matter of politics and policy, rather than an exercise of matching resources to the needs of children.

The complexity of children's needs and the serious limits on resources make planning for children in the care system a difficult task. Long-term strategic planning is needed to create adequate and sufficiently flexible resources locally so that children are placed in situations matched to their needs and to their capacity to accept care. When children and carers are given the help they often need, disruptions of placements lessen and continuity improves. Accurate and ongoing assessment of the needs of children and of carers should be a multi-agency task: reviews for looked-after children should routinely draw on appropriate resources in the health and social services, and in education. This approach is costly in time. The needs of many children cannot be met by brief interventions, and some young people and their carers will need support beyond the age when independence could otherwise be expected.

Pointers for change

Some of the poor outcomes described in this chapter could be avoided by the provision of well-directed help both for children and for carers. The problem is not lack of knowledge, but failure to focus on the child's needs or to provide appropriate resources for the carers. Early intervention and evaluation of attachment patterns and response to abusive experiences, together with careful planning of placement, could assist many more children towards healing. At present there is a gross imbalance between the large sums expended during the relatively brief period of children's entry into the care system, and the inadequacy of the resources provided to help them on their long and perilous journey through it. The answer is not to leave children in abusive situations in their families, but to make the care system better.

Acknowledgement

I am grateful to Veronica Milton, clinical psychologist, who helped with the germination of this chapter and has allowed me to use case examples from her practice in Cleveland.

CHAPTER 9

Pre-trial therapy for children who have been sexually abused

Tink Palmer

This chapter is based on my experience of managing a therapeutic unit for sexually abused children for five years. It argues that it is in the interests of justice that child victims of sexual abuse can receive therapeutic intervention prior to giving evidence in a criminal trial. The rationale for such intervention, the respective fears of prosecutors and therapists, and a model of working within an acceptable framework and protocol are described. The final section considers the research outcomes of offering therapy to child witnesses prior to their giving evidence in criminal proceedings. The research covers the period December 1994 to January 2000 (Webster, Palmer and Hughes 2001).

Connections with Cleveland

The therapeutic unit was initially established in 1987 as the Child Resource Centre in Middlesbrough General Hospital at the instigation of Dr Marietta Higgs, Dr Geoffrey Wyatt and Sue Richardson, 'in response to the crisis of referrals of children who had suffered sexual abuse within the Cleveland area' (Barnardo's 1998, p.7). Although it is a sad reflection that such resources are needed by children, the unit represents for me a vindication of the beliefs of those of us who were working in Cleveland circa 1987; namely, that there are many children in the community who have been and are being sexually abused, and who need rescuing by safe adults. It is still difficult for many children to speak out about their abusive experiences, but when they do, or an adult does on their behalf, they need help in making sense of what has happened to them. All children currently living in the Cleveland area can avail themselves of such a service from the Barnardo's unit.

The Barnardo's therapeutic unit

The work of the unit has evolved over a 13-year period. In 1989, the centre moved to the management of Cleveland Education Department and by 1992 the unit opened as a joint venture between Barnardo's and the local authority social services and education departments. The unit offers a range of individual and group-based services, which meet the needs of children and their families affected by sexual abuse. We also offer support to mothers and carers, individually in the first instance but with a view to offering them group work and joint work with their children. Invariably, the nature and security of the attachment between child and carer is damaged due to the dynamics of sexual abuse and it is essential for the future well-being and protection of the child that this is addressed. The need for support for carers should never be underestimated.

Children in both Group A and Group B (Richardson and Bacon 1991a) are referred to us. The former, who by definition have disclosed abuse, are the most significant proportion and are referred for therapeutic and counselling services. The latter, a smaller number, include children for whom there are concerns but who have not been in a position to disclose, and children referred for assessment due to their sexualised behaviour, the aetiology of which is unknown. The children who are the subject of this chapter belong to Group A, i.e. children who have made initial disclosures of sexual abuse and who were referred to the unit for therapy.

The case and rationale for early intervention

In practice, child witnesses have frequently been denied therapy pending the outcome of a criminal trial for fear, on the part of the prosecution, that their evidence could be tainted and the prosecution lost and, on the part of the therapist, that the unique and confidential nature of their work will be jeopardised and their case notes be demanded by the defence.

The concepts of safeguarding the interests of the traumatised child witness on the one hand and that of the defendant on the other do not lie easily with one another and are often seen as conflicting. Within the criminal justice system, the interests of justice and the rights of all accused persons to a fair trial are seen as paramount.

However, the rights of the child witness are often lost within this forum. Article 3 of the European Convention on the Rights of the Child makes it quite clear that 'in all actions concerning children, whatever body may undertake them, the best interests of the child shall be a primary consideration'. In January 1995, the British government was advised by the UN Committee on the Rights of the Child to implement more effective strategies to promote the physical, psychological and social recovery of the child victims of neglect, sexual exploitation and abuse.

There is long-standing recognition (Bentovim *et al.* 1988; Briere 1989; Finkelhor 1986; Jehu 1988) that the earlier therapeutic intervention takes place for an individual following trauma, the better the chance of healing and ameliorating the effects. Children are no exception to this. It is our experience that if children are left in a state of limbo and unable to make sense of their abusive experiences following disclosure, confusion and low self-esteem and low self-worth may well result in distress, self-harm or destructive behaviours.

The effects of sexual abuse are many. Children may feel grief, guilt and fear. They may display an inability to trust, cognitive confusion, lack of mastery and control, repressed anger and hostility, blurred boundaries and role confusion, pseudo-maturity and failure to complete developmental tasks, depression and poor social skills (Barnardo's 1998; Sgroi 1982). The degree of internalisation of abusive experiences is unique to each child and dependent on factors such as the nature of the abuse, the circumstances in which this occurred, the modus operandi of the abuser, the nature of the child's previous life experiences, the degree of support within the home environment and the child's natural 'in-built' resilience.

The trauma of disclosure is often underestimated. In order to cope, children need acknowledgement of their feelings and fears and need guidance. In all, experience tells us that in the aftermath of disclosure the child needs:

- to feel believed
- to be in a safe place
- to be protected from contact with the perpetrator
- to be offered therapy at the earliest time
- to be supported through the process of being a witness.

Many children remain in Group B and cope by blocking out their sexually abusive experiences, with long-term results that are now well recognised (Berliner and Conte 1995; Ferguson, Lynskey and Horwood 1996; Jones and Ramachandani 1999). For Group A children who have been able to disclose, it is in their best interests to be offered therapy as soon as possible after the disclosure. The longer the time between disclosure and starting therapy, the greater the likelihood of the child developing reinforced inappropriate responses and behaviours.

The *Memorandum of Good Practice* (Home Office and DH 1992, paragraph 3.44) states that after completion of the joint investigative interview, 'it should be possible for appropriate counselling and therapy to take place'. A study of the implementation of the *Memorandum of Good Practice* (Social Services Inspectorate/DH 1994) recognises the professional's wish for 'a damaged child to have the benefit of therapeutic help'. *Working Together under the Children Act 1989* (DH 1991) goes further and states that 'there will be occasions when the child's need for immediate therapy overrides the need for the child to appear as a credible witness in a crucial case', although revised guidelines (DH 1999) do not mention this issue.

Utting (1997, p.196) also recognised that 'it is important that children get as much help and support as possible and that the prospects of a successful prosecution are not affected'. He urged the Crown Prosecution Service to finalise the work on a code of practice on pre-trial therapy and to make it available as quickly as possible.

Concerns of the legal profession, law enforcement agencies and therapists regarding the provision of pre-trial therapy

Conflicting issues regarding the provision of therapy for traumatised child witnesses can be summarised as:

1. the interest of the child versus the interests of justice, i.e. ensuring that the accused has a fair trial

2. fears that the child's evidence may be tainted and deemed invalid

3. withdrawal of cases due to the court's perception that the child has been unduly influenced

4. myths held by members of the judiciary, legal profession and law enforcement agencies regarding children, i.e. that children tell lies, children may be coached in their evidence by adults, young children cannot express themselves adequately and that the witness experience may be too traumatic for them

5. views held by counsellors and therapists that children are no more likely to tell lies than adults, and are unable to maintain coaching, that young people are able to express themselves but do not use verbal communication as their only means of expressing themselves, and that

young people are able to survive the witness experience if properly supported

6. fears held by counsellors and therapists that the court may request their records and/or they may be summoned to give evidence, thus breaking the child's trust, which is pivotal to the therapeutic process.

The plight of traumatised child witnesses is being reviewed (Home Office 2000) and some new provisions will be implemented following the introduction of the Youth Justice and Criminal Evidence Act 1999. However, professionals are still faced with the dilemma of ensuring not only that the child's therapeutic needs are met but also that the court views the child's evidence as valid. In fact, the care professionals and the law enforcement agencies have a mutual interest in ensuring, wherever possible, that children receive pre-trial therapy and are still regarded as witnesses who will give reliable testimony. In addition, the therapist and child need to feel they can work within a safe, trusting relationship where confidentiality is maintained to the highest limit possible.

The Barnardo's unit's therapeutic process

There are clear criteria for referral of children and young people for therapeutic assessment and intervention. As a matter of general principle, the child should be:

- believed and supported by the carer with whom the child is living

- living in a stable environment with no imminent change of carer planned

- in a position where he or she has no contact, either direct or indirect, with any alleged perpetrator. This also applies to any person who may seek to pass messages from a perpetrator to the child, or influence the child on behalf of the perpetrator. The rationale for this stance is that the child needs to be released from the abusive messages, influences and experiences of the past in order to undertake therapeutic work

- escorted reliably to and from the unit by a consistent escort

- supported, along with his or her carer, by a social services or educational social worker, to whom the case will remain open during the period of intervention.

The key treatment focuses on the interconnection between how the child feels, thinks and behaves and our approach, although holistic, draws on cognitive and behavioural therapies.

Planning process

Prior to the initial planning meeting, all relevant documents are seen by the therapist. These will include the joint police and social services investigation report, the child's statement (video recorded and/or written), the perpetrator's statement and any additional reports from agencies involved with the child. Such information gathering is helpful in giving the therapist a view of the child's world, and is also often a useful adjunct to understanding the modus operandi of the perpetrator and the possible impacts that his abusive behaviours may have had on the child.

The planning meeting is attended by the child (if of an age and understanding), the carer(s), the nominated teacher, the social worker and the therapist, and chaired by the project leader or deputy project leader. The purpose of the planning meeting is fivefold:

- To confirm that the child is *choosing* to come to the unit.

- To ensure that the criteria for referral have been met.

- To confirm the unit's way of working and to offer any explanations that may be required by carers and children. Staff take a child-centred approach, work progresses at the child's pace and the child is facilitated to talk about abusive experiences should he or she wish to do so. There is no time limit to the child's attendance at the unit and the child's wishes and feelings are of paramount importance.

- To arrange a review date following the assessment of therapeutic need. This is normally eight weeks after the commencement of work.

- To explain the unit's confidentiality policy, i.e. all work at the unit remains confidential with one exception: if the child informs the therapist that he/she or another child has been or is being abused and this is new information, the therapist will, after discussion with the child, pass this information to the social services department. Therapists have clear written guidance on the management of new disclosures and procedures to be followed.

Following the planning meeting there is an eight-week assessment period when the child attends for one hour on a weekly basis. In order to offer consistency and security to the child, the session is held at the same time and on the same day each week. If there is more than one child from a family receiving a service from the unit, each child has a different therapist and each family member's work is reviewed independently. The objectives of the assessment period are:

- to clarify with the child the purpose of attendance at the unit

- to establish rapport and trust

- to establish the child's willingness to undertake therapeutic work

- to establish means of communication and methods of working

- to identify the main issues for the work during the next therapeutic stage. In particular, the social development, emotional and intellectual levels of the child are assessed, as are his or her sexual knowledge, behaviour and language. The main issues for therapeutic work are informed by the known impacts of sexual abuse. If it becomes clear that the child is displaying symptoms that indicate a mental health problem, consultation may take place with mental health professionals.

The therapist's written assessment and objectives for further work are shared with the child prior to a review meeting which is attended by all those who were present at the planning meeting. Subsequent review meetings are then held on a quarterly basis to review progress and a final review meeting is held on completion of the work. The therapist and the child make a joint decision when to end the work and the child is informed that he or she can return to the unit at a later stage if necessary. Children regularly take up this offer and their re-referral is treated as priority.

The unit takes a particular stance on what is termed 'safe and strong' work, i.e. where children are taught to 'say no and tell'. Our view is that safety is the responsibility of the whole community and in particular the adults involved in a child's life. Children and young people are not able to protect themselves against people in a position of power and authority over them, nor should there be an expectation for them to do this. Whereas they will be offered self-esteem raising strategies and awareness raising work as an integral part of their therapeutic work, no 'safe and strong' work is undertaken.

Preparation for the witness experience

Preparation for the witness experience is an integral part of the work at the unit. Testifying in court is known to be stressful and intimidating for both adults and children alike (Dent and Flin 1992; Goodman and Bottoms 1993). Many children who have been abused and are required to give evidence in criminal proceedings may already have suffered significant trauma from the abuse, been threatened with violence if they told, and experienced further trauma by the investigative process and medical examination. They may also worry about whether they are believed, whether they can remember the facts and whether they risk being rejected by those they love. One seven-year-old girl lived in fear following her disclosure because her stepfather had slit the throat of her pet rabbit in front of her and told her that this would happen to her mother if she disclosed his abusive behaviour. She had no cause to disbelieve him.

When preparing a child for the witness experience the worker must be clear about both the aims and components of witness preparation (Aldridge 1997). The aims identified by Aldridge are to:

1. educate the child witness about the legal process

2. address the child witness's fears

3. reduce anxiety.

The components of witness preparation are:

1. assessment

2. education

3. enhancing the child's ability to testify

4. enhancing the child's emotional resilience

5. involvement of child's carers

6. liaison and practical arrangements

7. debriefing.

At the unit a minimum of two one-hour sessions are offered, the timing of which is crucial. If they occur too soon, this can heighten children's anxieties and fears. On the other hand, if they are carried out at the last minute children feel rushed and can't always assimilate the information given. As with any good outcome, there is a need for careful planning – which includes co-ordination with the police and social services.

We have found that approximately two to three weeks prior to the giving of evidence is a helpful time to begin. Once the witness preparation is completed, the child is given the opportunity of a pre-trial visit to the court, accompanied by a police officer, carer and, sometimes, a social worker.

The children are also shown our video entitled *So, You're Going to be a Witness* (Barnardo's 1996) and use is made of the *Young Witness Pack* (NSPCC/ChildLine 1998). Each child is prepared individually to ensure that defence lawyers cannot suggest that collusion has occurred. In addition, carers and siblings may be included in the witness preparation process.

Because so many cases fail in the present criminal system, we have to make children aware that there are several possible outcomes:

- The defendant may plead guilty at the last moment, so the child won't need to give evidence.

- The defendant may change his or her plea.

- The hearing may be postponed.

- The defendant may be found not guilty.

- The defendant may be found guilty, but sentences vary and cannot be reliably predicted.

We have found that well-prepared witnesses can view the process as a positive experience, whatever the outcome, if they feel they have had the opportunity to be heard in court. This empowering effect takes place when young witnesses feel they have expressed themselves to the best of their ability.

Children also need an opportunity to express their feelings after giving their testimony. At the unit, we offer sessions to the child to debrief from the hearing and to assess any further counselling needs. One five-year-old girl attended the unit the day after she had been cross-examined and she was in a highly agitated state. The cause of this emotional disruption was the fact that the defence barrister had accused her of lying. Fortunately, her perpetrator was found guilty and received an eight-year custodial sentence. However, she required a further six therapeutic sessions to help her make sense of her witness experience.

Ensuring safe practice

Staff at the unit focus on ensuring a safe environment for the children. Accurate and prompt recording is a prerequisite of good practice. The session is recorded on the same day and written minutes are made of each meeting held. All files are regularly read and signed by the project leader or deputy project leader. The ethos of the therapeutic team is to challenge openly one another's practice, ideas and belief systems. Issues and concerns are regularly shared. In addition, there is a defined supervision structure that encompasses a two-hour monthly individual supervision session for each therapist, group discussions, weekly team meetings and ad-hoc daily availability of senior staff to offer support, advice and guidance.

Developing a framework and protocol for working therapeutically with children who are to give evidence in criminal proceedings

In 1994, a protocol was drawn up jointly by the unit manager, the officer in charge of the Cleveland Police Child Protection Unit and the director of the local Crown Prosecution Service in order to safeguard the best interests of the children and to ensure that they would be able to give evidence that was seen as reliable and valid by the court.

Initially, the nature of the therapeutic process and the way of working was shared with police and Crown Prosecution Service colleagues. Common myths about therapy were explored and the need to work at the child's pace and level of understanding was emphasised. An agreed framework for the therapy work was drawn up. This framework reflected the unit's normal way of working as outlined above.

However, there were two alterations to our normal practice. First, the therapist would not view the video of the joint investigation, nor read any police files prior to the child giving evidence. Second, our confidentiality policy was amended to include the fact that we would endeavour to keep all records confidential according to our stipulated criteria but would be unable to guarantee total confidentiality.

The agreed protocol reflects the balance between the therapeutic needs of the children and the need to ensure that their evidence is seen as valid in the criminal process.

Protocol

1. Before a therapist is allocated to the case, the project leader or deputy project leader liaises with the relevant police officer from the Police Child Protection Unit. This is to establish that there are no investigative matters outstanding and/or that there are no other issues that might militate against starting therapy.

2. The police officer informs the Crown Prosecution Service that the child has been offered therapy and ascertains if there are any contra-indications.

3. The police officer confirms with the project leader or deputy project leader that there is nothing to prevent therapy beginning.

4. Therapy can then start under the following conditions:

   (a) The child receives individual sessions with the same therapist.

   (b) The child is not involved in any group sessions prior to giving evidence.

   (c) The therapist makes immediate, factual, concise and accurate recording of the session following its cessation.

   (d) The therapeutic process stays within the agreed protocol and is child-led, i.e. no direct questioning of the child about his or her experiences occurs and sessions are conducted at the child's pace.

   (e) When or if a child chooses to talk about his or her abusive experiences for which the perpetrator is awaiting trial, the therapist should acknowledge what the child has said and make appropriate generalised comments but should not ask probing, investigative questions. It is recognised that children's disclosure rarely occurs as a 'one-off' event and is seen, in practice, as a process in which facts and details evolve over a period of time.

   (f) Should a child disclose further abusive experiences, the therapist should follow the unit's written guidance, which includes a referral under child protection procedures to the social services department with a view to a joint investigation being pursued.

   (g) The therapist completes a pro forma after each session on which the following data are included: the date and location of the session, name of therapist, names of anyone else present, length of session, confirmation whether records were made.

   (h) Just prior to the final hearing within criminal proceedings, the completed pro forma should be copied and the original should be given to the police who will place a copy on their file and forward the original to the Crown Prosecution Service. Another copy should be held on the therapy file.

Policy regarding disclosure of records

Concerns about confidentiality of the project's work with children led to the drawing up of a policy statement, with practice guidelines and staff guidance regarding disclosure of case records. This states that Barnardo's believes that case records of work undertaken with children and families are confidential and should not be disclosed, other than with the permission of the subject of the record, the person holding parental responsibility for the subject, for the protection of the child, or by order of a judge.

Thus the guidelines for therapists about requests for disclosure are clear. The policy of the Barnardo's unit is to resist all such attempts to gain possession of files by applying, in all cases, for Public Interest Immunity.

Safeguards for child witnesses

It can be difficult to offer children the safeguards they need regarding both the use of the protocol and the confidential nature of the work. At the planning meeting, the issues are addressed with both the child and his or her carers. Although it is not possible to ensure complete confidentiality in advance, we outline the action that we would take should there be a demand for the disclosure of our records.

The draft national guidelines on pre-trial therapy for child witnesses makes it clear that

> disclosure should not be viewed as a tool to enable the prosecution or defence to satisfy their curiosity. It is a principle that is designed to ensure that information which is of genuine relevance to a criminal case is available to the parties and the court. (Crown Prosecution Service, Department of Health and Home Office 2001)

A ruling by Mr Justice Sedley in June 1996 clarifies that the defence cannot seek access to files for the purpose of finding information that may assist their enquiries or discredit a witness. If they persist in a summons, despite the third party stating that they have no evidence to be submitted, and if the judge consequently decides that there is no admissible material, the defence put themselves at risk of a Wasted Costs Order (R v Liaqat Hussain Reading Crown Court 13 June 1996).

Evaluation of the joint working protocol

The project has been evaluated over a five-year period between December 1994 and January 2000 (Webster *et al.* 2001). During this time, 483 children were referred to the unit for therapeutic intervention following joint investigations by police and social services; 42 of these children would be required as witnesses in criminal proceedings at some future date.

It should be noted that once a crown prosecutor considers that there is a realistic prospect of conviction, the public interest must be considered. In cases when a child is the principal prosecution witness, the primary consideration for crown prosecutors is the best interests of the child. The decision not to prosecute the perpetrators of the vast majority of children referred to the unit is shared by the police and crown prosecutors, with the crown prosecutors making the final decision.

The Crown Prosecution Service sometimes appears to base its decisions that prosecution is not in the public interest on the following:

> the experience of testifying at trial is traumatic for children, the sole evidence is that of an inarticulate child who has not given a clear account of the abuse, corroborative evidence was generally lacking and/or a child who had delayed making a complaint, could be exploited by the defence. (Davis *et al.* 1999, pp.2–3)

Similarly, it is sometimes considered that the child is too vulnerable (e.g. because of learning difficulties or acute anxiety) to be put in the position of giving evidence in court.

The implications of such decision making are far reaching. The vast majority of children who have been sexually abused are faced with the bewildering knowledge that their disclosure, though believed by the investigating police officer and social worker, is not believable enough to be heard in a court of law. Perpetrators are not made answerable to the children and society for their abusive behaviour and, as such, remain a risk to children within the community.

The children

The ages of the 42 children who received therapy prior to giving evidence ranged from four years to 18 years. Their mean age was 11.6 years, with a standard deviation of 3.4 years. Of the 42 children, there were 36 girls and six boys. 39 were white Caucasian and 3 were of mixed race. At the referral stage, 13 children were reported to have some form of special need due to health, educational or behavioural issues, or due to physical disabilities.

The children had lived through some profoundly disturbing experiences and their perpetrators were charged with offences such as rape, unlawful sexual intercourse, indecent assault and actual bodily harm.

The vast majority of the children had been abused by somebody they knew – father, stepfather, mother, sibling, grandfather, close relative, family friend, babysitter or teacher. For many, their sexually abusive experiences occurred in the context of family dysfunction in which emotional abuse, domestic violence and, at times, chronic neglect were evident. For the majority of the children, their abuse took place over periods of months or years.

The legal process

Despite the fact that there was a government circular in 1996 (Home Office 1996) stating that all cases concerning child witnesses should be fast tracked and the benefits for the child in doing this, long waits, unexpected delays and adjournments are common. At least one-third of the 42 cases took more than a year to reach a final hearing and of these, five cases took over two years.

The two most common charges were indecent assault (34) and rape (11). In 15 cases the perpetrators were charged with more than one offence and in several cases there were three or more charges. Of the 42 defendants, 19 were found guilty two of whom have yet to be sentenced, 12 received custodial sentences ranging from less than one year to nine years, and 11 defendants were found not guilty. Of the remaining 12 cases, eight are pending a hearing, three have been dropped due to a decision by the Crown Prosecution Service that there was insufficient evidence to proceed, and one due to the fact that the child was too distressed to act as a witness.

Conclusion

There are a number of encouraging findings from this research. First, it is a striking fact that despite the previous stated concerns about this area of the work, in only two of the 42 cases were the therapist's records requested. In both cases the unit staff applied for Public Interest Immunity. On each application, the trial judge viewed the entire file and upheld their request completely in one instance and in the other asked for four sheets of recording to be submitted to the court. These sheets did not convey anything of a personal nature regarding the child and contained purely factual information.

Second, the fact that the children had received therapy was not raised as an issue of concern by the Crown Prosecution Service, defence lawyers or trial judges, and thus no cases were dropped due to therapeutic intervention.

Third, in the majority of cases it was clear that the project's intervention made a positive contribution to the children's confidence and self-esteem, which in turn enabled them to be assertive during the witness experience and is reflected in the high rate of convictions to date, namely 45 per cent.

There are, however, two further findings that continue to cause serious concern for abused children and those attempting to assist them. The unacceptable length of time some of the children in this sample had to wait before they were able to give their evidence was detrimental to their well-being. Although 483 children were referred for therapy during the five-year period under consideration, only 42 (i.e. 8 per cent) of their perpetrators were charged for their abusive behaviours. The investigating social workers and police officers had no doubt that all the children had suffered sexual abuse. This highlights the need for a re-examination of the way children's voices are heard and how their stories may be told in a judicial context, in order that perpetrators of abuse are brought to account both to the children and to society for their actions.

Professionals wishing to help abused children are still faced with a dilemma. On the one hand, children need therapeutic intervention as soon as possible. On the other, there are fears that the children will suffer further trauma if their perpetrators walk free, especially if this is due to the therapy being deemed to have tainted their evidence, or if the confidential relationship between the child and therapist has been broken due to disclosure of records.

This research shows that abused children can safely be offered therapeutic help prior to their giving evidence in criminal proceedings. There needs to be clear communication and understanding between the key professionals about all aspects of the process, both therapeutic and legal. Therapy needs to be offered on a sound, carefully thought out basis and to be accompanied by good supervision and recording processes.

At the unit we have tried to redress some of the imbalance that exists between the interests of the abused child witness and the interests of the accused. We consider that the trust that has built up between our unit and the other key agencies, i.e. the Crown Prosecution Service, police, social services department and judiciary, has made a very real contribution towards child-centred practice for one small group of children in the aftermath of Cleveland.

CHAPTER 10

Monsters and angels

How can child victims achieve resolution?

Maggie Ambridge

This chapter explores some thoughts about the extent and limits of intervention and therapy, from my own perspective as an art therapist specialising in child protection, and from discussions with colleagues. It looks at factors on the journey from abuse to resolution as they relate to children seen in a specialist project (see Bacon, Chapter 4) and considers how we may learn to offer more effective therapeutic help within child and adolescent mental health services.

The impact of Cleveland

This chapter is also an opportunity to reflect on and reassess personal and professional experience during the 'Cleveland crisis'. Living in Cleveland and working there as an art therapist with adult survivors meant that, although I was not directly involved, the issues were close enough to affect my life significantly. Through my work with adults beginning to talk about their experiences of abuse, and through that of other professionals close to me who were more directly caught up in what seemed a quagmire, I was witness to the toll taken on individuals and families. The experience affected both the victims of abuse, and those who worked with them or on their behalf. To me, it felt like a simultaneous combination of inclusion and isolation. That is, it brought a strange, unwanted and unsought inclusion in an exiled group.

When I visited other parts of Britain, I was struck by the impact of the 'myth' of Cleveland that had already taken root. Here were people like me, friends, colleagues, social workers, health professionals, who seemed curious, bemused, questioning, even seeming to want to keep the issue at arm's length lest they became contaminated. Sick jokes about Cleveland abounded at this time. They were usually either about Cleveland as the place where incest was the norm, or where social workers routinely kidnapped children and isolated them from their parents. These seemed to reflect a fear of guilt by association, which prompted people to dissociate themselves from what was going on there. Yet surely the same problems existed throughout the UK. Why were people who knew about child sexual abuse behaving as though it were an aberration that existed only in this specific area in the north east of England? Maralynn Hagood, an American art therapist who came to the UK in 1987, describes her own experience in this (tongue in cheek?) observation:

> Coincidentally, during that visit, the Cleveland Incident was splashed across newspapers all over Britain, and discussions on child sexual abuse were everywhere. Surely Cleveland had it wrong – there couldn't be so much child sexual abuse in the United Kingdom. (Hagood 1994, p.198)

The isolation of professionals in Cleveland at this time – not just by the media and public, but also isolation from peer support – can be compared with the situation of children when they encounter a disbelieving response to disclosure from parents and other trusted adults. The lack of a supportive environment makes it hard for professionals to recover or retain their integrity, just as it makes the child's hope of recovery and healing more difficult to achieve.

The privilege of working with adults abused in childhood was of primary importance for my practice at this time and had a profound influence on me. These women's own lives were vividly affected by the glare of publicity. Not only did this surround the same horrors they had been through in childhood, but also it unbelievably focused very publicly on their home area. It is hard to imagine just how exposing this situation was for them. It must have been like being caught in the beam of a huge spotlight, feeling that all the dreadful experiences they had kept concealed for so long were now made visible and revealed for all to see. At the same time, when their disclosures were met with disbelief, some doubted their own perception.

Yet, what was very striking was the simultaneous determination of the adults, many of whom were now mothers themselves, to proclaim loudly that what happened to them must not go on happening to future generations of children, that their voices must be heard. It was also not unusual for them to fear for their own children despite their protective stance, and to be very aware that they themselves could be misperceived as potentially abusive.

Cycle of abuse: myth or reality?

We are aware that adults abused in childhood may go on to become abusers or non-protective parents. What of the many who do not? The populist view is that victims are at risk of becoming perpetrators. While there is growing evidence that many offenders were sexually or otherwise abused as children (e.g. Vizard, Monck and Misch 1995), offenders are only a small proportion of those in the general public who have suffered abuse. Thompson (1999) suggests:

> This misconception – that sexual abuse victims are likely to go on to become sex offenders – grew out of research that asked adult offenders about their past, and discovered that the majority had been sexually abused as children. But the research asked the question of the wrong people. (Thompson 1999, p.20)

In considering the issue of recovery, we are immediately faced by more questions than answers. The first task is to find the right focus and ask the right questions. What of those abused children who never came to the attention of agencies and practitioners, of social workers or therapists? Those who go on to live lives which, while likely to be somehow affected by their experiences, are more or less stable; who form non-abusive relationships, develop self-esteem – in short, who live unremarkably? (See Cara's story in Ambridge, Henry and Richardson, Chapter 11.) Have they worked through their experiences and achieved resolution or do they have exceptionally strong support systems or personal resilience?

While there is growing evidence that many offenders were sexually or otherwise abused as children (Briggs *et al.* 1998; Finkelhor 1984; Wolfe 1984), it has been well documented (Alexander 1992; Finkelhor 1979; Russell 1986) that children are more severely affected by abuse, and are less able to achieve a good outcome, if the perpetrator is an attachment figure. Howe *et al.* (1999) comment that:

> When children's attachment figures become sexually active with them, attachment relationships become mixed with fears of pain, rejection and abandonment. This makes the conduct of all relationships problematic for these children. To form relationships with others implies sex, yet inevitably arouses fear, distress and anger. (Howe *et al.* 1999, p.151)

Within our project, these are the children we see who may already be becoming sexually aggressive and targeting other children. They may be the children who have no friends, who are bullied or feared; the children who are vulnerable to further predatory adults. As adults, they may continue to go through disastrous, abusive relationships until they are themselves parents who are, in turn, unable to attach securely to their own children. Although we are familiar with the assumption that abused children can go on to become abusers (if they are boys) or non-protective parents (if they are girls), this (as suggested above) should not be regarded as a foregone conclusion. We need to remember that those abused parents who recognise their experiences as abuse are more likely to break the cycle of abuse and not abuse their own children than those who feel that they were not abused (Hemenway, Solnick and Carter 1994). In addition, those who consider themselves as abused try to behave towards their children in a different way than their parents did, whereas the 'non-abused' child may identify with the abusive parent and act like her/him (Gara, Rosenberg and Herzog 1996, cited in Haapasalo and Aaltonen 1999).

The process of disclosure: what do we know?

Asking the right questions is particularly useful in addressing practice issues for the children who we are trying to access and help, both those who have disclosed (Group A: see Bacon, Chapter 4) and those who have not reached that point of trust and safety to be able to disclose (Group B: see Bacon, Chapter 4). It is important to check out early on the significance of various factors such as the context in which the abuse took place, the time scale or severity of the trauma, the gender of the abuser or victim. Is the key factor the response to disclosure, or being enabled to disclose, or even to find safety in a changed situation without disclosing? What are the effects of further life events? All of these variables interact with the underlying predisposition or individual resources of the child, making for a complicated picture. What differences might these considerations make for the child's journey towards resolution?

Disclosure in the context of attachment

Our project confirms the view that 'children classified as secure, avoidant, ambivalent and disorganised will show different behavioural reactions and proceed along different developmental trajectories in response to sexual abuse' (Howe et al. 1999, p.151). The first requirement for children in all these categories is safety. Herman (1992, p.154) contends, from her work with adults, that the central task of the first stage of recovery is the establishment of safety. Before a child can begin any form of therapy or start to address her internal hurt, the first step needs to be made to make her safe in a very real and concrete sense. That is, the abuse needs to have stopped and the child protected from further abuse. Sinason (1992a), in her work with abused handicapped children and adults, stresses the fact that abuse means a boundary has been broken. 'There was less room for inner fantasy at a time of trauma. The external event took up all the space and needed addressing and containing before the inner world could be strengthened' (Sinason 1992a, p.84).

Those concerned with the recovery of children in Cleveland in the late 1980s commented that 'disclosure is ... regarded as the first step in the healing process, despite the crisis it involves for the child, the family and helpers' (Richardson and Bacon 1991b, p.18). Even before this stage is reached, a degree of safety is usually a prerequisite for the child to be able to move up the continuum of disclosure (Richardson 1991b). Indeed, some older children and adolescents, having attracted sufficient concern to achieve removal into care, will delay disclosure until safety has been achieved.

Case example: Sarah

One such child, Sarah, a very intelligent girl, having engineered time out for herself, returned to the family home without making a disclosure, but now able to ensure her own safety, in order to protect her younger siblings. She did this, knowing that her presence could guarantee that the person who abused her would not harm the other children, whereas disclosure, while also protecting them, would have devastating repercussions for the family. Such solutions may not be what we would wish for these children, but offer a way they can cope with the situation – albeit at a cost. Sarah, along with others like her, gave up a promising academic future; she has sacrificed her immediate prospects to retain an uneasy stability.

The child's inclination to be wary of telling the whole story is understandable, especially if they are unsure of a parent's response. For example, Timmons-Mitchell and Gardner (1991) point out that:

Failure of the adults to validate the sexual abuse contributes to the child's difficulty trusting the self and others. Parents who fail to validate a daughter's experience of sexual abuse aggress against the child by discrediting the child as capable of accurate perceptions and judgements. (Timmons-Mitchell and Gardner 1991, p.333).

Supportive mothers and attachment figures

A significant factor for a positive outcome following disclosure is the way in which the disclosure is received and responded to. If the recipient of the disclosure is the child's primary attachment figure (usually the mother), her response and subsequent support may be the most positive external element of the child's recovery (Richardson and Bacon 1991b, p.22). Toth and Cicchetti (1996, p.39) point out that the variation in outcome for childhood victims of sexual abuse is likely to be a function of the perpetrator of the abuse and of the protection or lack thereof that the child perceives from their primary caregiver.

> In the context of child sexual abuse, mothers can be said to be the primary adult actors in child protection. … Their mothers' responses also form one of the key factors in children's recovery. Support from a non-abusing mother is one of if not the most significant factor(s) in uncoupling abuse from both short-term and long-term effects. (Hooper 1992, p.4)

Recovery can begin if the mother has the necessary internal and external resources to take on this task of validation for her child. Howe *et al.* (1999) indicate that the varied outcomes observed in victims of child sexual abuse can be accounted for by the type and quality of their primary attachment, and that good quality care giving is the most potent form of self-enhancement for children. Sometimes it seems that the negatives about abuse and its context can only be outweighed by the positives embodied in the caregiver and the quality of subsequent experience. The protective mother, then, has an awesome task to fulfil if she is to be the leading player in the recovery of her child.

Hooper (1992, p. viii) considers the responses of mothers and social workers, and notes 'increasing recognition of the importance of their mothers' support for children who are sexually abused'. She goes on to observe that 'the bulk of the work of child protection is done not by professionals but by children themselves, their friends and parents' (Hooper 1992, p.3), and refers to a study by Kelly, Regan and Burton (1991) which indicates that girls abused by adults are most likely to disclose to their mothers. Where the abuser is under 18, children and adolescents more often tell female peers.

Case example: sexual abuse in the context of secure attachment

> Two little girls, Rosie and Amanda, suffered serious, prolonged sexual abuse by their putative step-grandfather from the ages of 2 and 3. Because

of factors including the severity and duration of the abuse and the complexity of the relationship situation, disclosure was difficult and risky for the children and they didn't tell anyone what was going on until they were 6 and 7. The experience of these children might suggest a potentially negative prognosis. Factors included early onset, prolonged duration, serious sexual molestation, the perpetrator being someone perceived as a close family member, and silencing of the children by a complex system of threats and rewards. However, set against this, their mother's positive response of unqualified and immediate action to make them safe enabled the recovery process to begin. Further to this, and of equal importance, are the factors that enabled this mother to respond positively, and to continue interacting in a healing way with her children. Factors at play here include styles of attachment, internal resources, and external supportive relationships. It was fairly clear, from observation and history taking, that the girls had a secure attachment with their mother before the abuse. She, in addition, had good, secure supportive relationships with family friends, church and community that have contributed to her ability to sustain the security of attachments between herself and her children.

The girls' recovery process has been aided by their mother allowing and encouraging them to use creative and symbolic ways of overcoming the power of the abuser. This took place both at home, where they destroyed and ceremonially burned photographs of him, and within the project, through paintings and story making in art therapy sessions.

Acknowledging the abuse as a reality, which can then be moved on from, opposes the secrecy position of colluding with the abuser in the pretence that it didn't really happen or was insignificant.

In one of her therapy sessions, Rosie painted a powerful picture of herself, her mother and her sisters as a strong united group, standing tall with chins tilted upwards and gazing confidently forwards (see Figure 10.1). Continued contact with, and support from, other members of the family and key relationships which were established before the abuse confirms the sense of self and sustains the child through the difficult and painful process of healing – a process which can often have setbacks and needs 'holding'. Confidence in herself and her allies is an important factor to nurture at this stage as such qualities are effective in maintaining positive self-esteem when the way is hard.

This example illustrates Howe's point that 'children's ability to affect and influence the world around them, to believe that they can make a difference, to feel that they have some control over what happens, increases their sense of self-efficacy, a known resilience factor' (Howe *et al.* 1999, p.257).

Figure 10.1 Rosie's family

Non-supportive attachment figures

Not all parents are able or willing to give their children the unconditional belief that both protects them from further abuse and sets them on the path to recovery. The way a mother (or other primary attachment figure) responds to the revelation that her child has been abused is of paramount significance and importance. If she can maintain a close, supportive position alongside her child, recovery is greatly enhanced. However, a caregiver who is over-whelmed, emotionally unavailable, or who responds with anger, blame or disbelief, creates an environment in which the child experiences rejection and betrayal, and distress is intensified rather than alleviated. I have noted elsewhere that:

> Attachment theory addresses dyadic patterns of interaction; there is a fun-damental link between the study of sexual abuse and that of disrupted attachment, with dissociation being the third side of the triangle. There is a paradox in the cases of mothers of abused children who are both unable to protect, and at the same time determined to protect their children. (Ambridge 2000, p.74)

Case example: sexual abuse in the context of a dissociated mother

This case is particularly interesting because it illustrates differing experiences within the same family. It seems to show that 'good quality relationships at any time in life can help 'disconfirm' an insecure working model' (Howe *et al.* 1999, p.38). Parents who have themselves been victims of abuse are much more likely to be able to respond helpfully to their own children's trauma if the attachment with the child is secure. The prognosis is also better where the parent has achieved a good degree of resolution regarding their own experiences.

> Joan, the mother of a child referred to our project, had been sexually abused as a very young child by a female babysitter. As is often the case, Joan was unable to give a coherent account of her childhood. Joan described her childhood as ideal, with herself as a model child. In reality her childhood was chaotic and family life was based on violence. She recalls being smacked by her mother and also witnessing her stepfather attacking her mother. Joan did not know until much later that he was not her birth father. She says that he never hit her and she felt closer to him than to her mother. Relationships with both parents had been distorted. In her first marriage, Joan was re-abused sexually and physically, in a quite horrific manner. She found herself isolated and seemed unable to extricate herself from the relationship or to protect her 3-year-old son, Andrew, who was made to witness the abuse. Some years later, she is able to recognise that her own issues about not having been able to be a normal 3-year-old herself had led to her blocking off feelings and meant that she had insufficient resources to parent or protect Andrew at the same age.

> Andrew was referred at 8 years. His mother, Joan, now remarried, tells us that Andrew's behaviour has been regressing, he is giving his stepdad a hard time, and there has been a recent allegation of sexual behaviour towards a younger girl. Joan has another son, Will, who is 3 years old. Her relationship with her new husband, who is not abusive, has afforded her enough support to parent Will differently. While Andrew's problems include regression, sexualised behaviour and insecurity, Will appears to have a secure attachment with his father and a better one with his mother. Joan sees her younger son as very different from either herself or Andrew at the same age.

Case example: problems of a disorganised attachment

Problems can be more serious when sexual abuse plus disorganised attachment leads, as Howe comments, to children 'feeling depressed, uncertain and socially less competent. There is confusion about how to handle the self in relationships' (Howe *et al.* 1999, p.151).

> Flora made a clear disclosure of abuse by her father. Her mother, despite co-operating with the agencies involved, to the extent of accompanying her to a police video interview, did not want to believe that her husband could have hurt her child. She preferred to substitute alternative explanations for Flora's distress and behaviour. Flora, picking up on her mother's feelings, and needing to avoid rejection by her, retracted her original story following the video interview, saying that the story she had told was, in fact, a dream. Her mother was relieved to have an explanation that she could accept, which enabled her to retain her relationship with both her daughter and her husband. The price Flora paid was visible in increased symptoms for which her mother went on searching alternative explanations, while openly protecting her husband from even knowing that Flora's condition was a cause for concern. This mother is not alone in feeling relief at finding a more palatable (though false) explanation. After all, the concepts of the Oedipus and castration complexes, with their associated forbidden wishes and phantasies, 'replaced Freud's first idea that some actual occurrence such as seduction in childhood caused the later production of neurotic symptoms' (Mitchell 1996, p.13).

Supportive caregivers: the role of validation

If validation by the primary attachment figure is of singular importance, it is also a process that can be supported and strengthened in therapy. Treatment strategies for work with mother-daughter dyads focus on the teaching of trust. Timmons-Mitchell and Gardner (1991, p.333) comment that: 'The therapist who aligns with the client teaches trust by validating the client's perception of her previous experiences. ... Children feel supported and validated by the energy their parents exert on their behalf.' The treatment programme devised by Timmons-Mitchell and Gardner (1991) confronts the expectations that external agents will rescue the parent and child from victimisation, and focuses instead on supporting them to accomplish the transition from victim to survivor.

*Case example: the importance of a secure attachment in the resolution
of ritual abuse*

Sean, who had good early attachment experiences with his parents, struggled
in therapy to extricate himself from the internalised influence of organised
abusers who had used powerful techniques to distort the attachment and
supplant his parents in order to control him. The tug of war between the
primitive archetypes of good and evil, and his confusion about himself, is
played out through recurring images. Monster, angel and baby emerge as
aspects of himself, sometimes transforming from one to another. Several
sessions are spent constructing a clay mask, glazed black, and modelled to fit
his face. On donning it, in a subsequent session, he becomes first a 'monster
without a name', stripped of humanity and identity (qualities embodied in
secure attachment), then, 'an animal monster that plays and eats. Its favourite is
cookies and chips and fish for tea', clearly identifying the monster as a child –
himself.

> He tries to find an explanation for the origins of the monster – 'a friendly
> monster comes along, and then it grows up' or 'the angel makes it with a
> special machine'. This last is such an odd juxtaposition of spiritual and
> physical, earthly imagery that it could be straight out of the works of
> Dante or Blake, and seems to be a reminder that whatever changes have
> been imposed on him, the powerful primary experience remains as a pos-
> sibility to return to.

> 'The monster baby doesn't have a mum or dad', Sean says, describing the
> seemingly interminable period of being a 'lost boy', then goes on to say,
> 'but he does … he finds his parents in the end'.

> The constancy of the parental bond has been of paramount importance to
> Sean's progress and, like any child, he is intensely sensitive to the quality
> of their attachment to each other, displaying anxiety when the couple rela-
> tionship shows any sign of instability or conflict. A painting made by Sean
> in one art therapy session seems different from anything else he had done,
> but makes sense when seen in context of what was currently going on.

> He depicts a boy with his hands up in a gesture of surrender. On either side
> of him, a bull and a cow with steam coming from their nostrils face each
> other. 'They are cross', says Sean. 'The boy is frightened they will
> stampede and he would be dead. They are going to talk to each other.
> They might have a fight. They are arguing about who is having dinner
> first. The feeding trough is in the middle.'

Asked what would make the boy safe, Sean replies: 'If he went and climbed over the fence. I think the boy is going to jump over the fence and the cows will keep on arguing.'

This was at a time when Sean was being bullied at school in ways that echoed the circumstance of his abuse, and his parents again seemed unable to protect him. At the same time, there were arguments between his mum and dad, who were expressing some fundamental differences about their beliefs concerning what had happened to Sean. Only after his parents regained some stability in their own relationship, and it was safe to 'stay in the field', was Sean able to feel secure enough to continue his healing process and not 'jump over the fence'.

The absence of a secure base

The concept of safety is an important precondition for disclosure and thence the continuing process of recovery or healing. What, then, of the substantial subgroup who are unable to, or choose not to disclose (Group B2: see Bacon, Chapter 4)? A child cannot disclose until either a degree of actual, physical safety is achieved (for example, by separation from the abuser and having somebody to advocate and listen) or else there is sufficient security in the attachment relationship. Some older children and adolescents appear to consciously organise this process in a more sophisticated way. Individuals in this group, having alerted concerns, will sometimes delay actual disclosure indefinitely once physical safety has been achieved – by, for example, leaving home. Disclosure may or may not follow later, when the past abuse affects aspects of life that need to be addressed.

Case example: no secure base for disclosure

Shelley, an adopted child with an adopted older brother, manifested her distress in behaviour that included mutilation of dolls, fire-setting and, as she reached adolescence, frequent running away from home. In art therapy, she began to explore images that reflected her unhappiness and anger, and to develop a sense of herself as an individual. She verbally expressed a wish to have time away from her family, a request that was passed on to social services. At the same time she made a real effort to contain the situation by avoiding clashes at home. This lasted for a number of weeks but, when no respite was forthcoming, Shelley again disappeared. Eventually found, cold and sleeping out in the open, miles from home, Shelley was accommodated with foster parents, who, once she was living with them, attended to previously undiscovered physical injuries. In this setting more overtly sexualised behaviour emerged and, for a while, Shelley opted out of therapy, in which, it seems, she felt she was moving too close to issues she was still not ready (or safe enough?) to address.

There are clearly many other victims/survivors who choose to stay silent or who do not feel that they have a choice, making a private decision to stay silent. The following case example illustrates the significance of disorganised attachment for children trapped in silence.

Case example: chaotic/disorganised attachment

The process of disclosure is even more problematic for children like Jemima, whose early relationships were so disorganised that, at age 13, she was unable to give a clear account of who was or wasn't a family member, and it was difficult to identify a primary attachment figure. Neither her birth mother nor her stepmother had protected her from abuse by her father and by her brother, and her family continued to blame her for her father's imprisonment, leaving her depressed, socially disadvantaged, and confused about handling relationships.

After a year in a foster placement, Jemima has developed what can probably be best described as an anxious attachment with her foster mother whom she desperately wants to please. In her art therapy sessions, no matter what the verbal content, she consistently makes gifts and messages of love to her foster parents, especially mother. Following a disruptive period, during which Jemima had become physically abusive, her messages become more detailed and urgent, spelling out both her wish to stay with them for many years and her fear of rejection (see Figure 10.2).

Attachment and recovery

Several factors make for the most positive resolutions of the trauma of sexual abuse. Some are already inherent in the individual child, such as intelligence or creativity. Others relate to caregiving in early life and deficiencies in these areas may be 'topped up' by acquired or secondary attachment from accrued positive experience at any stage of life. Of all the factors that contribute to a favourable survivor outcome, the one that perhaps gives most cause for optimism is the quality of attachment that promotes resilience. The concept of the protective function of resilience is described by Bowlby (1989):

Figure 10.2 Jemima's messages of love

> my hypothesis is that the pathway followed by each developing individual
> and the extent to which he or she becomes resilient to stressful life events
> is determined to a very significant degree by the pattern of attachment
> during the early years. (Bowlby 1989, p.256)

The child's temperament can also be seen as contributing to the protective pot
of resilience available to an individual. We recognise such characteristics
within the unique person of every child, in his or her personality, humour, dis-
position and intelligence – the elements that make up a differentiated human
being. These factors interact with others residing in the child's relationship
with the parent (attachment figure) and, in turn, we are aware of the importance of the quality of the parent's own attachments and supportive relationships with others.

Fonagy *et al.* (1994) link a high reflective-self function to resilience
because it facilitates stepping back and reviewing what is happening in
complex interactions. For children in therapy, this function is often seen in
their visual or verbal images produced in artwork, play or stories. Rosie chose
to combine visual and tactile images in paintings and clay with written narratives – stories that progressed her recovery.

In her last art therapy session, having attended for a year, Rosie wrote a
self-evaluation, reflecting on the stories that had helped her.

Case example: Rosie's goodbye session

> The first time here it was strange and I was nervous about what it was
> going to be like. We were first looking for pieces of a jigsaw to put it in
> place [referring to a pattern of connecting shapes in her painting] and now
> we have put the jigsaw back together again. My first story that I wrote here
> is about somebody that is brave, a Head, and somebody that is bad, a
> Giant. The second was about someone who was frightened but with a bit
> of help was brave again. My next story was about a chipmunk that got
> scared of a lion because it was going to get eaten [trauma], so the
> chipmunk found a way to escape from the lion [accessing effectiveness].
> The next story, carrying on, was about a chipmunk that got happy again
> [psychological recovery].

The 'head' (referred to) had fallen off its clay body but was used as a character
in its own right – the brave, thinking self that could function to rescue itself
even though the body was helpless.

Rosie's 'goodbye session' illustrates how:

> The symbolic enactment and its product are subject to the mirroring
> process which carries its own subtle interpretive action. In contrast to
> 'acting out', which may be seen as a non-reflective event aimed primarily
> at reducing anxiety, this 'in-actment' is modified as it proceeds possibly
> through a series of images which mark the shifts in the child's under-
> standing of a traumatic event, or of aspects in a relationship. (Wood 1984,
> p.69)

Case example: Sean's goodbye

> Towards the end of a long period of therapy, Sean too, used a process of
> 'in-actment' and self-reflection that seemed to bring a completeness to the
> meaning of what had gone before. Sean spent most of this session playing
> (working) in the sand tray, creating a very complex story that he shared
> with me through an ongoing spoken narrative. The story involved all the
> elements of an exciting adventure drawing on traditional and modern
> myths and legends. There was a lot of tension as castles collapsed, treasure
> was lost and found, people were killed and came disturbingly to life again,
> and present day adventurers were pitted against medieval armies. Time
> and again it seemed that the 'baddies' would triumph and the world –
> Sean's world – was doomed to remain in the wrong time, replaying old
> disasters, and never achieving peace or resolution. However, much to my
> relief, with ten minutes to go, Sean brought the story to a conclusion. In

the end the people were saved and the ghosts of the past were laid to rest in their own time.

Sean washed his hands, left the sand tray and looked round the playroom. As though waking from a dream and seeing things with fresh eyes, he examined the toys, climbing on the rocking horse, then playing with the tea set and kitchen objects. Now absorbed in silent, solitary play, he knelt on the floor, looking like a much younger child. Then, for the last few minutes, after putting away the 'toddler' toys, he took out the toy cars for an enjoyable and age appropriate game of races.

Conclusion: the role of the therapist

We have learned within the project that the relationship with the therapist works alongside the qualities already residing in the individual child, young person or adult to build up their store of positive experiences. This can provide a secondary model of secure attachment.

We have also discovered that work with the mother–child dyad together has proved very effective in establishing a trusting, healing partnership. Similarly, relationship play groups for parents and young children that help parents actively to achieve strengthened attachments with their children can enable a greater degree of protective parenting.

Working with children like Sean and Rosie teaches us to trust in the child's sense of what they need to do. The therapist's role is to provide a holding, healing relationship, and the physical space and materials to enable the child to make progress. Most importantly, the therapist is there to bear witness, to reflect and make real (realise) the child's story, but from this to move on, neither trying to return to the same point as before the experience (denying the abuse) nor getting stuck at that point. Perhaps this is a journey that some are able to make alone, but there will always be many who cannot. We owe it to these children to continue, both to increase our understanding of the factors involved in trauma resolution, and to develop our skills in nurturing them. The key to effective working may be in linking what we now know about indicators for positive outcomes with a therapeutic process that employs personal resources to help children, parents and adult survivors.

CHAPTER II

Daleks and kerbstones

Surviving the aftermath of abuse

Maggie Ambridge, Cara Henry and Sue Richardson

> Someone once told me how Daleks can't go up kerbstones, so they have a choice of continually bashing against them, or looking for a new way of getting around. (Cara)

This chapter combines the perspectives of two practitioners who work therapeutically with adult survivors, and of one survivor who has integrated her experience into her work in the care field. It explores aspects of the healing process in both the presence and absence of therapeutic help. Through Cara's story, it illustrates the survivor's creative ability to construct a healing narrative and to develop a sense of self that does not have to be defined by the trauma of abuse.

Adults' accounts of the process of recovery

Adult survivors provide valuable information regarding the process of recovery. Talking with survivors can give clues to the continuing effects of trauma and how far it is resolved. As adults, some people who were abused as children report that they have been helped by individual or group therapy (Dale 1999; Etherington 2000; Meekums 2000). Others report that therapeutic approaches that are not sufficiently well attuned to the dynamics of child abuse trauma and to the survivor's own agenda can be stigmatising and unhelpful (Hooper and Koprowska 2000; Wolf 1998). The quality of therapeutic help depends a great deal on the extent to which it offers supportive companionable caregiving (Heard and Lake 1997; Hooper and Koprowska

2000). Allied to the equality, respect and capacity for empathic attunement that are integral to the latter, is the significance of an abuse-focused philosophy of treatment (Briere 1992). This regards the survivor's difficulties as solutions and treats with respect the context of trauma in which they have been devised. It can also be helpful to draw on a range of modalities, especially the creative arts therapies and non-verbal means of communication (Meekums 2000). Therapy may be most useful if offered incrementally, in the appropriate amount, at the times when the individual is most receptive and the therapy subject to their control. However, many adults, like Cara, feel that they have achieved just as much by themselves.

Retracing the experience of childhood and the subsequent journey to recovery through the hindsight of a grown-up survivor provides valuable insights. As Cara's story shows, the context of abuse, the early disclosure (or lack of it) of the child and how this was enabled, the nature of response, especially that of the mother or caregiver, and the subsequent experiences of the growing child are all areas of significance for the particular outcome for any individual.

Evidence from adults abused in childhood suggests that even those, like Cara, who have sufficient resilience to overcome the worst effects of abuse, are not necessarily symptom free (Herman 1992, p.110). Individuals report, for example, eating disorders and relationship difficulties as part of the picture along the road to recovery, whether or not these issues have been addressed in a therapeutic setting.

Many adults can function well in most areas of their life but still be affected by memories of abuse. As Howe et al. (1999) point out:

> Adults can have either a secure or insecure attachment organisation, but remain unresolved with respect to major loss or trauma. The disorganisation is only discernable in situations where distress, attachment related anxieties and traumatic childhood memories intrude into the present. (Howe et al. 1999, p.157)

Both the survivor's and the helper's ability to understand and to manage this dichotomy can be crucial to retaining a sense of the survivor's overall competence and developmental capacity.

Dissociation and attachment

Dissociation is 'a disruption in the usually integrated functions of consciousness, memory, identity or perception of the environment' (American Psychiatric Association 1995, p.489). It is a normal defence mechanism that occurs on a continuum of severity and a frequent coping response in the wake of trauma. Intrusive thoughts and memories may be blanked out either by dissociative 'absences' or, as for Cara, loss of some surrounding details. At other points on the dissociative spectrum, adults can resort to frenetic displacement activity and other strategies (such as drug use) to help with difficulty regulating affect. A repeated need to enter into dissociated state in childhood, particularly in response to trauma before the age of 6, can result in severe fragmentation and the formation of separate personality states as seen in dissociative identity disorder (Bagley *et al.* 1995; McElroy 1992; Putnam 1993; Steinberg 1994; van der Kolk, McFarlane and Weisaeth 1996).

The relationship between dissociation and attachment is a growing focus of the clinical literature. Dissociation is a way of resolving the dilemma of attachment to an abusive or non-protective caregiver (Blizard 1997a, 1997b; Blizard and Bluhm 1994; Liotti 1992; Ross 1997). The difficulty of maintaining proximity to a 'frightened or frightening caregiver' (Liotti 1992, p.198) can result in disorganised patterns of attachment in children that may have dissociation as its counterpart in adulthood (Anderson and Alexander 1996).

Like Cara, those survivors who are able to hold on to, rather than dissociate from, the knowledge of their trauma may be able to develop an integrated and coherent sense of self without recourse to professional help. An attachment-based approach to therapeutic work with severely fragmented inner states is explored by Richardson (2001). She emphasises the roles of empathic attunement and supportive companionable relating by the therapist as a way of developing the capacity for more secure relating within the survivor's internal system.

Attachment and reconnection

Work on attachment patterns across the life cycle (Fonagy 1998; Fonagy *et al.* 1995; Main 1991) argues for the power of reflexivity in the healing process. Summarising the work of Fonagy *et al.* (1995), Slade (1999, p.581) defines the reflective function as: 'what allows the individual to make sense of his or her own and others' psychological experience, to enter in to another's experience, to "read" another's mind'. The development of this capacity is one of the goals of therapy: it enables a different sense of self and others to be incorporated into internal working models and new meaning to be ascribed to past experience. Many survivors who embark upon their healing journey without professional help appear to have highly developed reflective capacities. This may be a characteristic of children and young people in Group A, one which enables them to take the decision to disclose. Cara's story provides a clear example of the reflective capacity in practice and how it can protect against the effects of trauma.

Herman (1992, p.197) proposes that 'helplessness and isolation are the core experiences of psychological trauma. Empowerment and re-connection are the core experiences of recovery'. The use of the traumatic experience as a source of contribution towards others or towards social change can be an important part of the healing process. Cara shares some ideas which she would like to take forward as part of her reconnection and which she has arrived at on the journey that she undertook for herself.

Cara's story: looking back, moving on
Reflections on Cleveland

> I felt lucky that my case was over before child abuse hit the headlines in Cleveland, because that would have brought questions about whether it had really happened. By then I was more aware of what was actually going on. I thought it was unfair that the seriousness of child sex abuse was being lost among stories of parents who were accused of abuse because their children wet the bed etc. I am sure there were a lot of abuse cases that got mixed up with cases that shouldn't have been there. One positive outcome was that sexual abuse was drawn to the attention of the media and it did help to give at least a small awareness of the problem. A lot of documentaries were made and most people, who had never thought that it might be happening in their street let alone their home, were forced to confront it as a fact of life.

Starting out

> I was an only child until I was 6½ and life seemed fairly uneventful. My earliest memory is being shouted at by my dad when I was about 3 because I had scraped the paintwork in the hall while riding my trike! Later, when my sister Melanie came along, she was dad's favourite. I didn't realise this until I was much older and mum pointed it out. Melanie and I fought a lot as children. We were on top of one another — literally, as we had bunk beds!

When I was 8, my parents bought the shop across the road from our house. Looking back, I realise that by that age I had taken on a parental role. I would be shouted at for not being responsible enough. You expect the comments, 'You're the older one you should know better!' but I lost a lot of my childhood trying to be an adult, trying to be responsible enough. Mum spent a lot of time looking after the shop, so my sister and I spent much of our time with each other for company in a small room above the shop.

When Melanie was a baby, if she hadn't woken by the time we had to go to the shop on an evening I would stay behind with her. When she woke, I would get her ready and ring mum to come out so she could see us over the road.

As we got older Melanie and I fought all the time, it seems. It's no wonder – we spent so much time together with no one else around. However, when we were too loud dad would come up and shout at me for being irresponsible, for not being quieter. He used to say as the older one, I should be more responsible. As time went on, things got worse. Eventually my dad would automatically assume that I was in the wrong without even asking what was going on. When he was my age his parents could leave him to look after his younger siblings, but I 'couldn't be trusted to keep my sister and myself quiet!'

I was made to feel that I was very irresponsible. However I now look back and wonder what he expected from a child between the ages of 7 and 13. In retrospect I think I did a good job, but it's only as an adult that I can see that. As a child I felt worthless as I had no template to work on as to what the average child of that age would be expected to do. Mum was working downstairs in the shop and I can't remember where my dad was most of the time.

Dad was very much an ogre at home as his word was final and law. I was not able to stay at the school disco to the end, because 'I couldn't be trusted'. They finished at ten o'clock, but I would have to leave at nine. I would have to be at the school front door waiting for my dad, or I would not get to go again! Before the last disco I ever went to at school mum had an argument with dad about it, so I didn't have to be at the front door until quarter to ten, but for the sake of fifteen minutes, he still wouldn't let me stay to the end of a disco.

But my dad could also be the nicest person going. He was always helping people. It used to take us hours to get to anywhere in the car. If anyone had stopped along the roadside, he would have to pull in and help them, so some car journeys were a lot longer than they should have been. He did do a lot of good work for people and was respected in the local community. At home, he would sit in his chair and demand. There were three of us who ran after him. Mum was, and is, very nice, but trusting and meek. She'd had a good upbringing and had never had to fight the way she would have had to in order to stand up to my dad.

The first loss I experienced was when I was about 17 (at least, the first loss that I count as a loss). This was Gran, my dad's mum. She was one of the few people I have respect for. We used to visit her and my granddad about once a year. My gran was a good person. She was always helping others. They'd visit us too, arriving unannounced which led to a stressful situation, but they always brought great toys that were just right without asking!

I didn't really ever talk to anyone. Sometimes I would talk to my sister, but only about things that we both had in common – such as when one of us had just been hit for misbehaving and we didn't think we deserved it. We had quite a support structure going on.

I didn't discuss any problems that were really important to me. If I am honest, I still don't. A problem is usually sorted at least with a solution in my head, but more likely a problem is done and dusted before I discuss it with anyone.

I do try to talk, but people have a way of trying to take control or judge. When I've given people control of my life before, they usually come up with solutions that are worse than mine. I feel a pressure to go with their solutions. As a child, if I hurt myself, I tended to cry in a heap away from people. If I turned to anyone it would be my mum. Sometimes she might get my dad who would say, 'You won't do that again', or 'You always have to learn the hard way' and so on. If I showed my mum, I got an audience. It was the same when I was sick. I liked an audience. Mum cared, but she didn't like sickness and couldn't really cope with it. (If someone threw up, mum felt an urge to join them. That's something I now relate to.)

I didn't cuddle as a kid. That changed when my little sister came along, then there was no choice – she used to force it on you! One of the best things she ever did was to teach me about love.

Disclosure at age 15

My dad never told me that I wasn't supposed to tell anyone else so I asked one of my friends, 'I don't know what to do about this – what do you reckon?' My friend wasn't sure either and she said, 'Shall we go and talk to one of the teachers – which teacher shall we talk to?' I said, 'Let's go and ask the music teacher'. I chose her because she was a really cool teacher – we were allowed to eat sweets in her class as long as we brought enough sweets for everyone. I ended up in the deputy headmaster's office and a policewoman came – she was really nice. Then we went home and the police told my mum what was going on. I wasn't happy with the situation but at the time I didn't know if I could do anything. I felt I was breaking up the family, that I was making a mess of everything.

Rejected and alone

My first real experience of rejection was when the sexual abuse came to light. While two of my dad's sisters were very supportive towards my mum, my sister and me, one of them sided with him. My dad never admitted what he did. He was innocent as far as he was concerned. He's always claimed he pleaded guilty so I didn't have to go to court, not because he was guilty!

I couldn't quite believe that people would swallow it; that he was pleading guilty to protect his child from having to go to court. If it were a lie, surely he would have wanted it sorted out. I didn't want to go to court – I was petrified. The day the summons arrived, I couldn't imagine telling a whole court the graphic details I had to go through with the police for my statement.

The policewoman who took my statement was lovely. She tried her best to make it as easy as possible. I felt so reassured when she said I just had to tell her and then I would never have to say it again. I felt lied to when the summons came and I was going to have to tell the court everything. I just wanted it over. The whole thing hung round me for just under a year, from disclosure to trial. That year was the longest of my life. It felt like a whole world came and went.

My Dad was sent down for two years, because I told the WPC the bare minimum. The only reason I said anything was because I had decided to leave as soon as I was 16, but wanted to protect my sister.

I can still recall most of what happened to me, but it's not raw any more; it's got sketchier. The important bits are still there but, as I haven't used those memories for years, I don't remember the dates anymore, just what the weather was like and so on.

Lack of professional help

I would say that I've had no help whatsoever. I chose my mum rather than a social worker to witness my police statement. I thought she should be there to hear it because I felt that if she wasn't there, it could create a barrier between us that I might never manage to heal. The realisation that if my mum wasn't supportive I could go into care was something that I learned as the interview went on. A week later I got a social worker. She took me from home to a day centre for somewhere neutral. My mum worked at the day centre and her boss was there, who cordially said hello to me by name! It didn't seem neutral. I would have been happier in my own house, but I wasn't listened to.

The social worker told me that if I didn't tell her what happened I would do it to somebody else, i.e. become an abuser. I was devastated. I felt that I was being condemned. She then asked me if I wanted counselling. I decided that if that's the way these people think I didn't want their help.

It took me a long time to accept that I wasn't responsible for the abuse. I felt guilty that in some way I had caused it to happen. I knew I wasn't responsible. People told me I wasn't responsible. However, I could not help thinking that in many ways I was to blame for destroying my family. Could I have been helped to that realisation sooner? I would probably have accepted help if I felt there had been any genuine help available, but I don't feel things have changed enough. At a social services course on sexual abuse in 1994, a trainer said, 'People who've been abused feel this way'. I was angry at being told how I should feel, or how anybody who has been abused should feel.

I don't believe social services have come on enough. Counsellors should listen in all situations to others. More importantly, how dare they tell people who have already gone through a nightmare how they feel? Telling vulnerable children that they should feel a certain way? You don't tell someone who has just been mugged in the street how to feel! You let them express it, and however they feel is right.

The same instructor also said victims should be told they're not on their own. I pointed out to her that if a woman is having a baby she knows that she's not the only one, but at that particular time she doesn't care!

Simply saying to someone, 'You're not on your own; we are here for you' more often than not highlights just how alone you are. Who trusts the man who keeps saying, 'Trust me'? It's the same idea. People with the same experiences react in different ways. I felt very depressed that night, having found that still not enough had changed, that children were still being told how they feel.

These days, I have begun to understand a lot of things that at the time I couldn't see. Things I now take for granted as being obvious.

I think my experiences with social services, and those of people who have approached me more recently, having been through the same channels, only reinforce my assertions that people are still not getting the help they need.

Most people I have met who have been abused seem to find their own way of abusing themselves until they get the hang of de-programming the years of abuse they have suffered and the wrong self-image it gives you. Some choose alcohol, some choose cutting themselves. I chose abusive relationships and eventually an eating problem. The abusive relationships backed me into a corner so the eating disorder gave me something in my life I could control. I could fill my life with it and it actually didn't 'kick in' until years later, or if it had started earlier it was certainly very minor.

My eating disorder came into play after I got food poisoning seven or eight years after my disclosure. I was living with a bloke in what I would now say was an abusive relationship, but at the time I was yet to come to that understanding. I felt I couldn't control anything in my life, that when I let anyone into my life they made a mess of me. We all need stability, and look for it in whatever form we can. I wanted a relationship, but I went for the wrong people. I sought them out because they weren't good for me. For a long time I didn't value myself. Through the disclosure I just kind of kept things together because my mum was falling apart. I didn't really think about me and how I felt until I got older. I'm not saying that I always got it right with my mum and sister but I don't think I had space for my needs as well.

My views have changed now – you work through things and get to better places. In the past, I used to feel that I was abused twice – once by my father and once by the system. However, now that I'm older I can see that the police really did the best that they could and in the light of that they were excellent – they did give me a lot time when I was really upset. My social worker wasn't so good and I was very relieved not to have anything to do with her – there are so many different ways she could have approached it. I thought, if this is help I don't want it.

Moving on

Looking back from an adult perspective, my mum didn't support me as fully as she could have, but then you can't make a wild horse run the Grand National. I don't think my mother had all the skills to cope with what was happening to us.

When everything became public I supported my mum because it was such a shock to her. I don't think she was aware. I think she didn't want to believe and I can understand that. I wrote an agony aunt a letter that I never sent. My mum found the letter and produced it for the police, but she thought it was just 'a teenager making things up'.

When I was a child she always went to the school plays, was always around, and I could always call on her, but she was overshadowed by my dad, and not allowed to stand up to him.

Even later we had difficulties seeing eye to eye on the issue of the past and my dad. When an invitation to my granddad's birthday arrived a few years ago, it led to a big discussion with my mum, because my dad was going to be there. She originally didn't want to go, but when I insisted I was going, she wanted to come with me and protect me. I wanted to go on my own. I didn't mind mum going, but I didn't want us to go together as I would feel that I had to support mum with her issues instead of dealing with my feelings and facing my demons. I wanted to take my boyfriend of that time, who was a big bloke. I told her I would be all right with him. I wanted to concentrate on what I was feeling and thinking. I think that was where the argument with my mum started.

Well, my dad was there. He went round the whole room and I was the last person he spoke to. He held out his arms, but I pushed my boyfriend forward and said, 'This is N'.

When I looked at him, I just thought how old he looked, and when he turned round I thought, 'Don't say how old he looks'. So out of my mouth flew, 'God you look round'. He did look fat, but I only meant to think it!

He started whispering in my ear about how he had not been in touch because of my mum. He hadn't changed. Everything was still someone else's fault. I refused to let him use this as an excuse. My cousin, who was standing next to me, said, 'What did you say?' so I just repeated it loudly so that everyone could hear!

Then dad said, 'I will give you my address so you can write to me', but I said, 'No, I'll give you my address so you can write to me'. I felt secure enough in him knowing where I lived because that would have been easy for him to find out anyway. I think if he really wanted to bridge the abyss he had put between us, he should do it, not me.

If I ever wanted more evidence that he hadn't changed, I saw it moments later. Because I had refused his address, he was soon shouting at his girl-friend.

I wanted to make sure that the ball was in his court. The reason we're not in touch is because he hasn't bothered, not because I wouldn't write. Having said that, I would have no qualms about not replying to him if he ever does write. If he were to choose to patch it up then I cannot say for definite I would refuse to let him try, but if he had been the kind of person who might have got back to me then I probably wouldn't have given him my address.

I feel this meeting really helped me to look at things differently. For the first time I'd actually seen him through adult eyes. We met as equals. The parent that I didn't dare say no to, the person who so frightened and con-trolled me, was nothing more than a middle-aged man, not as tall as I remembered, and I had the upper hand all the time. He couldn't back out with the usual, 'You're a child: I'll tell you when you grow up'.

This was a big thing for me, because I had done this for me, rather than thinking of my mother's needs. It was the first time I had put my needs first and it damaged my relationship with my mother for some time, but I believe we are stronger for it, both individually and in our relationship with each other.

More recently, I've had much better experiences with my mum. She once approached me wanting to know if I held her responsible for what happened. Whether I thought she could have done anything to help, whether she could have saved me from the pain.

I am afraid the answer has to be yes. While she didn't know of the sexual abuse, she did know the conditions we were all suffering, the emotional abuse that was being meted out. I understand she wasn't able to do anything, though. She was a victim of that abuse as well. I think I understood that at the time. You can't blame the person sitting next to you in the lifeboat; we all suffered.

I think the main thing that has restored the friendship with my mum is that she now gives me the respect that I deserve. Sometimes she's too scared of upsetting me. I hope with time things will level out.

There also comes a time when you realise you only have so long with your parents and very few things are perfect. I can discount dad, but mum is a nice person. She always tried her best, but she always knew her best would be overshadowed. As time went on, she stood up to him more and more. Latterly they always had fights. The more she stood up for herself and us, the worse the fighting got.

When I was about 8 she ran upstairs crying after a bad fight in the kitchen. I remember persuading her that she shouldn't leave us. When everything came out we knew we wouldn't be taken into care because she was there. She always looked after us. I guess I knew she was behind me, but I quite liked doing stuff on my own. At 15 I was independent, buying my own clothes.

I see myself as an insular person. I sort out my problems on my own usually. I'm scared of hurting anyone, of being responsible for someone else's pain, though I can accept that people get hurt. It's a fact of life. I just try to be more than fair so at least I can say I did my best not to hurt them.

I believe I am what I am because of what I've been through in my life, the things I've learned, the experiences I've had. Am I a survivor? I don't like the word because the person I was didn't survive. Having said that, I wouldn't be her again for all the tea in China! I spent a lot of years trying to move on, but people had a tendency of not letting me get away from it. This is a small town and people talk. I wanted to get away, as Snoopy from the *Peanuts* cartoon said, 'No problem is so big you can't run away from it'! I have moved past this now. I accept that I can't hide from my past. I now actively use my experiences to help others who have suffered abuse.

But I am more than the product of one set of negative experiences. Having ridden the storm and then been talked about, I felt that we were the ones serving the prison sentence. We were the ones who couldn't go out the door without someone saying something! People stopping, talking as you pass by.

The process of recovery

I've spent a long time looking for stability. I think a number of things have helped. It's helped having my own house, the ability to say who comes in and who doesn't.

Having males who are friends and who don't have another agenda helps. Having friends to whom it doesn't matter whether I'm male or female. I don't distrust males. I much prefer male company because they don't get so worked up on small things, like babies and what was on telly last night. Men don't get so involved.

I found Penny Parks (1989) helpful, though I couldn't get the hang of writing to the (inner) child. The visualisation as a way of helping the child is interesting. We tend with adult information to judge the child. Why didn't I say 'no'? As a child I didn't say 'no' because I didn't dare. This book has been very helpful, not only to me but to others I know. It's helped them to handle their problems and to allow their partners to understand what they feel and where they are coming from.

Now I am fiercely independent. Other people have had control over my life and stuffed it up. If I stuff it up now it's my own fault.

Recommendations and future goals

I still have goals. Children should have rights. Having information as a child would be a start. The campaign for 'Sarah's Law' (a campaign for public access to the Register of Sex Offenders in the wake of a child's murder) is horrendous – it's like witch trials. We don't do that any more. Yes, these people could be a danger to children, but the people who are actually going to be on the Register of Sex Offenders are only a small percentage of the people who are likely to abuse your children. You should judge for yourself if you can trust your children to be with someone, not make assumptions because they are not on a hopelessly short list of 'bad people' (usually men). It's more often the people they know well and not the people in the street.

I think it's going to be a long process for me – now I think I'm sorted when ten years ago I thought I was dealing with it, but the older I get the better I get. I have a book by Louise Hay (1988), which talks about having cancer and how it was basically a gift in that she'd learned so much from it that she never would have learned without it. I can agree with her on that because, while my problems were different (nobody ever wants abuse or cancer to happen). I've learned so much I've met so many people, and I've actually done something and can see things so much bigger than so many other people. Without the experiences I've had I just wouldn't be the person I am. I love life, when things are bad these days it's nothing to what I have lived through. I have a great life, fabulous friends, a supportive mother and sister in all I do, and a stable relationship with my partner from which to launch my dreams.

When a colleague of mine read this chapter, she thought it very sad and found it hard to connect the person she knows with the story. Being abused was a part of my history; I can never forget it, but I can move on from it. It's a part of me, not all of me.

CHAPTER 12

Maintaining awareness of unspeakable truths
Responses to child abuse in the longer term

Sue Richardson

This chapter explores the conditions in which awareness of child sexual abuse can be maintained and considers the defensive processes which lead to its exclusion. It asserts the potential for transformation: from the defensive exclusion of unspeakable truths to a mode of supportive companionable relating (Heard and Lake 1997) which can enable the fear aroused by this issue to be addressed. The ability to manage fear, to construct a coherent narrative of events and to promote healing and reparation are seen as key tasks for practitioners and their allies in organisations and the community.

Key issues and tensions

A key issue for the long term is how to keep knowledge of child sexual abuse at the forefront of general awareness so that it can remain part of the social and political agenda. A paradigm shift is taking place: from denial of the existence of child sexual abuse to a recognition, however gradual and limited, of its reality and widespread nature. World-wide, communities and the media are seized by shock, anger and demands for justice, especially in response to abuse which takes place outside the family, for example in care settings. Such responses arise from fear and high levels of anxiety and lead to the desire to lose awareness: they tend to be short term, punitive in nature and denying of complex reality.

A significant challenge is how to move on from short-term moral outrage to an informed response – one which avoids polarisation and loss of awareness in favour of a climate in which child protection can advance. This means overcoming an even bigger challenge – that of maintaining awareness of unspeakable truths long enough for that knowledge to be integrated and transformed into a long-term strategy. Without integration and transformation, the painful but unproductive cycle of angry eruptions which explode and then subside – for all but the witnesses and the survivors – until the next shocking discovery, will continue.

The history of child sexual abuse is marked by 'cycles of discovery and suppression' (Olafson, Corwin and Summit 1993, p.17). A constant tension between the willingness to know, and the desire not to know condemns awareness of child sexual abuse to a fluctuating and conflicting state, just like the memories of many individual survivors. None of us can be exempt from this tension. For example, alongside parents whose children had been abducted and murdered, I contributed to a seminar held in 1998 at the European Parliament in Brussels. I was invited as one of the pioneers in raising awareness of child sexual abuse in the UK, yet part of me was reluctant to attend. I was not sure if I could bear to hear of yet more atrocities to children. Part of me wanted to turn away and focus on something less emotionally demanding. I know that these reactions are not unique to me as an individual but take place at every level – psychological, social and political – in response to trauma.

Difficulty can be caused by this need to avoid awareness, even when justice is seen to have been done. Summit (1988) gives the example of 'Mr Friendly', a trusted teacher who had abused a large number of boys in one community. Despite the action taken at the time, in the longer term 'the active efforts of the public were directed toward containment, avoidance and erasure' (Summit 1988, p.43).

Responses to the crisis of discovery of child sexual abuse in 1987 in Cleveland are another example of the same process. The medical diagnosis of sexual abuse in 121 children led to major turmoil. Those events were a major breakthrough in the societal recognition of child sexual abuse. They also marked the start of the backlash in the UK. A conflict developed between, on one hand, the needs of truth and justice for children and, on the other, the desire to avoid conflict and forget the trauma. Public and professional concerns were deflected by setting up a public inquiry and by legislative and procedural changes that followed. These changes have not resolved the dilemmas that I and my colleagues faced in Cleveland of protecting children trapped in fear and silence (Richardson and Bacon 1991a). The truth of what happened to the children concerned was never properly established. The need of those in charge was to contain, control and suppress controversy and a process of silencing – both official and unofficial – developed.

Once begun, the process of closing down a painful debate became permanent: in the former Cleveland area the debate has never resumed. In 1997, a television documentary made to mark the ten-year anniversary of Cleveland encountered significant difficulty in reassembling the facts and finding people willing to appear (see Tate, Chapter 1). The programme makers were accused of reopening old wounds and staff in the child protection services were instructed not to take part.

The post-Cleveland situation developed as it did as a result of the attempt to move on without the truth being established, without addressing the local community's need for healing and consequently without any real closure. Inevitably, the authorities were fearful of continued criticism. As a result they were unable to be exploratory and adopted a strategy that came to focus on the management of controversy rather than child protection. Many of the cases were not pursued assertively and children, many of whom were believed by child protection professionals to have been abused, were returned home unprotected.

Removal of the 'witnesses', implemented by the agencies responsible for child protection, was a key strategy, and a key component of the loss of a coherent narrative of what had taken place. Butler-Sloss (1988) hoped that:

> the troubles of 1987 would recede for those concerned with the protection of children in Cleveland and that they will work together, to tackle the exacting task of helping children who are subject to sexual abuse to the lasting benefit of the children, the families and their community. (Butler-Sloss 1988, p.245)

However, as a result of pressures brought to bear, none of those who bore witness to the abuse of children were left in post in Cleveland. Neither they, nor any of the children or the parents concerned, were included in an official ten-year anniversary conference and an alternative event was arranged to give them a voice.

The legacy of unhealed wounds

The outcome of silencing, societal ambivalence and the absence of a healing process undermines all efforts to tackle this issue. The outcome is especially wounding for children and adults in the following groups:

1. Those children in Groups A and B whom the system is unable to protect (Richardson and Bacon 1991a. See also Bacon, Chapter 4; Brooks, Chapter 5; McLoughlin, Chapter 7).

2. Traumatised parents, usually mothers. This includes both those who believe their children have been abused and are not supported by the system and those who are aggrieved by intervention because they do not accept that abuse has occurred. The former group of mothers are discussed in Chapters 6 and 11 and in other studies such as Hooper (1992) and Trotter (1998). The plight of the latter group is illustrated by a mother in one of the Cleveland families who did not accept the medical diagnosis of sexual abuse made in respect of their three children ('We can't forgive those who tore us apart', *Northern Echo* 11 August 1997). She described how the family had been unable to discuss what had occurred until their daughter went to university and discovered that she could read about herself in the university library. The family felt that they suffered from an inability to forgive or forget. This family's story illustrates the individual cost of an unresolved situation in which eternal argument has threatened to hold sway.

3. Adult survivors who have not had justice, especially those who have taken time to move up the continuum of disclosure (Richardson 1991b) for example, survivors of abuse in care settings.

4. Wounded workers in this field who may be targeted by campaigns which argue against research and other evidence for abuse or who suffer 'vicarious traumatisation' (Pearlman and Saakvitine 1995) in the course of their work.

5. Immediate colleagues, other professionals or members of the community who feel helpless and may suffer from bystander guilt.

In any of these five groups, individual solutions may have to be resorted to for the sake of survival. These solutions can never be truly effective without a shift to a more supportive, enabling and inclusive climate which promotes our ability to work as allies.

Divided consciousness and the loss of connection

The long-term outcome of the repeated cycle of discovery and suppression is a deeply divided state of consciousness in society as a whole.

Following the Cleveland crisis, other shocking cases of child sexual abuse have come to public attention on a regular basis. Some cases, involving allegations of satanic ritual abuse, have been regarded as the creation of crusading or misguided professionals (La Fontaine 1998) or have suffered, as in Orkney, from a failure to answer the central question of what had happened to the children (Clyde 1992). The outcome of such cases has communicated to professionals that their efforts to protect children in this kind of scenario are at risk of being disbelieved and denigrated.

Other cases, such as those involving the abuse of children and young people in institutional settings, have led to the conviction of a number of perpetrators, to yet another major statutory inquiry focusing on abuse in children's homes (Waterhouse, Clough and le Fleming 2000) and to police inquiries into past abuse in children's homes throughout the UK.

Public attitudes, reflected in the media, are contradictory and confused except for two consistent features. First, hostility towards perpetrators of abuse. Second, the inability to make a connection from one case to another, each being treated as a discrete entity. Such loss of awareness creates a situation in which it is as if there is no collective memory of the past. For example, the shocked reaction of the Belgian people to the Dutroux case concerning child abduction, abuse and murder was reported throughout Europe without any reference to the case of Notary X. The latter was 'Belgium's child abuse cause célèbre' (Pyck 1994, p.72) some ten years earlier. By contrast, it had resulted in a public outcry against the professionals who had identified abuse in the case of a 6-year-old boy who had alleged abuse by his father – a man who held a respected public position.

This process of disconnection appears to act as a means of keeping the problem in manageable proportions. It allows a curious coexistence of rising awareness and desire not to know. For example, the 'white march', held in Brussels in 1996 in memory of abducted and murdered children, received wide coverage in the British press, which acknowledged the parents' and the public's grief and supported the need for justice. This was followed within 48 hours by a sceptical media response to the release of a report (NSPCC 1996) that up to 1 million children a year could be suffering abuse in the UK. Some tabloids called the report's credibility into question and damned it as 'the abuse of statistics' (Pinning down abuse, *Community Care* 28 November–4

December 1996, p.16–17). A broadsheet which chose to support the report's findings, nevertheless dismissed the existence of ritual abuse as a product of 'ill-thought-out ideology disguised as science' (*Guardian* 23 October 1996, p.4). By 1998, the testimony of the Belgian parents and a second white march met with minimal press interest. By 2000, the parents felt too unsupported to hold a march at all.

This kind of fragmented thinking mirrors the responses of many survivors of trauma. It results in a loss of that connectedness on which learning depends and it forms a barrier to a united response to child protection (Richardson 1991). It is vital that hearing the traumatic experiences of children acts to make this climate less divided in the longer term. Central to this is the role of the witness.

The role of the witness

The role of the witness of abuse in breaking silence is crucial to changing the climate of awareness. The issues are kept visible by keeping the witnesses visible. Sustaining this role is enormously taxing in the long term. The task is to repeat the same message over and over until it is heard. It is a long battle. Witnesses themselves need to recognise that they will get weary and will often be traumatised. The need to rest, or to move on, can be in conflict with the knowledge that the problem remains and continues to damage other lives. It is especially hard to turn away when there seem to be few others willing to take up where they leave off. For example, following Cleveland, the exhortation of some colleagues to 'pass on the baton' was well meaning but unhelpful when the same colleagues could not convey their understanding of the dilemmas of children in Group B (Richardson and Bacon 1991a) who are unable to disclose.

The witness as whistleblower

The witness to the unspeakable truth of child sexual abuse is by definition a whistleblower, whether or not this is their intention. Whistleblowing is now acknowledged to have an important role in ensuring the safety of children. Advice has been given (Utting 1997) that:

> all organisations which accommodate children should instruct staff that they have both a duty to their employer and a professional obligation to raise legitimate concerns about the conduct of colleagues or managers, and guarantee that this can be discharged in ways which ensure thorough

investigation without prejudice to their own position and prospects. (Utting 1997, p.159)

While Utting (1997, p.157) acknowledges the 'tangible anxiety', fear and 'real consequences' including 'ridicule in some cases, ostracism, and worse', he stops short of saying that whistleblowing has usually meant sudden career death.

Generically, the whistleblowing role has been so demonstrably difficult that it has been necessary to frame legislation and procedures to protect those who take it on. In respect of child sexual abuse, the risks to individuals have been especially marked. Out of the seven founding members of an international network of professionals involved in high-profile cases of child abuse from four different European countries, only two were able to continue to work normally (Richardson 1994). Taylor (1994, 1997) has spoken of the financial and emotional toll on her resources in the wake of blowing the whistle on abuse in children's homes in North Wales: her action resulted in rejection by her employer and in personal and professional vilification. For all of us in this position, the personal as well as the professional toll has been enormous.

Children and young people as whistleblowers

The concept of whistleblowing can be broadened to include disclosure by children and young people. We need to remember that disclosure is not the norm. The norm is the accommodation syndrome described by Summit (1983) consisting of secrecy, helplessness, accommodation, delayed or conflicted disclosure, often followed by retraction. It is therefore little short of a miracle that children and young people attempt to blow the whistle on abuse in their own way, usually indirectly.

Some of these children can be very young. For example, in the Orkney Islands, children whose father had previously been convicted of sexual abuse alerted social workers to the alleged abuse of other children in the community. An allegation from an older sister (Group A) of abuse by her brother led to the removal from home of seven younger children, none of whom had made any complaint about abuse (Group B). Whilst in a place of safety, a 4-year-old and her 8-year-old sister began to describe abusive experiences outside the family and named a number of other children, from four further families, as having been abused as well. These nine children in turn became the subjects of a large scale child protection investigation (Clyde 1991).

Children in Group B are the most difficult to protect and their cases can become controversial. They require an adult who can blow the whistle on their behalf and who can withstand conflict or controversy. In Scotland, an inquiry found that children in Group B had used indirect means to alert adults to their plight, such as running away and name calling (Marshall, Jamieson and Finlayson 1999).

Young whistleblowers in Groups A and B face particular obstacles. Marshall *et al*.'s (1999) Inquiry report highlights how hard it is for children to articulate their concerns, to be taken seriously and to be believed. Research (Bentovim 1998) indicates that disbelief has even more serious effects on long-term mental health.

The Orkney inquiry report highlights the disadvantages presented by the legal system to the child witness and the problems which continue to surround children's evidence (see also McLoughlin, Chapter 7). The inquiry judge described the decision to abandon legal proceedings as 'unfortunate…regrettably precipitate and from the practical standpoint of those caught up in the affair mistaken' (Clyde 1991, p.352, 134).

The plight of children suffering abuse in a care setting is brought to life most vividly by Fred Fever (1994). He gives a powerful description of his dilemma concerning disclosure:

> I thought long and hard about who I could possibly tell, for I was going out of my mind and desperately wanted to talk to someone who could sort the matter out. The police were my first option, but I thought that they would blame me … I just couldn't bring myself to trust the staff … I didn't even consider approaching my teachers at school. In most of their eyes I was nothing more than a troublemaker. (Fever 1994, p.173)

Neither could Fred Fever confide in a couple who were his prospective foster parents. He sums up the isolation of a child whose ability to join Group A is compromised in the absence of any adult support:

> In last-ditch desperation, I thought about telling my mates at school. I soon abandoned that idea, because of the thought of being misunderstood and labelled as dirty, or a 'poof' or pervert. I soon realised I could tell no one. I was in this alone with no one to help me … I was at the mercy of all adults and those in authority. (Fever 1994, p.174)

Protective parents as whistleblowers

The non-abusing carer, often the mother, has a key role in ensuring the child's safety. As illustrated by the mothers' accounts in Chapter 5, parents who believe their children and in good faith advocate on their behalf can themselves be dismissed in the adult world. In 12 American cases of alleged satanic ritual abuse in day care of children, mean age 3.6 years, parents were allowed to testify on their behalf in the criminal trials (deYoung 1997). Twelve out of 15 defendants successfully appealed their conviction, a common ground being 'the improper admission of lay testimony about the sequelae of abuse from the parents of the children' (deYoung 1997, p.90).

Adult survivors of abuse as whistleblowers

The testimony of adults, for example in cases of historical abuse, illustrates the phenomenon of adults in Groups A and B i.e. adults who can make spontaneous disclosure and adults who remain silent. For example, Marshall *et al.* (1999) comment on adults corresponding to Group A who had repeatedly tried to tell about their abuse in the care system, and on adults who had emerged from the equivalent of Group B in response to proactive police investigations. Many of the latter had immediately been able to move to Group A. An example is given of an adult who

> on answering the door to the police and being informed of their general inquiry, immediately gave the name of his abuser, even though he had spoken to no one of that abuse in the past and had not spoken the person's name for some twenty years. (Marshall *et al.* 1999, 5.53)

Staff in fields of health and social care as whistleblowers

Marshall *et al.* (1999) highlight how well access to a supportive adult can work, especially for witnesses who, as the report delicately puts it, 'had not previously been well disposed to the police' (Marshall *et al.* 1999, 3.85).

What helped in this investigation was the ability of the investigators to convey 'sympathy and understanding' and their 'rigour, zeal and commitment to the task'. The report comments that: 'Without that high degree of commitment, these grave offences would have gone unpunished and there would have been no recognition of the abuse perpetrated on former residents' (Marshall *et al.* 1999, 3.85).

However, other professionals who have played this kind of role have been condemned for having these very characteristics. For example, Alison Taylor, who was commended for her 'remarkable tenacity' (Waterhouse *et al.* 2000, p.727) in raising concerns about abuse in children's homes in North Wales, was labelled during the attempt as 'a blatant trouble maker, with a most devious personality' (Chair of Social Services Committee, quoted in Waterhouse *et al.* 2000, p.14).

Whistleblowers in the fields of health and social care fall into three subgroups. In the first are those whose cases come to high public profile such as Cleveland, Orkney and North Wales. In the second are those whose cases are unknown to the public and who do not have even the potential protection of being in the eye of the storm.

In the second group, concerns, if acted on at all, tend to be responded to in a way that aims to avoid public attention. Those who raise the concern can find themselves being disposed of quietly. Alison Taylor might have been one of this group had it not been for her own persistence: Waterhouse *et al.* (2000, p. 660) comments that responses to her complaints, such as being labelled as difficult, were 'classic examples of what happens to a whistleblower'. Despite increased protection for whistleblowers, it cannot be assumed that such cases are a thing of the past. For example the Huntingdon Support Group, set up in response to child abuse in Cambridgeshire, receives regular calls from staff in this situation from different parts of Britain (Heather Hogan, personal communication).

Just 'as with children', staff also 'may resort to behaviours which they hope others will pick up on when they feel unable to articulate their concerns' (Marshall *et al.* 1999, 3.33). For example, in Edinburgh there was a suggestion that three members of staff may have resigned to draw attention to concerns about how homes were being run.

What the first and second groups have in common is that, to date, survival in one's post, after being seen as carrying an unwanted message about child abuse, has not been feasible.

The third group is made up of people from different disciplines who are engaging with this issue in a committed and professional way. In effect, they are blowing the whistle on this issue. As a result, without supportive caregiving, they are likely to suffer from some of the factors affecting other whistleblowers such as high stress levels and professional isolation, and to operate in fear of becoming the next victim.

A model for understanding: the contribution of attachment theory

Attachment theory helps us to understand the nature of defensive reactions to unspeakable truths and the supportive environment in which they might be heard. A core issue is the need of the witness for supportive caregiving.

Any form of contact with child sexual abuse will tend to increase emotional arousal, ranging from the traumatic stress reactions experienced by the child or adult victim to the secondary traumatisation to which the helper and members of the community are exposed. Such distress will stimulate the individual's attachment system to respond by seeking proximity to an attachment figure for care, comfort and protection. Effective caregiving will be responsive, attentive, receptive, consistent and empathically attuned to the distress of the care seeker (Heard and Lake 1997). It will provide a secure base from which distress can be assuaged and from which exploratory behaviour can resume.

Heard and Lake (1997) propose that, in contrast to dominant and submissive (D/S) forms of relating, effective caregiving will be characterised by supportive companionable (SC) relating and will include interest-sharing. The concept of SC relating offers a way of changing defensive processes at individual, organisational and societal levels. It is an essential context for healing and recovery. As individuals and as a group, child and adult survivors and their witnesses are repeatedly confronted by responses based on the dynamics of dominance and submission, for example pressures to submit to the status quo by being silenced. Their pressing need is for a supportive environment in order to stay in SC mode when confronted with D/S patterns (see also Richardson and Bacon, Chapter 2).

The history of the discovery of child sexual abuse is characterised by the absence of supportive relating and informed caregiving. Survivors have felt betrayed, exploited and misunderstood by professionals. Professionals have mistakenly either idealised or pathologised the role of the survivor and have failed to work in partnership with them. Employers have failed to support staff working at the frontiers of discovery. The media and the general public have looked for scapegoats when anything has gone wrong.

It has been demonstrated that SC relating can be an effective approach at an individual level in work with dissociative processes (Richardson 2001) and in resolving the difficulties of traumatised staff groups (Richardson 1999). Intervention is needed into similar processes which operate at a societal level. Since awareness of child sexual abuse goes in cycles (Olafson *et al.* 1993), some loss of collective awareness and loss of memory of what we have so painfully become aware is inevitable. To counteract this, we need to respond actively by honouring the truth and by promoting a healing process, not only for the individuals involved but also for the community as a whole.

The pressing need of all systems is to have models of SC relating to draw on. A danger in this field is that supportive alliances can be misconstrued or seen as threatening. For example, the charge of 'collusion and conspiracy' (Butler-Sloss 1988, p.166) made against professionals in Cleveland has been difficult to dispel, despite the fact that the inquiry found that there was 'no evidence whatsoever' (Butler-Sloss 1988, p.166) to support this view.

Cleveland as an example of failed supportive companionable relating

Prior to the Cleveland crisis, the awareness and study of child sexual abuse was informed by the work of interest-sharing peers led by survivor groups and feminist networks, and followed by pioneering clinicians. Such peers were able to provide a sufficiently SC context within their particular groups or network to remain exploratory. The wider environment was often hostile or unaware. In this climate, the SC relating enjoyed within these three groups did not necessarily extend to anyone outside them. On occasion, there could be painful D/S interactions between the groups themselves, for example, survivors who felt marginalised by the growth of a 'child abuse industry' (Armstrong 1996) led by professionals; feminists unhappy with systemic approaches to intrafamilial sexual violence (MacLeod and Saraga 1988).

Butler-Sloss (1988, p.13) was satisfied 'with the arrangements and the inter-disciplinary working of the main agencies in Cleveland in their response to child abuse other than child sexual abuse'. In other words, there was effective, companionable interest-sharing in most areas of practice. In respect of child sexual abuse, there was a long-running dispute between police surgeons and paediatricians regarding joint medical examinations and it had not proved possible to reach agreement on procedures for case management. Efforts to resolve this impasse resulted only in polarisation and many instances of the dynamics of dominance and submission.

The Cleveland crisis led to a flight from interest-sharing within the profes-sional system. For example, the pioneering multidisciplinary team in Leeds decided to play down the fact that they shared the dilemmas faced by their counterparts in Cleveland. In making this strategic choice, the Leeds team were considering the interests of children by deciding to protect their ability to continue making the medical diagnosis. This transferred the conflict and led Butler-Sloss (1988, p.199) to conclude: 'There were times during the medical evidence when it seemed to the inquiry that the professional dispute over the diagnosis and research of the Leeds team was being fought out in the arena of Cleveland'. Wynne's account (Chapter 6) shows how difficult it has proved to resolve the dilemma which arises for the paediatrician in respect of the medical diagnosis of child sexual abuse.

In the wake of the crisis, a community group, Cleveland Against Child Abuse (CAUSE) was formed to support professionals on the basis of a shared interest and concern for the protection of children (Cashman and Lamballe-Armstrong 1991). This group explored ways in which professionals and the community could work together in pursuit of 'a society which cared enough about its children to protect them from sexual abuse' (Cashman and Lamballe-Armstrong 1991, p.120). This combined endeavour was acknowledged as likely to give rise to conflict within the group itself:

> Abuse survivors, for instance, may have criticisms of professional practice. Professionals may feel misunderstood. Lay members may feel undervalued. Group members may use different kinds of language and have to struggle to understand each another. (Cashman and Lamballe-Armstrong 1991, p.133)

Such inherent tensions are likely to lead to defensive relating at times. In the short term, the group was experienced by beleaguered professionals as supportive. In the longer term, CAUSE faced the challenge of sustaining a supportive companionable mode in the absence of any source of caregiving for the group as a whole.

What is needed in the long term: the development of supportive companionable relating

A model for future action can be based on the restoration and promotion of supportive companionable relating. This depends on the availability of enlightened caregiving which is well informed about the dynamics of secondary traumatisation and can attune empathically to the conflicts and distress experienced by the witness.

Key goals of supportive companionable relating

Supportive companionable relating in the field of child sexual abuse can promote three key goals. First and foremost, breaking the silence about the reality of abuse and making the problem visible. Second, the provision of an exploratory forum for the sharing of experience on which to base recommendations for action and explore creative ways to respond. Breaking the silence and a forum for survivors are especially important because the testimony of the survivors and their allies is the essential data on which to base change. There can be no real change until they are heard and the real problem acknowledged (Nelson 1998). Third, bringing together the witnesses to the truth – survivors, parents and professionals – as allies against child abuse i.e. moving to joint ownership of problems and solutions.

The task of allies: changing the past legacy of organisations

Most organisations can operate in a supportive companionable way only in the absence of conflict or controversy. The effects of fear make it difficult for them to provide a secure base from which to explore the new and anxiety-provoking territory of child sexual abuse. The legacy of fear is characterised by the following factors:

- trauma-organised systems
- professional scapegoating and silencing
- legislative and procedural attempted solutions
- a backlog of yesterday's children
- loss of credibility by the childcare system.

Trauma-organised systems

Bentovim (1992, 1998) uses the term 'trauma-organised systems' to conceptualise the way in which traumatic events, by their nature overwhelming, are defended against and accommodated to by individual and family systems. The trauma response cycle (Duncan and Baker 1989) can be used to explore the way in which the reverberations of trauma can inform responses to abuse on a societal and organisational level (Richardson 1993a; Richardson and Bacon, Chapter 2).

A key characteristic of trauma-organised systems is anxiety. Parton *et al.* (1996, p.82) describe how, post-Cleveland, the entire focus of child protection shifted from 'child abuse to risk insurance'. Campbell (1997) sees the recommendations of the Butler-Sloss Inquiry (1988) concerning disclosure interviewing as concerned, in the context of adult anxiety about what they may have to say, with 'controlling the conditions in which children may speak' (Campbell 1997, p.238). In her view, as a result of government responses to the controversy, the legacy of Cleveland is an 'adversarial atmosphere' and a 'criminalised culture of child protection' (Campbell 1997, p.247).

The report on Edinburgh's children (Marshall *et al.* 1999) also comments on organisational defensiveness in the wake of public disclosures of past abuse and the dilemma of how to find the confidence to move beyond measures designed by the organisation to cover itself.

It can be concluded that the issue of child sexual abuse is hard for organisational systems to own and causes 'disruption to the developmental stages which help to keep change manageable' (Richardson 1989, p.120). Polarisation and scapegoating are among the results.

Professional scapegoating and silencing

Nelson (1998) emphasises the enforcement of professional silence as a key defence by organisations in response to fear of embarrassing publicity or other difficult consequences of work in the abuse field. She considers this practice to be unethical, unjustifiable and unacceptable and expresses concern about the fate of professionals who act as whistleblowers. Scapegoating and silencing can be seen as symptoms of anxious, unsupportive caregiving. They mirror the style of communication chosen by some ministers when addressing directors of social services departments. For example, there was a storm of protest after Paul Boateng MP accused the latter of being 'complicit' in the sexual abuse of children ('Boateng in clash over child abuse', *Guardian* 28 January 1999, p.4). This incident highlights the difficulty of establishing companionable approaches to a perceived threat.

Legislative and procedural attempted solutions

Many organisations have drawn up procedures to provide a framework for staff to raise concerns and whistleblowers are now protected by legislation. While these developments are to be welcomed, I have reservations: neither takes into account the dynamics of trauma which affect responses to child abuse in general and child sexual abuse in particular; the procedural emphasis is on keeping whistleblowing in-house and may simply operate as a means of containment.

Attempted solutions to a problem which is still emerging can be dangerous. For example, there are contrasting views (La Fontaine 1998; Sinason 1994) regarding the existence of satanic ritual abuse. Recommendations for action should provide for continued exploration, rather than opt for what has been referred to as 'feel good legislation' (Freeman-Longo 1996) – for example, public notification of the release from prison of sex offenders – which may assuage anxious or vengeful feelings but fails to provide real solutions.

A backlog of yesterday's children

This backlog carries with it a legacy of unhealed wounds. Examples of the damaging effects of child sexual abuse are given by all of the contributors to this book.

In responding to Utting's (1997) grim findings concerning the care system, the Health Secretary, Frank Dobson, acknowledged 'a woeful tale of failure at all levels to provide a secure and decent childhood for some of the most vulnerable children' (*Guardian* 16 February 2000). But although he announced measures to ensure better protection for children living away from home in future, the needs of those who had already suffered were not mentioned.

The latter's difficulty of obtaining redress is enormous. Many childcare organisations are in the invidious position of having to refuse to settle the compensation claims of former children in their care. In addition, as Butler-Sloss (1988), Waterhouse *et al.* (2000) and other sources such as Hooper and Koprowska (2000) attest, there is a pressing need for trauma-orientated therapeutic and counselling services.

Loss of credibility by the childcare system

The strength of disillusion is highlighted by survivors like Fred Fever (1994) and Cara (see Ambridge, Henry and Richardson, Chapter 11), as well as by protective parents such as members of LASA (see Brooks, Chapter 5). The vulnerability of children in care (highlighted by Bacon in Chapter 8) heightens concern. The message of Waterhouse *et al.* is that

> The Children Act 1989 has provided a springboard for many improvements in children's services but the need for vigilance and further positive action remains if the ever present risk of abuse is to be minimised. (Waterhouse *et al.* 2000, p.825)

Changing the legacy: towards a secure base

A secure base can be built via caregiving which is supportive and companionable and which enables the professional and the community to be exploratory rather than defensive.

Supportive companionable relating can enable the trauma response cycle to be understood and worked through. Individuals, organisations and society as a whole can opt for a cycle of resolution of the normal reactions of anxiety, guilt, anger and grief. Each point on the cycle would then represent a normal stage of development but stages only, none of which would dictate strategy. Any backlash or denial would be seen as part of a learning curve. Attempts at killing the messenger would be understood as a symptom of the absence of a solution and an attempt to preserve the status quo. It would be possible to own with Summit (1988, p.45) that: 'Anyone who tries to encourage unwanted awareness becomes a target for censure. Unlike ordinary frontiers of discovery, sexual abuse provokes an authoritarian insistence for obscurity over enlightenment'. It would ensure a collegial response to the silencing and victimisation of whistleblowers

No individual whistleblower or professional group should face backlash alone and unsupported. The backlash, something which is engendered by all social movements (Myers 1994), needs to be responded to in an authoritative and organised way by professional groups and organisations, and with the kind of committed advocacy described (Marshall *et al.* 1999) as so crucial to the testimony of Edinburgh's children.

The task of reparation

A huge repair process is called for in the wake of what we now know about the reality of child sexual abuse. My experience of a small-scale mediation and reparation exercise in a staff team (Richardson 1999) shows how a breakdown of communication and functioning can be addressed in stages by adapting the tools of mediation to fit the needs of secondary trauma. We need to address this on a much larger scale. There has as yet been no healing in the wake of any of the so-called child abuse scandals – not for the individual survivors, the organisations concerned, the professionals currently working within them, the whistleblowers who brought it to light and the community at large.

There are several alternative models that can be explored as a means of promoting healing and repair. In some parts of the world, a political commitment to promoting recovery from past trauma has taken the form of a Truth Commission. In response to the emergence of past abuse in childcare settings, the Irish government has adopted a similar model by setting up a national forum (Bertie Ahern, An Taoiseach, press release 11 May 1999).

The purpose of a Truth Commission is to allow society to establish an undeniable, commonly accepted public record of what has happened. An authoritative public recognition of the truth produced in this way provides an agreed foundation for future action to prevent past crimes being repeated. It reduces the possibility of future denial or forgetting. It is a process described by Archbishop Desmond Tutu as 'opening the wound in order to cleanse it, so that it does not fester' (quoted in Hird 1997, p.11). It enables the survivors to speak out and for their voices to be heard. Sharing their suffering helps survivors to ensure that they have contributed to the prevention of similar trauma in the future. Being heard also helps to provide the survivor with a sense of justice and dignity. This approach may provide, at all levels, sufficient strength and containment for traumatic responses to be worked through, to promote interest-sharing and to promote supportive companionable relating.

The statutory inquiry is another approach to establishing the truth and to using the experience of the injured for future good. An official inquiry is often a goal desired by survivors and others. For example, families bereaved in traumatic incidents such as the sinking of the *Marchioness* river boat on the Thames, the Clapham rail disaster and following surgery for heart defects on babies in Bristol have all pressed for, and succeeded, in obtaining official inquiries. However, this approach to testing the truth tends to be adversarial. Official inquiries do not necessarily operate on an SC model, especially when, at the point of announcing their findings, they are disbanded and cannot oversee the outcome. The hopes for truth and justice to prevail and for the assuagement of painful feelings of hurt, anger and loss invested in the process by the participants can be gravely disappointed by the findings.

Effective responses honour the truth, promote resolution of long-term dissension and help to heal wounds, both individual and societal. They incorporate the principles of restorative justice which re-empower the victim, restore harmony and community (Braithwaite 1996) and dispose of 'integrated' rather than 'fragmented forgiveness' (Meriweather 1999).

Components of a supportive companionable approach to healing and reparation

Honouring the truth is the first and most crucial step. The truth has an intrinsic value which can heal individuals and the community. For example, what the majority of survivors of historical abuse want most from the organisations whose care failed them is an admission of the truth and an apology.

Agreed ways of remembering the past need to be in place. Rituals of memory are important in healing all grief. There need to be ways of keeping the experience part of the public consciousness and underlining the message 'never again'. This contributes to an ongoing process of education, awareness raising and rediscovery and is better than strategies based on 'transformed denial' (Richardson and Bacon 1991b), which seek to reassure us that the problem is solved when it is not.

For the long term these activities should not be the task of the witnesses alone even when supported by public opinion. There needs to be a clear political agenda backed up by political will.

The task of the caregiver

Sensitivity to the long-term needs of the witness is crucial. It is unavoidable that the witnesses will still be living with their pain long after the immediate response to them has died down. In my experience as a witness, it is very hard in the long term to cope with others' fears that I might constitute a threat to their well-being, manifested in things like persistent targeting by campaign groups and isolation from colleagues. Well-meaning suggested survival strategies usually involve submission. These can include advice to flee the area, to change one's name or career or to become a bystander and give up the fight for one's own peace of mind. Equally, in my experience, it can be tempting for others to exhort the witness to carry on when time out for rest and recovery is needed. Most difficult of all is the sense of professional exile, abandonment and the ongoing task of negotiating the professional continuum of survival (Richardson and Bacon 1991c; see also Richardson and Bacon, Chapter 2).

The following are suggested as the positive tasks of the caregiver who wishes to support the witness during times of despair as well as hope:

1. Help to cope with and mourn losses on several fronts such as the loss of the support and companionship of peers; the loss of professional role and identity; the loss of self-confidence and self-esteem; the loss of opportunity to contribute from the experience.

2. Help to process and metabolise the effects of 'vicarious traumatisation' (Pearlman and Saakvitine 1995). This might include support for professional exploration and study of the experience by the witness.

3. The provision of a specific transitional space for the necessary processing. In my opinion, this needs to be distinct from normal supervisory arrangements.

4. Help with the creative transformation of the experience. This is helped by the active provision of the means and the opportunity for the witness to contribute from his or her experience. For example, in contrast to the isolation of pioneering professionals in Europe, colleagues in the USA are often invited to share their experiences at conferences and seminars.

To fulfil the above tasks, caregivers need to be able to:

- recognise the limitations of their own experience

- attune to the personal and professional distress of the witness

- provide continuity

- understand that the situation is often long term and ongoing in the present rather than simply in the past

- see the experience of the witness as a potential source of growth, self-development and contribution

- deal with their own 'survivor guilt' or past role as bystander

- recognise that, to be adequate to the task, existing models of practice may need revising or new ones devising

- recognise that everyone, including themselves, is having to adapt to a changed environment

- understand the significance of attachment issues, for example the impact of losses such as relationships with colleagues

- be willing to work with those who are the focus of key events to co-construct the learning which can take the field forward.

These are the kinds of components which might best facilitate a return to SC relating where this has existed previously, or to introduce it as part of a culture change. They encourage the whole system to construct a narrative of events which is coherent and meaningful because it is shared.

Learning to be allies: messages from experience

Alliances can replace the strategic management of controversy. Actively seeking alliances between whistleblowers of all kinds and organisations responsible for the care and protection of children can promote a healing integration which can enable us to hold on to and to honour the truth in the longer term. A demonstration of respect and a desire to work in partnership will do more to promote a whistleblowing culture than mere whistleblowing training.

It is a tragedy when potential allies remain bystanders. In Cleveland, this resulted from a mixture of lack of information, confusion, anxiety, ambivalence, fear and hostility. Some bystanders distanced themselves. Some were critical. Others gave support in private but not in public. Some felt helpless and were inactive. Others lacked a forum to make their views known. Some needed to resolve their ambivalence, for example Campbell (1988, p.7), who began her research into the Cleveland case from a place of 'restless discomfort for the people who had decided to do something about the evidence before their own eyes'. Others felt bound to support the status quo – it couldn't happen here!

What can allies do to respond in a more supportive and companionable way? An understanding of the tasks of the caregiver (above) can be helpful. Above all, allies can provide a peer relationship, based on reciprocity, mutual respect and shared problem solving. This allows the witness to be an ally too and to contribute to resolving some of the difficult issues such as the dilemmas of children in Group B. Allies can help to maintain exploration and promote debate. It is essential for progress to have a continuing debate on what Butler-Sloss (1988, p.243) called 'new and particularly difficult problems'. The necessary debate cannot take place when everyone is in a state of siege and feels their interests to be threatened – exploration can happen only in a supportive environment. Seeing the value of their role can enable allies to make active choices. They can ask themselves: what does it mean to be an ally on this issue? How might the chances of being a good ally be sabotaged? How might they be increased?

These general principles can help to prevent the unhelpful polarisation between the idealisation of the witness as heroic and their denigration as wreckers. They move towards restoring the connection between humans which is broken by trauma. They provide for all individuals in this field to be committed to healing their own wounds. Telling one's own story of hurt and oppression means that the feelings of anger, powerlessness and helplessness, which can get in the way of being effective, need not operate in the present. This includes personal and professional experiences, as part of everyone's task of formulating a coherent narrative of events.

Lastly, allies need to prepare to be mistreated too: no one escapes this issue unscathed. However, my assumption is that mistreatment is likely to lessen the more we ally together. Everyone engaged in this issue can affirm and celebrate their own capacity for courage.

Learning to be allies: messages for organisations

All childcare organisations are facing an unprecedented challenge of confronting the reality and extent of abuse of children entrusted to their care in the past, making recompense to survivors in the present, and ensuring that services are safe in the present. How those challenges are faced will determine their fitness to provide services. In addressing these challenges, organisations need as many outspoken witnesses as possible as their allies, since this issue and the survivors are not likely to go away.

Organisations who want to be good allies need to think about four things. First, negotiate openly about what it would mean to have those who have been witnesses to the truth work with you or for you. Conflicts of interest should not arise if all are committed to the welfare of children: where they do, the aim should be to be inclusive of the witness. In particular, employers should not demand that becoming a bystander should be the price of staying in a job.

Second, accept that all staff in this field are in the difficult role of witness to the truth – it comes with the territory. Reflect on your duty of care in the light of that and the vulnerability of your staff. Third, inform yourselves about the dynamics of abuse and the backlash to avoid becoming a trauma-organised system. Fourth, consult the witnesses about what support is needed. This also means providing resources to ensure that responses are inclusive and flexible. There is a tension around the financial cost of inclusion of individuals and voluntary groups who are unfunded.

Conclusion: clear choices

Organisations, individuals and communities have a clear choice to make, based on the knowledge which has been gained so painfully. The future can be one in which everyone continues to get buffeted by fresh storms and fearful responses. Alternatively, there is the more rewarding and successful route of supporting one another as allies in the exploration of some of the tough issues which cause controversy in the public arena.

As shown in Figure 12.1, societal awareness of child sexual abuse fluctuates in response to conflicting pressures. Societal denial has among its key features silencing, isolation and a political consensus of avoidance or containment. It is a process of disconnection characterised by an absence of sup-

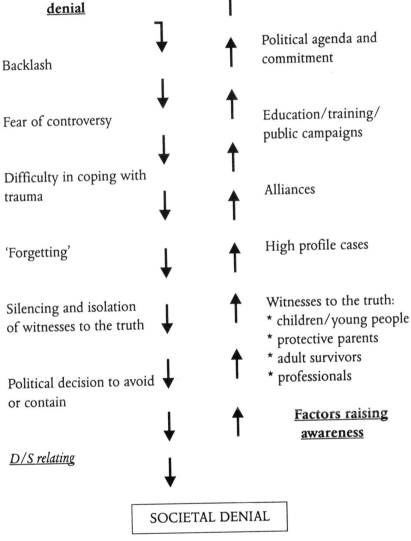

Figure 12.1 Awareness of child sexual abuse

portive companionable relating. Societal recognition is promoted by testimony, alliances and a political commitment. It is a process of integration promoted by supportive companionable relating.

Despite the power of all that we feel, despite our resolve to remember and testify to all that we have heard, we need to acknowledge that pressures to be silent and to rejoin a consensus of denial, disconnected from what we actually know, will crowd in on us again. Honouring the truth in the testimony of survivors, and actively seeking alliances of survivors, relatives and professionals in all areas can provide a healing integration. Individually and socially integrated, we can maintain awareness of the unspeakable truth of child abuse, can combat its violations and seek to heal the trauma it creates.

Acknowledgement

This chapter is based on a paper given by the author at the seminar, Trade in People, Abductions and Abuse of Children in the European Union: Problems and Solutions, European Parliament, Brussels, 15–16 October 1998.

The contributors

Maggie Ambridge is a state registered art therapist who has substantial experience of working with adult survivors of childhood sexual abuse, as well as with children and families. She is employed by an NHS trust where she works in a specialist child protection project embedded in a child and adolescent mental health team. She has previously written on the subject of art therapy and child abuse, and is currently engaged in research in the area of trauma resolution in relation to art and literature. She also endeavours to progress her own personal artwork.

Heather Bacon is a clinical psychologist committed to working on a multi-agency basis to assist abused children. She has specialised in the area of child protection since being involved in the Cleveland crisis. She works in the child and family mental health team of an NHS trust, and also acts as an independent expert witness on behalf of children in the courts. Primarily a clinician, she is interested in combining practice with research into children's attachments, and the resolution of sexual abuse trauma. She is a regular contributor to training and conferences and is the co-editor and co-author of *Child Sexual Abuse: Whose Problem?* (Venture Press, 1991) and other published papers.

Isabel Brooks is a pseudonym for the founder member of the League Against Sadistic Abuse (LASA). She is a graduate who has had a successful career in education and commerce. She founded LASA after her adult daughter disclosed that she had been sadistically abused by her father throughout her childhood. Isabel has forged links between LASA and parent groups and child protection agencies in France, Belgium and the Netherlands.

Frank Cook is Member of Parliament for Stockton North. He is a Deputy Speaker in Westminster Hall (House of Commons) and a Vice-President of NATO's Parliamentary Assembly. A trustee of the Faithfull Foundation, he has been concerned about the issue of child sexual abuse for many years. As a local constituency MP, he gave evidence to the Butler-Sloss inquiry in Cleveland in 1987.

Cara Henry is a pseudonym for a social worker who has gone through a process of self-analysis and self-discovery since being abused as a child. She is committed to using her experiences to educate and inform professionals and policy makers about the needs of abused children.

Pat McLoughlin has a background in social work in both the voluntary and public sectors. She has worked as a guardian ad litem in Leeds and Bradford since 1991. Her current interests are working with sexually abused children with a special focus on the injustice that children experience through the court system, and the implications of this for human rights.

Tink Palmer has been in social work practice since 1973. Between 1984 and 1991 she was a guardian ad litem and concurrently tutored at the University of York and offered consultative and therapeutic services. In 1992 she was appointed Principal Officer (Child Care) for Cleveland Social Services Department. In March 1995 she took over the management of the Barnardo's unit in Middlesbrough, a therapeutic unit for children and their families where sexual abuse is an issue. At present, she is in a Department of Health seconded post with a brief to develop a strategic response to the abuse of children through prostitution. She continues to act as a consultant and is an associate member of the Home Office Committee on Child Evidence and a member of the National Working Group for Children who are Sexually Exploited.

Sue Richardson is an attachment-based psychoanalytic psychotherapist with almost 30 years' experience in the helping professions. During her former social work career she was a key figure in the 1987 Cleveland child abuse crisis and a key witness at the subsequent Butler-Sloss inquiry. She is a part of an international network of professionals who have pioneered awareness of child sexual abuse. She is a regular contributor to national and international conferences, co-editor and co-author of *Child Sexual Abuse: Whose Problem?* (Venture Press, 1991) and a number of published papers. Sue is in independent practice where she has integrated her skills and knowledge into creative work with adults abused in childhood. She acts as an expert witness in this field in which she also provides training and consultancy.

Tim Tate is an award-winning documentary film-maker, journalist and author. He has produced and directed films for Channel 4, ITV, Discovery Channels and the A & E Network: many have investigated the abuse of children by adults and the wider politics behind the policing of paedophilia. His work has been honoured by awards from UNESCO, the New York Film Festival, the US Cable Academy and Amnesty International. In addition to writing for many national newspapers and magazines and contributing to other people's books, he has published five works of non-fiction examining the law, child pornography, ritual abuse and the policing of murder. His most recent book, *The Murder of Childhood* (with Ray Wyre, Penguin, 1995) has also been published in translation in Japan and China. His documentary film reassessing the 1987 Cleveland child abuse crisis (*Cleveland: Unspeakable Truths,* Channel 4, 1997) was short-listed as a finalist in the Royal Television Society's Current Affairs Film of the Year award. Married with six children, he lives in Yorkshire.

Jane Wynne is a retired community paediatrician. Her interest in child abuse began as a medical student and she has worked in paediatrics since 1973. In 1984 she was appointed consultant and senior Lecturer in child health at the University of Leeds. Since then she has lectured and taught in the UK and abroad. She is the author and co-author with Chris Hobbs and Helga Hanks of a standard textbook for paediatricians on child abuse and many articles and chapters on this subject. With the Leeds team, she gave evidence to the Butler-Sloss inquiry and their data was included in the Inquiry report. She has been awarded an honorary doctorate by Leeds Metropolitan University for her work with abused and neglected children.

Bibliography

Ainsworth, M.D.S., Blehar, M., Water, E. and Wall, S. (1978) *Patterns of Attachment: A Psychological Study of the Strange Situation*. Hillsdale, NJ: Erlbaum.

Ainsworth, M.D.S. and Eichberg, C. (1991) Effects on infant–mother attachment of mother's unresolved loss of an attachment figure, or other traumatic experience. In C. Murray Parkes, J. Stevenson-Hinde and P. Marris (eds) *Attachment across the Life Cycle*. London: Routledge.

Aldridge, J. (1997) Preparing Children for Court. In H. Westcott and J. Jones (eds) *Perspectives on the Memorandum*. Aldershot: Arena.

Alexander, P. (1992) Application of attachment theory to the study of sexual abuse. *Journal of Consulting and Clinical Psychology 60*, 2, 185–195.

Ambridge, M. (2000) Using the reflective image within the mother-child relationship. In J. Murphy (ed) *Art Therapy with Young Survivors of Sexual Abuse - Lost for Words*. London: Brunner-Routledge.

American Psychiatric Association (APA) (1995) *Diagnostic and Statistical Manual of Mental Disorders, Fourth Edition, International Version*. Washington, DC: APA.

Anderson, C.L. and Alexander, P.C. (1996) The relationship between attachment and dissociation in adult survivors of incest. *Psychiatry 59*, 240–254.

Armstrong, L. (1996) *Rocking the Cradle of Sexual Politics: What Happened When Women Said Incest*. London: Women's Press.

Bacon, H. and Richardson, S. (2000) Child sexual abuse, accommodation and the continuum of disclosure. In C. Itzin (ed) *Home Truths about Child Sexual Abuse*. London: Routledge.

Bagley, C., Rodberg, G., Wellings, D., Moosa-Mitha, M. and Young, L. (1995) Sexual and physical child abuse and the development of dissociative personality traits: Canadian and British evidence from adolescent child welfare and child care populations. *Child Abuse Review 4*, 99–113.

Barnardo's (1996) *So, You're Going to be a Witness! (Video)*. Essex: Barnardo's.

Barnardo's (1998) *Bridgeway Annual Report 1997–1998*. Essex: Bridgeway Project, Middlesbrough, c/o Barnardo's .

Bedingfield, D. (1998) *The Child in Need: Children, the State and the Law*. Bristol: Family Law.

Bentovim, A. (1992) *Trauma Organised Systems: Physical and Sexual Abuse in Families*. London: Karnac.

Bentovim, A. (1998) Children are liars aren't they? An exploration of denial processes in child sexual abuse. In V. Sinason (ed) *Memory in Dispute*. London: Karnac.

Bentovim, A., Elton, A., Hildebrand, J., Tranter, M. and Vizard, E. (eds) (1988) *Child Sexual Abuse within the Family: Assessment and Treatment*. London: Wright.

Berliner, L. and Conte, J. (1995) The effects of disclosure and intervention on sexually abused children. *Child Abuse and Neglect 19*, 371–384.

Bibby, P. (ed) (1996) *Organised Abuse: The Current Debate*. Aldershot: Arena.

Birchall, E. and Hallett, C. (1995) *Working Together in Child Protection*. London: HMSO.

Blizard, R.A. (1997a) The origins of dissociative identity disorder from an object relations and attachment theory perspective. *Dissociation X*, 4, 223–229.

Blizard, R.A. (1997b) Therapeutic alliances with abuser alters in dissociative identity disorder: The paradox of attachment to the abuser. *Dissociation X, 4*, 246–254.

Blizard, R.A. and Bluhm, A.M. (1994) Attachment to the abuser: Integrating object relations and trauma theories in treatment of abuse survivors. *Psychotherapy 31*, 383–390.

Bowker, L.H. (1988) *Wife Beating and Child Abuse*. Newbury Park, CA: Sage.

Bowlby, J. (1969) *Attachment and Loss, Vol. 1, Attachment*. London: Hogarth Press.

Bowlby, J. (1973) *Attachment and Loss, Vol. 2, Separation, Anxiety and Anger*. London: Hogarth Press.

Bowlby, J. (1989) The role of attachment in personality development and psychopathology. In S.I. Greenspan, and M.D. Pollock (eds) *The Course of Life, Vol. 1, Infancy*. Madison, CT: International University Press.

Braithwaite, J. (1996) Restorative Justice for a Better Future. Dorothy J. Killam Memorial Lecture, Dalhousie University, 17 October, forthcoming in *Dalhousie Law Review*.

Briere, J. (1989) *Therapy for Adults Molested as Children*. New York: Springer.

Briere, J. (1992) *Child Abuse Trauma: Theory and Treatment of the Lasting Effects*. London: Sage.

Briggs, D., Doyle, P., Gooch, T. and Kennington, R. (1998) *Assessing Men Who Sexually Abuse*. London: Jessica Kingsley Publishers.

Briggs, F. and Hawkins, R. (1996) A comparison of the childhood experiences of convicted male child molesters and men who were sexually abused in childhood and claimed to be non-offenders. *Child Abuse and Neglect 20*, 3, 221–235.

British Association of Community Child Health (BACCH) (1995) *Child Health Rights*. London: BACCH.

British Psychological Society (1995) *Recovered Memories*. Leicester: British Psychological Society.

Butler-Sloss, Rt Hon. Justice E. (1988) *Report of the Inquiry into Child Abuse in Cleveland 1987*. London: HMSO.

Calder, M. (1999) Managing allegations of abuse against carers. In A. Wheal (ed) *The R.H.P. Companion to Foster Care*. Lyme Regis: Russell House Publishing.

Campbell, B. (1997) *Unofficial Secrets: Child Sexual Abuse – The Cleveland Case*. 2nd Edition. London: Virago.

Cashman, H. and Lamballe-Armstrong, A. (1991) The unwanted message: Child protection through community awareness. In S. Richardson and H. Bacon (eds) *Child Sexual Abuse: Whose Problem? Reflections from Cleveland*. Birmingham: Venture Press.

Cassidy, J. and Shaver, P.R. (eds) (1999) *Handbook of Attachment Theory, Research and Clinical Applications*. London: Guilford press.

Cleaver, H., Wattam, C. and Cawson, P. (1998) *Assessing Risk in Child Protection*. London: NSPCC.

Clyde, Lord J.J. (1992) *The Report of the Inquiry into the Removal of Children from Orkney in February 1991*. Edinburgh: HMSO.

Cohen, J. Berliner, L. and Mannerino, A.P. (2000) Treating traumatized children: A research review and synthesis. *Trauma, Violence and Abuse 1*, 1, 29–49.

Colclough, L., Parton, N. and Anslow, M. (1999) Family support. In N. Parton and C. Wattam (eds) *Child Sexual Abuse: Responding to the Experiences of Children*. Chichester: NSPCC/Wiley.

Collier, F. (1998) *BAAF Action Plan to Improve Adoption Services*. London: BAAF.

Cooklin, A. (1999) Children abused in families: Is the criminal law the only redress? Workshop 6: ChildLine conference 'Hearing children's voices', London 13 May.

Cresswell, T. (2000) Why are paediatricians so vulnerable to abuse? Presentation to symposium, Walking the Touchline: Doctors and Child Abuse, BASPCAN Fourth National Congress, Meeting Children's Needs: The Opportunity for Change in Child Protection, York 17–20 September.

Crittenden, P. (1988) Family and dyadic patterns of functioning in maltreating families. In K. Browne, C. Davies and P. Stratton (eds) *Early Prediction and Prevention of Child Abuse*. Chichester: Wiley.

Crittenden, P. (1995) Attachment and psychopathy. In S. Goldberg, R. Muir and J. Kerr (eds) *Attachment Theory: Social, Developmental and Clinical Perspectives*. Hillsdale, NJ: Analytic Press.

Crittenden, P.M. and Ainsworth, M. (1989) Child maltreatment and attachment theory. In D. Cicchetti and V. Carlson (eds) *Child Maltreatment: Theory and Research on the Causes and Consequences of Child Abuse and Neglect*. Cambridge: Cambridge University Press.

Crown Prosecution Service, Department of Health and Home Office (2001) *Provision of Therapy for Child Witnesses Prior to a Criminal Trial: Practice Guidance*. London: CPS Communications Branch.

Dale, P. (1999) *Adults Abused as Children: Experiences of Counselling and Psychotherapy*. London: Sage.

Davies, G. (1995) *Videotaping Children's Evidence: An Evaluation*. London: Home Office.

Davies, G. and Noon, E. (1991) *An Evaluation of the Live Link for Child Witnesses*. London: Home Office.

Dent, H. and Flin, R. (1992) *Children as Witnesses*. Chichester: Wiley.

Davis, G., Hoyano, L., Maitland, L. and Morgan, R. (1999) The admissiblity and sufficiency of evidence in child abuse prosecutions. *Research Findings 100*. London: Home Office.

Department of Health (1991) *Working Together Under the Children Act 1989: A Guide to Arrangements for Interagency Co-operation for the Protection of Children from Abuse*. London: HMSO.

Department of Health (1999) *Working Together to Safeguard Children: A Guide to Arrangements for Interagency Co-operation for the Protection of Children from Abuse*. London: HMSO.

Department of Health (DH) (1988, 1991, 1999) *Working Together under the Children Act*. London: HMSO

Department of Health (DH) (1995) *Child Protection: Messages from Research*. London: HMSO.

Department of Health and Social Security (1986) *Child Abuse – Working Together: A Draft Guide to Arrangements for Interagency Co-operation for the Protection of Children from Abuse*. London: HMSO.

Department of Health and Social Security (1988) *Working Together: A Guide to Arrangements for Interagency Co-operation for the Protection of Children from Abuse.* London: HMSO.

deYoung, M. (1997) Satanic Ritual Abuse in Day Care: An Analysis of 12 American Cases. *Child Abuse Review 6,* 84–93.

Duncan, S. and Baker, A. (1989) Assessing the child's therapeutic needs. Presentation to Conference, Not One More Child, Reading, 18–20 September.

Egeland, B., Jacobvitz, D. and Sroufe, L.A. (1988) Breaking the cycle of abuse. *Child Development 59,* 1080–1088.

Egeland, B. and Susman-Stillman, A. (1996) Dissociation as a mediator of child sexual abuse across generations. *Child Abuse and Neglect 20,* 11, 1123–1133.

Esterson, A. (1972) *The Leaves of Spring: A Study in the Dialectics of Madness.* Quoted in J. Rowan (1981) The Leaves of Spring by Aaron Esterson: An appreciation. In P. Reason and J. Rowan (eds) *Human Inquiry: A Sourcebook of New Paradigm Research.* Chichester: Wiley.

Etherington, K. (2000) *Narrative Approaches to Working with Adult Male Survivors of Child Sexual Abuse: The Client's, the Counsellor's and the Researcher's Story.* London: Jessica Kingsley Publishers.

Fahlberg, V. (1991) *A Child's Journey through Placement.* London: BAAF.

Faller, K.C. (1998) The spectrum of sexual abuse in daycare: an exploratory study. *Journal of Family Violence 3,* 283–298.

Farmer, E. and Pollock, S. (1999) Mix and match: Planning to keep looked after children safe. *Child Abuse Review 8,* 6, 377–392.

Ferguson, D.M., Lynskey, M.T. and Horwood, L.J. (1996) Childhood sexual abuse and psychiatric disorder in young adulthood. *Journal of the American Academy of Child and Adolescent Psychiatry 35,* 1402–1410.

Fever, F. (1994) *Who Cares? Memories of a Childhood in Barnado's.* London: Warner.

Finkelhor, D. (1979) *Sexually Victimised Children.* New York: Free Press.

Finkelhor, D. (1984) *Child Sexual Abuse: New Theory and Research.* New York: Free Press.

Finkelhor, D. (ed) (1986) *A Sourcebook on Child Sexual Abuse.* London: Sage.

Finkelhor, D. (1990) Early and long-term effects of child sexual abuse: An update. *Professional Psychology Research & Practice 21,* 325–330.

Finkelhor, D. and Browne, A. (1986) Initial and long-term effects: A conceptual framework. In D. Finkelhor (ed) *A Sourcebook on Child Sexual Abuse.* London: Sage.

Fonagy, P. (1998) Attachment, the development of the self, and its pathology in dissociative disorders. *Bulletin of The Menninger Clinic 62,* 147–169.

Fonagy, P., Steele, H., Leigh, T., Kennedy, R., Mattoon, G. and Target, M. (1995) Attachment, the reflective self, and borderline states: The predictive specificity of the Adult Attachment Interview and pathological development. In S. Goldberg, R. Muir and J. Kerr (eds) *Attachment Theory, Social, Developmental, and Clinical Perspectives.* London: Analytic Press.

Fonagy, P., Steele, M., Moran, G.S., Steele, H. and Higgit, A. (1991) The capacity for understanding mental states: The reflective self in parent and child and its significance for security of attachment. *Infant Mental Health Journal 2,* 200–216.

Fonagy, P., Steele, M., Steele, H., Higgit, A. and Target, M. (1994) The theory and practice of resilience. *Journal of Child Psychology and Psychiatry 35,* 2, 231–257.

Freeman-Longo, R.E. (1996) Invited commentary: Feel good legislation – Prevention or calamity. *Child Abuse and Neglect 20,* 2, 95–101.

Frothingham, T., Barnett, R., Hobbs, C.J. and Wynne, J.M. (1992) Child sexual abuse in Leeds before and after Cleveland. *Child Abuse Review 2,* 23–34.

Gallagher, B. (1999) The abuse of children in public care. *Child Abuse Review 8,* 6, 357–366.

Gallagher, B. (2000) Ritual and child sexual abuse. *Child Abuse Review 9,* 5, 321–327.

Gara, M.A., Rosenberg, S. and Herzog, E.P. (1996) The abused child as parent. *Child Abuse and Neglect 20,* 797–807.

General Medical Council (2000) *Confidentiality Guidance.* London: GMC.

Gil, E. (1993) Etiologic theories. In E. Gil and T. Cavanagh Johnson (eds) *Sexualized Children: Assessment and Treatment of Children who Molest.* Rockville, MD: Launch Press.

Glaser, D. (2000) Child abuse and neglect and the brain: A review. *Journal of Child Psychology and Psychiatry 41,* 1, 97–117.

Golier, J. and Yehuda, R. (1998) Neuroendocrine activity and memory-related impairments in post-traumatic stress disorder. *Development and Psychopathology 10,* 857–869.

Gonzalez, L.S., Waterman, J., Kelly, R.J., McCord, J. and Oliveri, M.K. (1993) Children's patterns of disclosures and recantations of sexual and ritualistic abuse allegations in psychotherapy. *Child Abuse and Neglect 17,* 281–289.

Goodman, G.S. and Bottoms, B.L. (eds) (1993) *Child Victims, Child Witnesses.* New York: Guilford Press.

Gough, D. (1996) An overview of the literature. In P. Bibby (ed) *Organised Abuse: The Current Debate*. Aldershot: Arena.

Haapasalo, J. and Aaltonen, T. (1999) Mothers' abusive childhood predicts child abuse. *Child Abuse Review* 8, 231–250.

Hagood, M. (1994) Group art therapy with adolescent sex offenders: An American experience. In M. Liebman (ed) *Art Therapy with Offenders*. London: Jessica Kingsley Publishers.

Hanks, H.I.G. and Wynne, J.M. (2000) Females who sexually abuse: An approach to assessment. In M. Calder (ed) *The Complete Guide to Sexual Abuse of Females*. Lyme Regis: Russell House.

Hay, L. (1988) *You Can Heal Your Life*. London: Eden Grove.

Heard, D. and Lake, B. (1997) *The Challenge of Attachment for Caregiving*. London: Routledge.

Hemenway, D., Solnick, S. and Carter, J. (1994) Child-rearing violence. *Child Abuse and Neglect 18*, 1011–1020.

Herman, J.L. (1992) *Trauma and Recovery: From Domestic Abuse to Political Terror*. New York: Basic Books.

Heron, J. (1981) Philosophical basis for a new paradigm. In P. Reason and J. Rowan (eds) *Human Inquiry: A Sourcebook of New Paradigm Research*. Chichester: Wiley.

Hewitt, S. (2000) She's too young to talk so she probably won't remember anyway. Presentation to BASPCAN Fourth National Congress, Meeting Children's Needs: The Opportunity for Change in Child Protection, York, 17–20 September.

Hinchliffe, M. (1989) The role of the Official Solicitor in child abuse cases. In A. Levy, (ed) *Focus on Child Abuse: Medical, Legal and Social Work Perspectives*. London: Hawksmere.

Hird, C. (1997) *The Terror and the Truth*. London: BBC.

Hobbs, C.J. (1991) Paediatric Intervention in Child Protection. *Child Abuse Review 1*, 1, 5–17.

Hobbs, C.J., Hanks, H. and Wynne, J. (eds) (1993) *Child Abuse and Neglect: A Clinician's Handbook*. Edinburgh: Churchill Livingstone.

Hobbs, C.J. and Wynne, J.M. (1986) Buggery in childhood: A common syndrome of child abuse. *Lancet ii*, 793–796.

Hobbs, C.J. and Wynne, J.M. (1987a) Child sexual abuse: An increasing rate of diagnosis. *Lancet ii*, 837–841.

Hobbs, C.J. and Wynne, J.M. (1987b) Management of sexual abuse. *Archives of Diseases in Childhood 62*, 1182–1187.

Hobbs, C.J. and Wynne, J.M. (1990) The sexually abused battered child. *Archives of Diseases in Childhood 65*, 423–427.

Hobbs, G., Hobbs, C.J. and Wynne, J.M. (1999) Abuse of children in foster and residential care. *Child Abuse and Neglect 23*, 12, 1239–1252.

Hollander, N.C. (1998) Exile: Paradoxes of loss and creativity. *British Journal of Psychotherapy 15*, 2, 201–215.

Holmes, J. (1993) *John Bowlby and Attachment Theory*. London: Routledge.

Home Office Circular 1996; Statement of National Standards of Witness Care in the Criminal Justice System. London: Home Office.

Home Office (2000) *Achieving Best Evidence in Criminal Proceedings: Guidance for Vulnerable or Intimidated Witnesses, including Children*. London: HMSO.

Home Office and Department of Health (1992) *Memorandum of Good Practice on Video Interviewing of Child Witnesses*. London: HMSO.

Hooper, C.A. (1992) *Mothers Surviving Child Sexual Abuse*. London: Routledge.

Hooper, C.A and Koprowska, J. (2000) Reparative experience or repeated trauma? Child sexual abuse and adult mental health services. In U. McCluskey and C.A. Hooper (eds) *Psychodynamic Perspectives on Abuse: The Cost of Fear*. London: Jessica Kingsley Publishers.

Howarth, V. (1999) Unpublished presentation at ChildLine Conference 'Hearing Children's Voices', London, 13 May.

Howe, D., Brandon, M., Hinings, D. and Schofield, G. (eds) (1999) *Attachment Theory, Child Maltreatment, and Family Support: A Practice and Assessment Model*. London: Macmillan.

Howes, N., Richardson, H., and Robinson-Fell, B. (2000) Coping strategies and consequent behaviours in traumatised/abused children. Presentation to BASPCAN Fourth National Congress, Meeting Children's Needs: The Opportunity for Change in Child Protection, York, 17–20 September.

Hudson, P.S. (1994) The clinician's experience. In V. Sinason (ed) *Treating Survivors of Satanist Abuse*. London: Routledge.

Hunt, J. and MacLeod, A. (1997) *The Last Resort*. Centre for Socio-Legal Studies, university of Bristol.

Itzin, C. (ed) (2000) *Home Truths about Child Sexual Abuse: Influencing Policy and Practice – A reader.* London: Routledge.

Ivaldi, G. (1998) *Children Adopted from Care.* London: BAAF.

James, B. (1994) *Handbook for Treatment of Attachment-Trauma Problems in Children.* New York: Lexington Books.

Jehu, D. (1988) *Beyond Sexual Abuse: Therapy with Women who were Childhood Victims.* Chichester: Wiley.

Johnson, C.J. (1989) Female child perpetrators: children who molest other children. *Child Abuse and Neglect 13*, 4, 571–585.

Jones, D.P.H. and Ramachandani, P. (1999) *Child Sexual Abuse: Informing Practice from Research.* Oxford: Radcliffe Medical Press.

Kelly, L. (2000) Disconnection or connections: or will we ever learn? In P. Cox, S. Kershaw and J. Trotter (eds) *Child Sexual Assault: Feminist Perspectives.* London: Palgrave.

Kelly, L., Regan, L. and Burton, S. (1991) *An Exploratory Study of the Prevalence of Sexual Abuse on a Sample of 16–21 Year Olds.* London: Polytechnic of North London Child Abuse Studies Unit.

Kelly, L., Regan, G. and Burton, S. (2000) Sexual exploitation: A new discovery or one part of the continuum of sexual abuse in childhood? In C. Itzin (ed) *Home Truths about Child Sexual Abuse: Influencing Policy and Practice – A Reader.* London: Routledge.

Kempe, J. and Kempe, C.H. (1978) *Child Abuse.* London: Fontana.

Kolvin, I. (1988) Child sexual abuse: Principles of good practice. *British Journal of Hospital Medicine 39*, 54–62.

La Fontaine, J.S. (1994) *The Extent and Nature of Organised and Ritual Sexual Abuse: Research Findings.* London: HMSO.

La Fontaine, J.S. (1998) *Speak of the Devil: Tales of Satanic Abuse in Contemporary England.* Cambridge: Cambridge University Press.

Lindsay, D. and Read, J. (1994) Incest resolution: Psychotherapy and memories of childhood sexual abuse. *Applied Cognitive Psychology 8*, 281–338.

Lindsay, M. (1999) The neglected priority: Sexual abuse in the context of residential care. *Child Abuse Review 8*, 6, 405–418.

Liotti, G. (1992) Disorganised/disoriented attachment in the aetiology of dissociative disorders. *Dissociation 5*, 4, 196–204.

Liotti, G. (1995) Disorganised/disoriented attachment in the psychotherapy of the dissociative disorders. In S. Goldberg, R. Muir and J. Kerr (eds) *Attachment Theory, Social, Developmental, and Clinical Perspectives.* Hillsdale, NJ: Analytic Press.

London Borough of Brent (1985) *A Child in Trust: The Report of the Panel of Inquiry into the Circumstances Surrounding the Death of Jasmine Beckford.* London: London Borough of Brent.

Lyons-Ruth, K. and Jacobvitz, D. (1999) Attachment disorganisation: Unresolved loss, relational violence and lapses in behavioural and attentional strategies. I.J. Cassidy and P.R. Shaver (eds) (1999) *Handbook of Attachment Theory, Research, and Clinical Applications.* London: Guilford Press.

McElroy, L.P. (1992) Early indicators of pathological dissociation in sexually abused children. *Child Abuse and Neglect 16*, 6, 833–846.

McFadyen, A., Hanks, H. and James, C. (1993) Ritual abuse: A definition. *Child Abuse Review 2*, 35–41.

McFadden, E.J. and Ryan, P. (1992) Preventing abuse in family foster care. Presentation to Ninth International Congress on Child Abuse and Neglect, Chicago, 29 August–3 September Detail from B. Gallagher (1999) The abuse of children in public care *Child Abuse Review 8*, 357–365.

MacLeod, M. (1999) Don't just do it: Children's access to help and protection. In N. Parton and C. Wattam (eds) *Child Sexual Abuse: Responding to the Experiences of Children.* London: Wiley.

MacLeod, M. and Saraga, E. (1988) Challenging the orthodoxy: Towards a feminist theory and practice. *Feminist Review 28*, 16–55.

Main, M. and Goldwyn, R. (1984) Predicting rejection of her infant from mother's representations of her own experience: Implications for the abuse-abusing intergenerational cycle. *Child Abuse and Neglect 8*, 203–217.

Main, M. (1991) Metacognitive knowledge, metacognitive monitoring, and singular (coherent) vs. multiple (incoherent) model of attachment: Findings and directions for future research. In C. Parkes, J. Stevenson-Hinde and P. Marris (eds) *Attachment across the Lifecycle.* London: Routledge.

Main, M. and Hesse, E. (1990) Parents' unresolved or frightening experiences are related to infant disorganised attachment status: Is frightened and/or frightening parental behaviour the linking mechanism? In M. Greenberg, D. Cicchetti and M. Cummings (eds) *Attachment in the Preschool Years.* Chigaco: University of Chicago Press.

Main, M. and Solomon, J. (1986) Discovery of a new insecure-disorganised/disoriented attachment pattern. In M. Yogman and T.B. Brazelton (eds) *Affective Development in Infancy*. Norwood, NJ: Ablex.

Marshall, K., Jamieson, C. and Finlayson, A. (1999) *Edinburgh's Children: The Edinburgh Inquiry into Abuse and Protection of Children in Care*. Edinburgh: Edinburgh City Council.

Masson, J. (1999) *Out of Hearing: Representing Children in Care Proceedings*. Chichester: Wiley.

Meekums, B. (2000) *Creative Group Therapy for Women Survivors of Child Sexual Abuse*. London: Jessica Kingsley Publishers.

Meriweather, V.J. (1999) The sword of forgiveness: Clinically integrating truth, justice, prudence and the relationship of love. *Treating Abuse Today* 9, 1, 6–23.

Mitchell, J. (ed) (1996) *The Selected Melanie Klein*. London: Penguin.

Mollon, P. (1998) *Remembering Trauma: A Psychotherapist's Guide to Memory and Illusion*. London: Sage

Myers, J.E.B. (1994) *The Backlash: Child Protection under Fire*. London: Sage.

Nelson, S. (1998) Time to break professional silences. *Child Abuse Review* 7, 3, 144–153.

NSPCC/ChildLine (1998) *Young Witness Pack*. London: NSPCC/ChildLine.

Olafson, E., Corwin, D.L. and Summit, R.C. (1993) Modern history of child sexual abuse awareness: Cycles of discovery and suppression. *Child Abuse and Neglect* 17, 1, 7–24.

O'Neill, T. (1997) The Memorandum and the guardian ad litem: Whose rights, needs and interests? In H. Westcott and J. Jones (eds) *Persectives on the Memorandum*. Aldershot: Arena, Ashgate Publishing Limited.

Papadopoulos, R.K. (1999) Storied community as secure base: Response to the paper by Nancy Caro Hollander, 'Exile: Paradoxes of Loss and Creativity'. *British Journal of Psychotherapy* 15, 3, 322–332.

Parks, P. (1989) *Rescuing the 'Inner Child': Therapy for Adults Sexually Abused as Children*. London: Souvenir Press.

Parton, N., Thorpe, D. and Wattam, C. (1996) *Child Protection, Risk and the Moral Order*. London: Macmillan.

Parton, N. and Wattam, C. (eds) (1999) *Child Sexual Abuse: Responding to the Experiences of Children*. Chichester: NSPCC/Wiley.

Pearlman, L.A. and Saakvitine, K.W. (1995) *Trauma and the Therapist: Countertransference and Vicarious Traumatization in Psychotherapy with Incest Survivors*. London: W.W. Norton.

Perry, B. and Pollard, R. (1998) Homeostasis, stress, trauma and adaptation: A neurological view of childhood trauma. *Stress in Children: Child and Adolescent Psychiatric Clinics of North America* 7, 1, 33–51

Pigot, T. (1989) *Report of the Advisory Group on Video Evidence*. London: Home Office.

Prior, S. (1999) *Object Relations in Severe Trauma: Psychotherapy of the Sexually Abused Child*. Northvale, NJ: Jason Aronson.

Putnam, F. (1993) Dissociative disorders in children: Behavioural profiles and problems. *Child Abuse and Neglect* 17, 39–45.

Putnam, F.W. (1997) *Dissociation in Children and Adolescents: A Developmental Perspective*. New York: Guilford Press.

Pyck, K. (1994) The backlash in Europe: Real anxiety or mass hysteria in the Netherlands? A preliminary study of the Oude Pekela crisis. In J.E.B. Myers (ed) *The Backlash: Child Protection under Fire*. London: Sage.

Richardson, S. (1989) Child sexual abuse: The challenge for the organisation. In P. Carter, T. Jeffs and M. Smith (eds) *Social Work and Social Welfare Yearbook 1*. Milton Keynes: Open University Press.

Richardson, S. (1991a) Making the connections: Overcoming barriers to learning in child protection work. *Child Abuse Review* 5, 2, 11–12.

Richardson, S. (1991b) The continuum of disclosure. In S. Richardson and H. Bacon (eds) *Child Sexual Abuse: Whose Problem? Reflections from Cleveland*. Birmingham: Venture Press.

Richardson, S. (1993a) Community responses to child abuse: Understanding the backlash against professionals. *ENBAR Newsletter 1*.

Richardson, S. (1993b) Scapegoating professionals: What does it mean for the field? *The Link 2*, 1, 5.

Richardson, S. (1994) Professional survival in the child protection field: An international perspective. *The Whistle 4*, 11–12.

Richardson, S. (1995) Cycles of loss and renewal: A presentation of difference. In The Annette Berg-Goodman Memorial Presentations 1995 and 1996. London: CAPP.

Richardson, S. (1999) Transforming conflict: Mediation and reparation in a staff team. *Child Abuse Review 8*, 133–142.

Richardson, S. (2001) Will you sit by her side? An attachment-based approach to work with dissociative conditions. In V. Sinason (ed) *The Shoemaker and The Elves: Working with Multiplicity*. London: Routledge.

Richardson, S. and Bacon, H. (eds) (1991a) *Child Sexual Abuse: Whose Problem? Reflections from Cleveland*. Birmingham: Venture Press.

Richardson, S. and Bacon, H. (1991b) A framework of belief. In S. Richardson and H. Bacon (eds) *Child Sexual Abuse: Whose Problem? Reflections from Cleveland,*. Birmingham: Venture Press.

Richardson, S. and Bacon, H. (1991c) Questions not answers: Progressing the debate. In S. Richardson and H. Bacon (eds) *Child Sexual Abuse: Whose Problem? Reflections from Cleveland.* Birmingham: Venture Press.

Rose, K. and Savage, A. (1999) Safe caring. In A. Wheal (ed) *The R.H.P. Companion to Foster Care.* Lyme Regis: Russell House Publishing.

Ross, C. (1997) *Dissociative Identity Disorder.* Chichester: Wiley.

Rowan, J. (1981) The Leaves of Spring by Aaron Esterson: An appreciation. In P. Reason and J. Rowan (eds) *Human Inquiry: A Sourcebook of New Paradigm Research.* Chichester: Wiley.

Royal College of Physicians (RCP) (1991, 1997). *Physical Signs of Sexual Abuse in Pre-Pubertal Children. Report of the Working Party of the RCP.* London: RCP.

Russell, D. (1986) *The Secret Trauma: Incest in the Lives of Girls and Women.* New York: Basic Books.

Rutter, M. (1989) Intergenerational continuities and discontinuities in serious parenting difficulties. In D. Cicchetti and V. Carlson (eds) *Child Maltreatment, Theory and Research on the Causes and Consequences of Child Abuse and Neglect.* Cambridge: Cambridge University Press.

Saradjian, J. (1996) *Women Who Sexually Abuse Children: From Research to Clinical Practice.* Chichester: Wiley.

Schneider-Rosen, K., Braunwald, K., Carlson V. and Cicchetti, D. (1985) Current persectives in attachment theory: Illustration from the study of maltreated infants. In I. Bretherton and E. Waters *Growing Points of Attachment Theory and Research,* Monographs of the Society for Research in Child Development No. 209, 50, Nos. 1–2.

Sgroi, S. (1982) *Handbook of Clinical Intervention in Child Sexual Abuse.* Lexington, MA: Lexington Books.

Silberg, J. (1998) *The Dissociative Child: Diagnosis, Treatment and Management.* New York: Sidran Press.

Sinason, V. (1992a) *Mental Handicap and the Human Condition: New Approaches from the Tavistock.* London: Free Association Books.

Sinason, V. (1992b) Paper presented to Child Abuse Interest Group, January, 1992 in Study Day on Abuse of Children with Disability.

Sinason, V. (ed) (1994) *Treating Survivors of Satanist Abuse.* London: Routledge.

Sinason, V. (ed) (1998) *Memory in Dispute.* London: Karnac.

Slade, A. (1999) Individual psychotherapy: An attachment perspective. In J. Cassidy and P.R. Shaver (eds) *Handbook of Attachment Theory and Research.* London: Guilford Press.

Smallbone, S.W. and Dadds, M.R. (2000) Attachment and coercive sexual behaviour. *Sexual Abuse: A Journal of Research and Treatment 12,* 1, 2000.

Smeyers, L. (1999) Kindermishandling. Presentation to ChildLine Conference, Hearing Children's Voices, London, 13 May.

Smith, H. and Israel, E. (1987) Sibling incest: A study of the dynamics of 25 cases. *Child Abuse and Neglect 11,* 101–108.

Smith, M. (1995) *Parental Control within the Family: The Nature and Extent of Parental Violence to Children. Child Protection (Messages from Research).* London: HMSO.

Social Services Inspectorate/Department of Health (1994) *The Child, the Court and the Video: A Study of the Implementation of the Memorandum of Good Practice on Video Interviewing Child Witnesses.* London: HMSO.

Sorenson, T. and Snow, B. (1991) How children tell: The process of disclosure in child sexual abuse. *Child Welfare 70,* 1, 3–15.

Speight, N. and Wynne, J. (1999) Is the Children Act failing severely abused and neglected children? A discussion paper. *Archives of Diseases in Childhood 82,* 192–196.

Spencer, J.R., Nicholson, G., Flin, R. and Bull, R. (eds) (1989) *Children's Evidence in Legal Proceedings: An International Perspective.* Papers from an International Conference, Selwyn College, Cambridge, 26–28 June.

Stark, E. and Flittcraft, A. (1988) Women and children at risk. *International Journal of Health Services 18,* 1, 97–118.

Stein, J., Golding, J., Siegal, J., Burnham, M. and Sorenson, S. (1988) Long-term psychological sequelae of child sexual abuse. In G. Wyatt and G. Powell (eds) *Lasting Effects of Child Sexual Abuse.* London: Sage.

Steinberg, M. (1994) *Interviewer's Guide to the Structured Clinical Interview for DSM IV Dissociative Disorders (SCID-D).* Washington, DC: American Psychiatric Press.

Stern, D. (1985). *The Interpersonal World of the Infant.* New York: Basic Books.

Summit, R.C. (1983) The Child Sexual Abuse Accommodation Syndrome. *Child Abuse and Neglect 7,* 177–193.

Summit, R.C. (1988) Hidden victims, hidden pain: Societal denial of child sexual abuse. In G. Wyatt and G.J. Powell (eds) *Lasting Effects of Child Sexual Abuse.* London: Sage.

230 CREATIVE RESPONSES TO CHILD SEXUAL ABUSE

Swann, A. and Ralston, I. (1991) The importance of the child's account in the validation of child sexual abuse. Turning Research into Practice, BASPCAN First National Congress on the Prevention of Child Abuse and Neglect, University of Leicester, 16–19 September.

Taylor, A. (1994) Child abuse: Politics and power. *The Whistle 4*, 10.

Taylor, A. (1997) Brought to book. *Community Care 25*, 30 January–5 February.

Thompson, A. (1999) When children abuse in community settings. *Community Care 29*, July–4 August 20–21.

Timmons-Mitchell, J. and Gardner, S. (1991) Treating sexual victimisation: Developing trust-based relating in the mother-daughter dyad. *Psychotherapy 28*, 2, 333–338.

Timms, J. (1992) *Manual of Practice Guidance for Guardians ad Litem and Reporting Officers*. Department of Health. London: HMSO.

Timms, J. (1995) *A Guide for Guardians ad Litem in Public Law Proceedings under the Children Act*. Department of Health. London: HMSO.

Toth, S.L. and Cicchetti, D. (1996) Patterns of relatedness, depressive symptomatology, and perceived competence in maltreated children. *Journal of Consulting and Clinical Psychology 64*, 1, 32–41.

Trotter, J. (1998) *No-one's Listening: Mothers, Fathers and Child Sexual Abuse*. London: Whiting and Birch.

United Nations (1992) *Convention on the Rights of the Child Adopted by the General Assembly of the United Nations on 20 November 1989*. London: HMSO.

Utting, W. (1997) *People Like Us: The Report of the Safeguards for Children Living Away from Home*. London: HMSO.

van der Kolk, B.A., McFarlane, A.C. and Weisaeth, L. (eds) *Traumatic Stress: The Effects of Overwhelming Experience on Mind, Body and Society*. London: Guilford Press.

Vizard, E., Monck, E. and Misch, P. (1995) Child and adolescent sex abuse perpetrators: A review of the research literature. *Journal of Psychology and Psychiatry 36*, 5, 731–756.

Wade, A. and Westcott, H. (1997) No easy answers: children's perspectives on investigative interviews. In H. Westcott and J. Jones (eds) *Perspectives on the Memorandum: Policy Practice and Research in Investigative Interviewing*. Aldershot: Arena.

Walrond-Skinner, S. (2000) Transgenerational family therapy musings. *Context: the Magazine for Family Therapy and Systemic Practice 49*, 2–3.

Waterhouse, Sir R., Clough, M. and le Fleming, M. (2000) *Lost in Care: Report of the Tribunal of Inquiry into the Abuse of Children in Care in the Former County Council Areas of Gwynedd and Clwyd since 1974*. London: HMSO.

Wattam, C. (1999) Confidentiality and the social organisation of telling. In N. Parton and C. Wattam (eds) *Child Sexual Abuse: Responding to the Experiences of Children*. Chichester: NSPCC/Wiley.

Webster, A., Palmer, T. and Hughes, M. (2001) *Children Who Have Been Sexually Abused: Therapy before Evidence*. Journal of Clinical Psychiatry

Westcott, H. and Jones, J. (1997) *Perspectives on the Memorandum, Policy Practice and Research in Investigative Interviewing*. Aldershot: Arena.

Wieland, S. (1997) *Hearing the Internal Trauma*. London: Sage.

Wolf, R. (1998) Becoming real: The story of a long journey through psychiatry, counselling and psychotherapy. In Z. Bear (ed) *Good Practice in Counselling People Who Have Been Abused*. London: Jessica Kingsley Publishers.

Wolfe, S. (1984) A multi-factor model of deviant sexuality (presented paper). Cited in T. Morrison, M. Erooga and R. Beckett (eds) *Sexual Offending Against Children: Assessment and Treatment of Male Abusers*. London: Routledge.

Woodward, C. and Fortune, D. (1999) Coping, surviving and healing from child sexual abuse. In N. Parton and C. Wattam (eds) *Child Sexual Abuse: Responding to the Experiences of Children*. Chichester: NSPCC/Wiley.

Wyatt, G. and Higgs, M. (1991) The medical diagnosis of child sexual abuse: the paediatrician's dilemma. In S. Richardson and H. Bacon (eds) *Child Sexual Abuse: Whose Problem? Reflections from Cleveland*. Birmingham: Venture Press.

Wyre, R. (2000) Paedophile characteristics and patterns of behaviour: Developing a typology. In C. Itzin (ed) *Home Truths about Child Sexual Abuse: Influencing Policy and Practice – A reader*. London: Routledge.

Subject Index

Author Index

Aaltonen, T. 170
Ahern, B. 213
Ainsworth, M.D.S. 44, 45
Aldridge, J. 8, 159
Alexander, P. 46, 169, 185
Ambridge, M. 8, 12, 13, 52, 54, 61, 74, 82, 138, 167–96, 212, 221
American Psychiatric Association 184–5
Anderson, C.L. 185
Anslow, M. 70
Armstrong, L. 208

Bacon, H. 8, 12, 13, 23, 29–84, 121, 133–51, 153, 167, 170, 171, 172, 178, 199, 200, 202, 207, 210, 212, 215, 221
Bagley, C. 185
Baker, A. 33, 210
Barnardo's 152, 154, 160
Bedingfield, D. 107
Bell, S. 25
Bentovim, A. 47, 50, 140, 154, 204, 210
Berliner, L. 149, 154
Bibby, P. 133
Birchall, E. 101
Blizard, R.A. 185
Bluhm, A.M. 18
Boateng, P. 211
Bottoms, B.L. 159
Bowker, L.H. 108
Bowlby, J. 34, 50, 75, 179, 180
Bracewell, Justice 126, 128
Braithwaite, J. 214
Briere, J. 154, 184
Briggs, F. 55, 169
British Association of Community Child Health 117
British Psychological Society 51
Brooks, I. 12, 13, 54, 8599, 125, 200, 212, 221
Browne, A. 47, 49
Buchanan, M.F.G. 104
Burton,S. 172
Butler-Sloss, Rt Hon. Justice E. 11, 12, 19, 20, 25, 29, 31, 32, 37, 38, 40, 41, 63, 70, 100, 105, 106, 107, 117, 131, 199, 208, 210, 212, 217

Calder, M. 148
Campbell, B. 12, 210, 211, 217
Carter, J. 170
Cashman, H. 209
Cassidy, J. 45

Cawson, P. 103
ChildLine 160
Cicchetti, D. 172
Cleaver, H. 103
Clough, M. 201
Clyde, Lord J.J. 201, 203, 204
Cohen, J. 146
Colclough, L. 70
Colledge, P. 8
Collier, F. 149
Conte, J. 154
Cook, F. 9–10
Cooklin, A. 68
Corwin, D.L. 198
Cresswell, T. 116
Crittenden, P. 44, 45, 47, 143, 148
Crown Prosecution Service 163

Dadds, M.R. 46, 49
Dale, P. 183
Davies, G. 105. 114
Davis, G. 164
Delaney, C. 8
Dent, H. 159
Department of Health 37, 70, 102, 105, 114, 118, 122, 123, 155, 163
deYoung, M. 205
Diamond, A. 5–16, 17
Dobson, F. 212
Duncan, S. 33, 210

Egeland, B. 45, 55, 64
Eichberg, C. 44
Esterson, A. 32
Etherington, K. 183

Fahlberg, V. 142
Faller, K.C. 148
Farmer, E. 135, 148
Ferguson, D.M. 154
Fever, F. 204, 212
Finkelhor, D. 47, 48, 49, 55, 63, 154, 169
Finlayson, A. 204
Flin, R. 159
Flittcraft, A. 109
Fonagy, P. 54, 76, 79, 180, 185
Fortune, D. 32
Freeman-Longo, R.E. 212
Frothingham, T. 112, 115

Gallagher, B. 109
Gara, M.A. 170
Gardner, S. 171, 176
General Medical Council 108
Glaser, D. 44
Goldwyn, R. 52
Golier, J. 48
Gonzelez, L.S. 32